PRAISE

PRAISE FOR *BACK FROM THE BRINK*

"The autobiography of Tim Chan, a young man with severe autism, provides a powerful theme of the unrelenting struggles in pursuing inclusion for a meaningful and productive life. He comes face to face with daunting obstacles of autistic challenges, as well as non-acceptance and stigmatisation in the wider world. Tim's insights into these challenges are testament to his resilience. His unstinting efforts in finding strategies to overcome them pave a way to understanding autism from an insider's perspective and address issues of inclusion and social justice.

Additionally the story includes the voice of Tim's greatest supporter and advocate – his mother, Sarah – and her tireless endeavours to help translate the world to Tim and help Tim translate himself to the world. We see Tim through her eyes – compassionate, insightful and ever ready to explore ways for Tim to develop mentally, emotionally and socially."

Anne Carson
Awarded Poet, Author, Artist, Editor

"*Back from the Brink* is a must-read book for many:

For people with autism and other vulnerabilities, Tim provides the voice of a peer with insights. He shares the pain, the elation and the resilience that provides a path to guide especially when the times are tough.

For families of people with disability, Tim and his mother Sarah provide a roadmap identifying the setbacks and the breakthroughs and offering insights for people discouraged by the 'system'.

For anyone who works or hopes to work with people with vulnerabilities, Tim shows the impact of suppression of voice and the way in which staff attitudes and values can fundamentally respect or deny personhood and enable or hinder opportunities that others take for granted.

Tim Chan has a great deal to offer – a thinker, a researcher, a motivational speaker, a peer worker. This book is a taster and a testament to the power of voice."

Belinda Epstein-Frisch OAM
Disability Consultant and Advocate

"The book, a thoroughly enjoyable and gripping 'read', is the biography of Tim, a young Melbournian with Autism, and of Sarah his indefatigable mother, who generates and marshals support for Tim with perseverance and skill that match those of our most admired military generals.

In it you will encounter some of the remarkable people whose expertise is drawn by Sarah into providing the support for Tim and the family. If you have ever wondered what it's like living with autism, or what must and can be done, by family and community members or by professionals, to support someone with autism, this book is essential reading.

Tim and Sarah's story is at times bleak, but it is, from beginning to heart-warming conclusion, spellbinding and moving. What impressed me most about this unusual book are the thought-provoking, often deeply moving insights emerging from the interplay of Tim and Sarah's mutual perspectives. Resurfacing after the last page is turned was an effort. This is a compelling read, at times heartbreaking, invariably uplifting and intellectually stimulating."

Dr Mike Steer, AM
Director of the NSW Office on Disability, Senior Lecturer, Sensory Disability, RIDBC Renwick Centre & The University of Newcastle, NSW

"I reread many passages, some because they are so perfectly evocative and moving; I want to fix them in my memory, to influence my thinking moving forward. Others are very visual and provide strong sensory connection. I think the encounter at the end is most significant to fully comprehend the story in its entirety, with a richer perception for the reader. I really love this book; it made me smile in parts, wince and cringe in others and cry at times. It is very rich in so many ways as it comes from a deep awareness and sensitivity."

Amanda Marshall
CEO, Kevin Heinze Grow, 2006-2017

∼

"Tim is determination personified! He has great depth to his writing and his written voice is an authentic one."

Chris Varney
CEO and Founder, I Can Network

BACK FROM THE BRINK

STORIES OF RESILIENCE, RECONCILIATION
AND RECONNECTION

TIM CHAN

SARAH CHAN

Edited by
ANNE M CARSON

Copyright © 2019 by Tim Chan and Sarah Chan

All rights reserved.

No part of this book may be reproduced in any form or by any electronic or mechanical means, including information storage and retrieval systems, without written permission from the author, except for the use of brief quotations in a book review.

This book is dedicated to people who, in one way or another, are not using speech to communicate, as well as their families and social support networks.

In addition, the efforts of people who have risen to their challenges to become shining examples of courage and resilience are celebrated.

CONTENTS

Foreword   xi
Introduction   xiii

1. Glimpses of the Road   1
2. Preparing for the Road   8
3. Taking the Road   13
4. Scaling a Summit   23
5. On the Road Less Travelled   31
6. If Fishes Had to Climb Trees (Doors to Learning)   38
7. Finding the Way through the Maze   46
8. Against the Odds   55
9. Uncommon Courage   65
10. Into the Arena   80
11. Warrior for Justice   91
12. Speaking Louder than Words   100
13. Storming the Citadel   108
14. High School Shambles   117
15. The VCE Shuffle   128
16. Back from the Brink - One Quotation at a Time   141
17. Man with Heart   156
18. Wonder in a Water Droplet   163
19. Earth Magick   172
20. Connections along the way   177
21. Changing Lives   185
22. Into the Night   192
23. Work in Progress   211
24. Hope Springs Eternal   219
25. Korea: Resilience in Action   225
26. Finding Our Voice   233
27. Hope Revisited   240
28. Champion for Communication   247
29. An Unexpected Encounter   255

Epilogue 266

Acknowledgments 269
Additional Resources 271
More about Tim 273

FOREWORD

This book is a unique narrative by two authors, a mother and son, who share their experiences of living with autism, and is a testimony to "where there is the will there is a way". Tim writes movingly about his autistic challenges, in particular, intense anxiety and extensive sensory overload. Despite being "written off" by persistent misunderstanding and dogmatic mindsets surrounding disability, and suffering the pain of social isolation and exclusion in various forms, Tim has persevered in his endeavours and triumphed to achieve outstanding success.

No one, apart from a person with lived experience could express such profound insights and perspective on autism. In challenging some of its myths, a lens is provided for fresh exploration and re-discovery of this enigmatic condition.

The book is also a tribute to the various professionals who were willing to assume competence, in believing and accepting unconditionally Tim's innate intelligence, thus enabling a sensitive non-speaking young man communicate his deep insights in a potent voice. His mother's constant love and support are palpable throughout his journey.

This book is a valuable resource for a diverse range of people, including parents and those in the teaching and allied health professions. From the signposts in commitment, knowledge and strategies found abundantly in Tim's story, additional competence can be attained for enhancing the lives of vulnerable individuals.

I am excited by *Back from the Brink*; Tim's story illustrates the vital importance of the right of every person to use a means of communication of their choice as outlined in *UN Convention on the Rights of Persons with Disabilities*. With communication, Tim becomes a **PERSON** with a voice. In confronting and exposing the glaring discrepancies and shortcomings of the system, one individual, with perseverance and courage, can strive to achieve an education for a productive future. I see this work as a ground breaking example to bring **REAL** changes for opportunities in attaining a purposeful education and a meaningful life for many.

Emmy Elbaum
Educator, Disability Advocate, Chairperson
Just Learning Inc.

INTRODUCTION

I was 14 years old when I entertained serious thoughts about suicide. I was only prevented from carrying out my self-destruction because of my severe autism. Not having full control of my body, I didn't know if I would end up in the morgue or permanently on life support or in a wheelchair. Already without speech, having huge hyper-sensory issues, movement difficulties, proneness to being overloaded, I didn't want to add immobility and other challenges to my list in case I didn't succeed in killing myself.

I wasn't aware that I was depressed. At 14, in Year 8 at High School, I only got the sense that life was grinding me down. I was totally out of place in a mainstream high school where no one seemed interested in me, and people walked past me as if I didn't exist. I was utterly powerless, had no speech, and was denied my usual means to communicate by typing with support. I felt the world would be better off without me.

What is it like to live with autism? From my own experience at the severe end of the spectrum, autism is like a life sentence of being trapped in a body that refuses to be controlled by your mind, like you are residing in an abode with structures that shift constantly without warning. When you try to talk, all you can manage is a high-pitched screech with no resemblance to speech. When you move your hand to write, you produce an illegible scrawl no matter how precisely you try to form the letters. When you try to read or listen to words, all you see or hear are their shapes or sounds which override their meaning. Within the prison of autism are other tortures; a nervous system so highly tuned that every sensation comes with unbearable intensity.

New clothes scratch like steel wool, lamp-light burns into your eyes, or hands clapping are akin to the deafening roar of pistol shots from the firing range. You live in a state of constant alert, never at peace, in an inner world of chaos and disconnection while trying to fend off the onslaught of overwhelming sensory input. Because of the lack of bodily equilibrium, the outer world can appear strange and terrifying without a ready point of reference. In addition, because you don't have an easily accessible system of meaning, people and their behaviour can be beyond comprehension, and activities and events can be complete mysteries. On top of everything else, nobody seems to understand your problems, and with no ready means of communication when you do not speak, you are isolated and confined to the confusion of your own contorted reality. It is hard to imagine a more fearsome ogre than living within autism's stranglehold.

Over the years since dipping to the lowest levels of self-loathing and despair from repeated encounters with a lack of understanding and of discrimination, I have chosen the path, with the help of my support network, to get at the root of my problems, and to explore what sets me and therefore my journey apart from other people. In this present attempt to acknowledge and write about my experiences, I have several purposes, firstly, recounting the crucial stages in my life which shaped me into the sum of who I am, secondly, to examine my engagement with life in all its aspects from the added perspective of hindsight, and lastly, to explore the kind of person I aspire to be, drawing on the people in my life who have inspired me in one way or another. Thus, I will begin with one of my favourite past-times.

I love to ride on trains, it doesn't have to be any special kind of train, like the famous Puffing Billy, with a steam locomotive, it can be just your everyday train that runs from the city to the suburbs, and back, carrying commuters from station to station. I board the carriage and choose a seat, hopefully a window seat; one as far from the doors as possible, with fewer distractions with the comings and goings of commuters. For the next hour or so, as my errant body relaxes to the constant motion of the rollicking carriage, I would press my face against the window. This way I would watch the cars and traffic on the roads, see the trees and poles whizz past, and catch a glimpse of the backyards of houses along the train track. I could see the vegie gardens, cubbies, clothes lines and occasionally, swimming pools. With body soothed, my mind also shifts gear, lulled by the ever-changing scenery. Mental agitation gives way to a certain lightness of being that endures for the ride.

Living with autism is like getting on a train, you can't control how fast or slow it is going, or whether the ride will be smooth or jerky. You share your ride with other commuters, and for a little while, they occupy your world as you watch them embark. Some sleep, eat, read, talk, play games or text on their mobile phone, or from time to time you catch snippets of people's conversations. Then they disembark, and traces of them fade into the background of awareness. You see, these commuters remind me of different parts of me, parts that feel like strangers, parts I can't control, yet these parts that appear so foreign are actually bits of myself that I don't understand or have trouble identifying with. My body, for instance, sometimes feels as if it doesn't belong to me. When I feel unable to connect with my own body, there is a sense of going through the motions without being able to actually carry out my intended purpose. For example, like wanting to say yes, but what comes from my lips is a no, or vice versa. Then again, more often than not, people's speech flits through my mental landscape and fades from view. If I don't make a conscious effort to recapture the essence of the intentions behind their talking, they are lost to me, and I can't make sense of what people are doing.

There is the larger world as the train meanders its way towards its destination. Watching from my vantage point on a moving train, through the insulating layer of thick glass, this external world can only be observed, never touched. The pictures of the world in my mind's eye are fleeting isolated instances of an existence outside my own experience, one that I cannot engage with or be part of. Growing up with autism, this feeling of being an observer, isolated behind thick glass, is ever pervasive.

One of my favourite activities which Mum and I love sharing is to walk through the Botanic Gardens to the Shrine of Remembrance. The Shrine was built in the 1930s after our soldiers returned from the carnage and trenches in Europe in World War 1. Mum and I have always been interested in the memorial services, photographic and audio-visual displays, and other exhibitions to commemorate the patriotic and heroic acts of our soldiers in various military involvements. I became hooked on war stories as I have always been fascinated by how soldiers are able to turn their fear into courage to face the enemy, no matter what the odds. One of the most celebrated engagements of war comes on 25th April, and this date in 2015 is the centenary of the disastrous landing at Gallipoli, where thousands of young Australian soldiers lost their lives. Despite knowing that they were outnumbered, out-maneuvererd and at a huge disadvantage, these young soldiers marched forward to face injury and death with great heroism and determination. The ANZAC spirit of courage and perseverance in the face of enormous challenges live on through these soldiers' stories, their diary entries, correspondence and the news from the front.

Our stories are the living legacies of our experiences and sharing these stories is empowering. I am often reminded that courage can be found anywhere. What is inspiring is that heroism exists in our everyday life, amongst ordinary people whom we meet when they care enough to put themselves on the line.

Because of my experience as a fringe dweller, especially at high school, I am keen to understand the mindset and strategies of the people who had come back from the brink to a life worth living. I want to learn the secret of their heroic efforts to find the path to re-engagement and reconciliation with themselves and their world. I also find that the people who come into my life at certain stages are instrumental in helping me understand certain aspects of my world and also of myself. In the process I become more able to handle the curved balls that life throws at me. Using this perspective, I have interwoven my story with those of the people I have found inspiring, who one way and another throw me lifelines.

1
GLIMPSES OF THE ROAD

Tim speaks

It is well-nigh impossible to capture my first impressions of the world because they are made up of fleeting images. These images are like snippets of videos that came into view, then disappeared without any sense of control on my part and were lost to me until something similar triggered the memory of them. I remember a pervasive and urgent need to make sense of a chaotic world. From an early age, there was a constant barrage of sensations, people, sounds, everyday objects and other things which demanded attention. Worse, all these pieces of information came as separate bits bombarding me without any underlying patterns or connections. It was like thousands of disparate pieces of a giant jigsaw puzzle, which were thrown at me, unaccompanied by the overall picture. I would be quite exhausted mentally trying to piece together all kinds of things to try to get an idea of what was happening around me. For example, I have a memory of our kitchen table where the family would sit and eat, or do other things. From about nine months old to a year and a half I often sat, strapped in a high chair at my place. At this stage, that table would appear as separate bits, the table top, all the things on it, plates, bowls, food, the legs which came into view as I was lifted up or down, and the sensations of sound and touch coming from setting the table and eating our meals. I would immerse myself in the pattern of wood grain in the table top which was a comforting sensation, as this helped me to block out other sensations, like the sudden noise of the spoon hitting the bowl or when cups or plates banged together, that felt like hitting a raw nerve. But this would also come as another separate bit of information.

As a baby I was admired for being cute, and as the youngest, doted on by the whole family. My eldest brother, who was kind, was already a teenager when I started to be more active. He would put me on his shoulders, but I would be scared if he walked around with me hoisted up. From this height, things looked different and I couldn't make the connection that I was seeing the same place but from a different vantage point. I always feel a lack of control when I am not on my own feet, but there was no way to let people know at that time.

For quite some time, I thought I had two mothers, my mum and my elder sister, who took care of me in many ways; talking, singing and playing with me. My second sister was more of a playmate, as she was closer in age. I liked looking at what she did and trying to make sense of her activities, like playing school with her stuffed toys. She would line these up in front of a board to teach the lesson for the day. I would follow her when I became more mobile, and laughed to see her doing things. It was hard for me to use my voice, though, as I didn't always have control over it. Laughing and humming came quite naturally, I don't know why, but I could always find something to laugh at as a young child. Maybe it is because I found our family hard to understand, such as my sisters playing with miniature replicas of animals, people or objects, making them talk, dance and eat. Anyway, laughing always made me feel more in control.

At the beginning, no one suspected that I was anything but healthy and full of life. I was lively to the extent that I had great difficulty sleeping. It was a miracle if I slept during the day, or fell asleep before midnight, even when I woke at the usual time of 5am. During the night, I would often wake up and stay awake. This sleep pattern carried on from birth until well past my twelfth birthday. As a result, Mum would suffer from a disrupted sleep cycle herself for many years.

From the inside, my early life was a series of sensory bombardments – intense light, sound, movements which battered me on every side. As much as I tried, I couldn't do much to stop this constant invasion of the outside world in a concentrated form. As soon as I opened my eyes in the morning, the sunlight would stream in like a mini-explosion that hurt my eyes, the clatter of noise from Mum preparing breakfast in the kitchen, my sisters' chatting, or my brother getting ready for the day were shockwaves of sound that could not be avoided. I would close my eyes, move my head away from the window, snuggle deeper into the blankets, but still the light and noise found a way of pushing through. When I was taken out from bed, the bedlam of sensations would increase as I also found touch and movement overwhelming.

The one way I was able to get a sense of control was to close my eyes, put my hands over my ears and block out the outside world by humming. Later I found solace in the patterns of light made by spinning objects. I would also lie on the floor to try to get away from the assault of over-stimulation. This is something I like to do even to this day, although I often need to control this urge and refrain as it is socially unacceptable in most situations.

When I was about nineteen months old, my family went back to Hong Kong where both my parents were born and raised, for a three-week visit. We stayed mostly at my uncle's (Mum's only brother) home. There is still a large extended family on both sides in Hong Kong, uncles and aunts, plus cousins galore. My brother and sisters enjoyed the trip. We went out every day and they had fun visiting relatives they never saw before, eating delicious food in different restaurants and in people's houses, or going to famous spots such as the Peak, Repulse Bay, and Clearwater Bay where my Mum's cousin lives.

But I found it extremely difficult. Instead of engaging with people or the toys I was given, I would spend long stretches of time gazing at the ceiling fan, trying to block out what was happening around me. When we went out, I would invariably seek out an escalator and kept riding on it until I was stopped, after the umpteenth time. I was also cranky, frustrated to the point of banging my head on hard surfaces. I can now see that my behaviour had to do with the unfamiliarity of people and places, constant hustle and bustle as well as unbelievably hectic life in an environment I was not used to. The noise, crowds, traffic, in addition to the busy activities of catching up with relatives and friends, shopping, dining out, and sight-seeing were all contributing to the intense overload on my hypersensitive systems. As a result I was like an engine that has overheated and is in danger of implosion.

Sarah speaks

It was in Hong Kong, outside of our regular environment, that I was able to see Tim more clearly and perceive that not all was well with his development. I had noticed during the second half of Tim's second year, his tendency to focus on spinning objects, as well as a reluctance to maintain eye contact. This was exaggerated in Hong Kong as there was so much that was new and unfamiliar. However, our time was occupied with the whirlwind of activities and visits to relatives and friends I had not seen for close on twelve years, I again put my worries aside and resolved to follow this up when we got back home.

∽

Tim is the last of my four children. Tim's siblings, my eldest son and elder daughter were born twelve and nine years earlier, and my second daughter was four at the time of Tim's birth. It was time consuming to meet the needs of this diverse age group, but Tim seemed to – or had to – fit into our busy routine. The Chinese word for good, 'hao', is made of the characters of son and daughter, and now, we have a pair of each, two 'hao' for our family.

My pregnancy with Tim was uneventful, and he was born almost on the expected date, without any complications, weighing a healthy eight and a half pounds (over four kilograms), big in comparison to his siblings at birth. His Apgar score (a quick method to assess the health of newborns) was nine out of ten, and he was alert and responsive. In his first weeks of life, everything appeared to be going well. The family, especially his siblings, was thrilled to welcome its latest member.

In some ways, Tim's alertness posed a challenge during the first year as he would not settle or sleep easily. His milestones were also delayed, not sitting up until he was eight months old. He never crawled, but took time in standing up, around fourteen months, and walked two months later. Tim's communication was a little late, but came along with babbling around twelve months, which progressed to single words not long after. I remembered thinking that unlike the his siblings, whose first word was 'ma', mother, Tim's was 'dang', light, which he seemed to look at more often than usual, but he also said, 'gor' for elder brother, and 'jie' for elder sister, when he saw them. Because Tim was happy and appeared to be comfortable with being part of family routines and activities, and because of the huge demands on my time and effort as a parent, I was not too concerned about the baby of the family at this stage.

On the other hand, I noticed that the explosion in language acquisition, which followed first words for his siblings, did not come with Tim. Apart from the occasional word, he was not a talker. Actually, even, worryingly, single words disappeared when he was fourteen months old. However, there was no problem with his hearing. My elder daughter had begun violin lessons at this point and used to practice in the hub of the house, the kitchen/family room where Tim often sat at the table. In the first few weeks of her practice, Tim would start to cry, but in the ensuing weeks when his sister began to get more proficient, he seemed content to remain at close quarters. Tim's love for music, good music, was apparent from this early age.

The pang of concern I felt when his few words disappeared I managed to rationalise; Tim was otherwise healthy and happy, eating well and showing initial signs of interest in family interactions, toddling around the house with his siblings and laughing when they played with him. I made the mistake of deciding to wait for further development.

I also told myself that these first tell-tale signs could point to lack of appropriate things to interest and engage him, and also that he could be a late bloomer who would catch up. That is, although I had an uneasy feeling about Tim's differences, it was hard to acknowledge that my baby could be afflicted with a serious condition, and my busy life with the rest of the family provided plenty of excuses for running away from reality.

As the months rolled on, the effects of Tim's delayed development became more obvious, manifested by his lack of speech, inability to understand or follow directions, obsessive rituals and inexplicable meltdowns. I sought the opinions of friends, and most of their comments were reassuring. Finally, a family friend of my parents, a speech pathologist, told me her fears after spending some time with Tim when he was two and a half. Yet, I still thought that she could be wrong. Impossible, I felt, as autism has not been found in the immediate or extended family. I was intensely conflicted and confused as I turned down her kind offer to accompany me to get some learning material for Tim. However, autism has reared its head, and I finally had to face this fearsome spectre.

2

PREPARING FOR THE ROAD

Sarah speaks

Finally, when Tim was around two and a half years old, I could deny Tim's difficulties no longer and it was now with a sense of urgency that I took the initial steps to contact health professionals. After a wait of several months, we were able to go for an appointment with a multi-disciplinary team at Austin Health for an assessment. After spending an afternoon with a pediatrician, a speech pathologist and a psychologist, we were told three weeks later that Tim had Autistic Disorder. I had never felt more hopeless.

It was with great difficulty that I started to come to terms with Tim's autism. In addition to the professional expertise and advice we received, I felt a compelling sense to help Tim lead the kind of life I had envisaged for him. Although my experience with autism was minimal, because of my training in the allied health professions, I felt less intimidated by the jargon and the huge and diverse body of research and literature in this area. To this end, I resolved to do my best in letting Tim, through his behaviour, guide me in what I needed to know to help him.

Tim speaks

Gradually, laboriously, after much trial and error, I began to be able to bring some of the disparate pieces of my world into relationship with each other. For instance, with the kitchen table I became more able to assemble some of these bits together to get an essential idea of what that table was used for and its place in the room. Not understanding the relationship between things is why I often got frustrated and discouraged as I tried to make sense of my world, and the people in it. However, I was determined to make the attempt to understand these mysteries, and put all available energy to do this. I had my feelers out for anything that would help me explain the world in ways I could make sense of, probably accounting for my alertness. My difficulty in falling asleep, in early infancy till late childhood, was related to the never ending bombardment of sensations and information as my mind continually tried to assemble the pieces of puzzles out of any information coming my way. As was my reluctance to stand; I hated the extra load of sensory input that an upright position and any movement entailed.

With my mind reeling from the vast array of sensory, speech and other information, I was still trying to figure out ways to deal with this onslaught. I continued to retreat into the effects of blinking lights, spinning objects and soft rhythms – they helped to calm me, and I spent hours seeking out these soothing sensations. I fixated on different types of fans, bubbles from which light reflected, and anything with predictable patterns of movement, spin, sound or light effects.

Yet, I longed for connection to people, and desperately craved understanding and acceptance. Being noticeably different, with flapping hands, little eye contact, constant humming, and no useful speech, this quest for connection was like climbing Mt. Everest, extremely challenging, insurmountable at times, but I just kept trying. For years to come, getting people to understand what I thought and felt was a monumental struggle.

∼

Sarah speaks

In the early days when Tim was just diagnosed, among the professionals we consulted, autism was seen in terms of a deficit model with many of the associated behaviours deemed as inappropriate or dysfunctional. As parents, we were told that these behaviours stood in the way of learning and we should therefore try our best to train Tim to substitute more appropriate or 'normal' ways of acting. For instance, when Tim repetitively picked up tanbark in the playground, and pushed these down the slide, the early intervention teacher gave him toy cars as substitutes. I did follow this well-meaning advice for a time, although I was also able to see in Tim, an innate spark of intelligence as well as a personality that shone through the constant ritualistic or self-stimulatory behaviour. I began to question the edict that parents should actively discourage or extinguish such autistic behaviour. I also embarked on my own learning path about autism, as I found that my observations and reading helped enormously to redirect my energy into forging positive ways to see the needs of my special child. As I learned to see beneath the surface of Tim's challenging behaviour, despite my initial despair at the gloomy prognosis, I started to get a feel of less conventional paths that might just provide some answers.

There is a school of thinking, called functionalism, which proposes that all behaviour has a purpose and develops as a result of best adaptation to a situation or environment. Seen in this light, Tim's behaviour began to make sense. His use of play material was repetitive and compulsive; lining up toy cars or blocks, endlessly spinning the wheels of overturned trikes and bikes. I began to see this way of playing as a need to assert some control over an environment which he had little understanding and minimal control, and also as a way to calm his over-taxed nervous system. In addition, Tim's humming, covering his ears or lying on the floor in busy or unfamiliar environments was a way to deal with the sensory assault from a hypersensitive nervous system prone to overloading. To distract, divert or discourage these autistic behaviours was at best unhelpful and at worst damaging. Instead, Tim's behaviour needed to be seen as coping strategies in his effort to learn how to navigate a challenging environment, because his body works differently. Parents and professionals may overlook this aspect in their concern for the child.

An anecdote recounted by Donna Williams, inspirational author, speaker, teacher and autism consultant who is on the spectrum herself, illustrates this point well. Donna was working at an autism residential unit when she saw a young woman resident being held down and fed by two support workers because this resident was not eating her lunch. On further investigation, Donna saw the underlying reason for refusing food was because the woman was trying to rub her arms with her hands which interfered with other tasks, like eating. When Donna started to rub the resident's arms, to give her the tactile stimulation she needed, the woman started to feed herself.[1]

With my new-found perspective, I also began to work on ways of reaching Tim, especially to support him learn the necessary skills and concepts to claim a place in our world.

Tim speaks

At three years of age, I was not aware that anything was different or wrong with me. But after we got back from the second visit to the hospital for feedback after the assessment, Mum and I started to spend more time together. Mum would take me to the Toy Library or to playgroup. These outings were all quite overwhelming with a large number of unfamiliar people and different environments. I hid around the shelves of puzzles and books at the Toy Library while Mum looked for things that we could use. At the playgroup, we were only able to spend probably 20 minutes before I needed to go home. Because of all the noise and movement from about six to eight kids and their parents, I seldom ventured out from my spot at the far corner of the room, nor took part in any of the joint activities.

At home, we would go through picture books or do activities like beating out rhythms with musical instruments to songs, throw and catch beanbags, similar to the kind of things I did at Remedial Gymnastics which I joined when I was about two years old. I still couldn't work out why we were doing what we were doing, but I liked Mum doing things with me.

---

1. Williams, Donna. (1994). *Somebody somewhere*, UK: Jessica Kingsley.

3
TAKING THE ROAD

Sarah speaks

My life began to revolve more and more around Tim. I spent most of the day in obtaining the intervention he required to catch up on all areas of development and in providing his day-to-day, hour-to-hour supervision and care. Although I tried my best to juggle the needs of the rest of the family, especially his second sister who was only four years older, I found that the intensive efforts and time required to support Tim's needs required most of my focus and sapped much of my energy. I rationalised that in giving Tim what he needed from an early age, both he and the rest of the family would be more able to reap the benefits at a later stage. Because of my refusal to see Tim's obvious challenges earlier on, my devotion to Tim's needs also assuaged my own guilt for my delay in making sense of his differences and doing something about this. It was with regret that I looked back on the times when I was impatient with the demands of my other children, especially Tim's second sister. But at that stage, my obsession with doing what I could for Tim became paramount. From my observations of the older children, it was a great blessing to see them develop in maturity, independence and resilience, taking on responsibility to help me around the house and care for Tim. In some ways, coming face to face with adversity early also helped Tim's siblings grow into the wonderfully caring and nurturing adults they are today. It is also gratifying that their achievements, educationally and professionally, have been grounded in an early start to find positive ways to deal with a sibling who is different.

When Tim was first diagnosed, the behavioural program known as Applied Behavioural Analysis (ABA) was in vogue, and we were told that this was the best way forward for children on the spectrum, with sound supporting evidence from both research and practice. It is a program based on intensive drills to teach basic social and educational skills for a recommended 40 hours per week. The highly experienced psychologist, our program consultant, had done some modification and put in additional drills for individualised learning for Tim, but he still had great difficulty in mastering numbers, receptive and expressive language, and basic concepts. Apart from the initial assessment to establish a baseline of what Tim could or could not do, the consultant was not able to give reasons for the drills that Tim found challenging, despite numerous trials. For example, when Tim failed to discriminate colour, or master one-to-one correspondence in counting after months of daily doses of these drills, her typical response was to substitute a different version of similar drills in which Tim again had difficulties. We were bewildered.

Tim speaks

On the home front, I was seeing Chris, a speech pathologist, who showed Mum what to do. I didn't know at the time that this was based on what they called Applied Behavioural Analysis or ABA. In addition to the other things we did, Mum would go through these new drills with me. I was able to match pictures, but when it came to drills requiring me to point to things when Mum said a word, I couldn't figure out what I was supposed to do, and it became sort of hit and miss. After a couple of months, Mum got another person, an ABA therapist, to work with me. Nora had a loud voice, but she also gave me piggy back rides and happily jumped with me on the trampoline. Mum arranged a work space for us with small table and chairs in the lounge. Soon afterwards, a psychologist Chris recommended came on board to supervise the program, and Nora was joined by several other ABA therapists. I also spent time every week with Chris for speech therapy.

Pretty soon my days at home were chock full of things I had to do. In the morning, after going with Mum to drop my brother and sisters off to school, I would do drills in the lounge room for two hours with a therapist. After lunch, this would be repeated with another therapist. Mum took over when the others left off, and we usually spent time on different activities, going for walks, or to the playground. Even then, she would coach me, including counting things we saw or playing throw and catch with a ball. Sometimes Mum would do the drills, but her ways were less strict, as she didn't always follow the manual exactly which suited me fine.

Sarah speaks

The ABA program had appeared so sound at first but it presented many problems which made me question its basic assumptions, including breaking up tasks into steps and mastering these (discrete trial training) to be incorporated into the whole afterwards (forward or backward chaining). I also drew on my experiences with my older children and my previous work with other students. For instance, Tim's second sister learned in unconventional ways. Because of older siblings whom she wanted to emulate, she was mastering many concepts considered advanced for her age. She had an extensive repertoire in language as well. Because of early exposure to books read aloud to her older siblings before bedtime, she was extremely keen to learn to read herself. However, when I made attempts to expose her to material more suitable for early readers when she was around four, she didn't seem very interested. When I switched to reading her classic children's books such as *Charlotte's Web*, progressing quickly to *The Hobbit*, *The Secret Garden* and *Watership Down*, I found that she had already taught herself to read at five. Furthermore, her self-taught style of reading differs from most children which can be illustrated with an example. When she was nine, her teacher had given the class a chapter book for silent reading. Midway through the 50 minute lesson, she went back to tell the teacher she had finished, but was told to go back to her desk and read the book properly.

From my experience, my second daughter devoured books and often came back with a stack of thick tomes from the library which she finished in the space of an afternoon. When she reads, she appears totally focused, and not only understands but remembers nearly everything. I can only conjecture that instead of reading word for word, she literally imbibes the ideas and details from books using a combination of different modalities including aural and visual. From this, I realised that learning involves the opportunity for children to use the resources around them to construct meaning from their experiences, and each child's method for making sense of the world and learning to use the tools of our culture, such as reading, would be as individual as that child him/herself. With a method that assumes all children learn in a linear, progressive way in which material are often rigidly transmitted as water poured into empty vessels, those students who learn differently would be 'uneducable' by their standards.

Because of my deference to authority as a result of my early experience in traditional education within the Chinese culture, I didn't question an evidence-based method that involved following a strict protocol on how a child should be given instructions, with the child's responses reinforced accordingly as measures of learning. But I was not blind to the fact that this approach was not reaching my child with special needs. As the behavioural program continued, I protested silently by varying things a little, adding in, subtracting out or simply doing the drills in a more natural way. From what I could see, Tim's learning didn't suffer from my different interpretation and implementation.

∽

Tim speaks

Drills which involved matching with pictures or blocks were no trouble, but I didn't think I was learning much when it came to drills that relied on language. Against the backdrop of all the things that flooded my awareness, words were just fleeting sounds which carried no meaning whatsoever. What I learned was to figure out ways to get the answers the therapists wanted from me, and in doing so, I also learned a bit more about people, specifically, about how each of the therapists worked. For example, when a therapist said, 'touch red' or 'touch blue', I had to touch the red card or the blue card when two or more colour cards were put on the table. With colour and other simple drills, I learned to work out the answer by how the cards were put down. The correct card, the one I needed to touch, would be laid out a bit more deliberately. Although it was just a fraction of a second longer, this gave me the clue I needed. But after doing the drills for a while, they complicated things by adding other instructions, for example, 'put the ball in front of the box', and this was when I floundered as I didn't understand what I had to do. Language was still a total mystery to me.

I also found that each of the three therapists did things differently. Sally was the best teacher, and she kept up my interest, so she got more out of me. Nora was getting results because she kept on doing the simpler drills, the ones I already understood. I was also scared of her as she could be quite rough and I got hurt a few times. When I lay on the floor, she would come and drag me by the arm to the table to work. She also forcibly pulled my hands down and kept them at my side to stop me from putting my fingers up my nose. Enza was Nora's complete opposite, a softie, and I could tell she felt sorry for me. When I got frustrated or just plain tired, I would try and get away with working by hitting her thigh. At first, she tried to stay cool and just gave me time-out, but when she got me back to the table to do another drill, I would look for another opening and hit her again, and when this happened a few times, she didn't know what to do. Once I got her so mad, she walked out of the session because I kept hitting her. Because I was getting so sick and tired of drills that I couldn't decipher, and because I felt so helpless, I was trying to get back at people. It wasn't the best move on my part, but I felt like I'd won my first battle with a sense of being able to control some of what went on around me. Because I knew I was getting nowhere, I felt sad and angry. I didn't like most of what I had to do, but I wasn't able to let people know this.

Sarah speaks

After three expensive and frustrating years I found myself once again questioning the efficacy of a regimen based on rote learning. Despite all the effort we had put in, Tim was still not speaking or making significant progress in understanding language and other basic skills. In those three arduous years, Tim had learned to sit at the table and do some simple tasks like matching, sorting, or rote counting, but the mastery of other basic tasks including understanding one step instructions, colours or numbers were still beyond him. The teachers/therapists who ran the drills also reported differing results. Tim was able to show mastery of the same drills with some of them, but not others. Tim himself was getting increasingly frustrated when he sensed that he was not succeeding. The intensity of the program was another problem; with my input whenever Tim was not working with the therapists, Tim was spending more than thirty hours per week at table-top tasks, with little time for enjoying simple childhood pleasures. The occasions when Tim refused to cooperate, lashed out, especially with one particular teacher/therapist, were becoming more frequent. After such high hopes for this much lauded therapeutic intervention, we were at an impasse. It was difficult to move forward as Tim was dragging his feet in following the daily schedule, and I was immensely conflicted to see his lack of progress and mounting recalcitrance.

Meanwhile, I had been spending many hours exploring the literature on autism and related methods of treatment. This, combined with Tim's lack of progress helped me look for answers to help Tim based on my growing library of authors in the field, including those on the spectrum. I also began to rely a little more on my own experiences and perceptions, skills in research and as a trainee educational psychologist, and in my parenting of Tim's older siblings. But most importantly I began to trust in a dawning insight that I ought to be guided by Tim as well. Hence the first tentative steps were taken in devising a suitable program based on a supportive environment as well as active participation from Tim himself to set the foundation for his learning. I reasoned that children on the autism spectrum would learn in similar ways as neurotypical children, but due to hypersensitivity, sensations from their body and from the environment may be too intense for comfort. Hence, the learning materials had to take this factor into account. Since children with autism have challenges in *accommodation*, I sought to provide material to fit as closely as possible to Tim's strengths as well as preferred style for *assimilation* to take place. I also needed to utilise Tim's hypersensitivity in all modalities, sight, hearing, olfactory, touch, taste and vestibular (sense of body in space) to set the parameters. The program also needed to be as flexible as possible, for Tim to lead and for me to walk in step with him.

I aimed to cater for his love of music and rhymes, and use his 'strengths' or autistic differences such as his love of watching light patterns, spinning objects, movement, touching different textures and hearing the noise he made with banging objects together. The debacle of the ABA Program helped me as well. Their method of presenting material in a very rigid and uninteresting way did not whet Tim's curiosity. For example, with learning colours, Tim had to pick the red colour card, presented with a distractor card of a different colour when the teacher/therapist said the word 'red'. As children learn by play and creative exploration in addition to instructions, the manipulation of material is essential for a sense of control which would lead to the mapping of the objects into concepts. In learning about colours, for example, I used objects such as red apples or yellow bananas with the gradual introduction of coloured blocks which he could play with. We would also be reading books, and singing and dancing to songs on colour.

I now see this as a crucial stage that I needed to go through to find the courage to be guided by Tim himself. In particular, I was able to see that how our children learn or fail to learn often gives us the most important information for catering to their individual ways of learning. Tim's despondent and rebellious attitude towards ABA drills was his way of telling me that I needed to look for better ways to reach him. I also began to have grave misgivings about the program's premises. There was an overriding assumption that the child's mind was a blank slate to be filled with the required information rigidly imparted by instructors, with the replication of such information forming the basis of learning. The program itself was limited: it focused on remediation of what a child could not do, and, when repeated trials failed to produce the desired results, was unable to offer solutions.

Furthermore, I felt that there was not much respect for the child as a learner. For instance, when Tim did not succeed in giving the correct answer, the instructor would prompt or present the same material in a simplified form as a repetitive drill until the right answer was reached, without helping Tim to understand the reason underlying these answers. Even when the correct answers were given, no further explanations were forthcoming to assist Tim in understanding the underlying principles. The intrinsic satisfaction resulting from the child's mastery of concepts was also overlooked. Instead, *reinforcement* in the form of edible treats (primary reinforcement) and/or high-fives and "awesome, great job" (secondary reinforcement) repeated *ad nauseam* from the instructors were used. It was obvious the tenet, that education should start with our children's strengths and work on ways to engage their curiosity and drive to learn, has very much fallen by the wayside.

In addition, I became enthralled by first hand accounts of autism written by people on the spectrum who give an insider's viewpoint on how autism affected them. I found the autobiographies of Temple Grandin and Donna Williams, two highly intelligent and perceptive authors on the Spectrum, especially illuminating. I was still struggling to deal with Tim's diagnosis of a life-long debilitating disorder without any known medical cure, so the work of these authors came as a refreshing change from the writings of professionals. Their accounts provided me with much needed hope for Tim and his future because these give a different perspective on some of the symptoms of autism. These authors' first hand experiences of their challenges provide insights and explanations for the often baffling behaviours accompanying autism which can be attributed to hypersensitive nervous systems, anxiety, related issues with understanding people and difficulty with language. These authors are obviously able to use their considerable gifts for a unique understanding of the disorder. I also love learning their strategies of coming to terms with autistic challenges and their debilitating effects, especially working with their strengths to become highly qualified and acknowledged professionals in their chosen fields. These courageous and committed autism spokespeople provide me with the necessary impetus to explore other ways to reach Tim.

4

SCALING A SUMMIT

Sarah speaks

I often found myself wondering what kind of life lay ahead for Tim. I could see that chances for an independent and rewarding life were far from certain. However, I was determined to explore the best way forward in terms of treatment and intervention. Still, it was extremely hard to accept that Tim's condition precluded him from living in active and fulfilling ways. My feelings at the time was to forge our path to give him all the necessary support to take his place in the family and later to find a niche in the wider world.

After losing faith in ABA, I took the leap to begin our own brand of educational activities at home for Tim. I wanted to assist him to catch up on different areas of learning with the help of instructors (with a couple of ABA therapists who stayed on with us). We began to incorporate some of the ABA drills which were modified to make these activities as naturalistic and age-appropriate as possible. For instance, the coloured blocks for the sequencing drill were used as the material for Tim to build a house or bridge, which he copied from home-made templates. The ABA picture vocabulary cards were used for a card game of picking up matching pairs. Whenever Tim played this game with me, he would win hands down because of his visual memory strength. There were also songs, rhymes and story books for enacting.

We also investigated other types of programs. We started Tim with Early Intervention at a special setting with a small group of children at the same time as Mainstream Kinder. I sensed it was important for Tim to have experiences in mainstream Kinder with his peers. Not unexpectedly, it was another challenge for him as I watched with trepidation his struggles with grasping things that typically developing children integrated easily.

For example, in the beginning, Tim refused to line up to go to the toilet before morning tea, and when we explored this issue further, we discovered that the noise of the hand dryer used by other children scared him. Luckily, this problem was easily resolved with our team's brainstorming. Tim went to the toilet after the other children finished, and played at the sink afterwards as reinforcement; he had no further issues. On the other hand, when other children participated happily in novel events such as party celebrations or visits from secondary school students who came to spend time as Kinder buddies, Tim found these changes to the routine challenging. No amount of explanation or visual schedules seemed to help and Tim would hum incessantly, or lie down on the floor and cover his ears during such times. Even with the Kinder assistant's and/or the Aide's support, Tim did not easily fit in. However, it was heartening to see the other children accepting Tim, with some of his classmates even seeking his company to take part in activities and during free play.

In the meantime, the severity of Tim's condition led us to investigating other forms of treatment. His father, a pharmacist, is keen to instigate biochemical treatments and when Tim was five he was put on a gluten free, casein free diet which has continued. To ameliorate deficiencies, he also received supplementation of vital minerals, vitamins and other nutrients, as well as probiotics. During the next several years, based on several biomedical models of autism, Tim underwent treatments with an anti-candida regime, the Pfieffer treatment of metallothionein supplementation, Methyl B12 injections, enzyme supplements as well as complementary and alternative medicine including homeopathy, chiropractic, acupuncture, and qigong, in addition to educational and other forms of therapy. The various methods have helped in one way or another to some degree, but it would take some time to come up with definitive ways for Tim to acquire the basic skills that continued to elude him during these early years.

Tim speaks

It is difficult to pinpoint when I actually began to think of myself as being part of the greater world. For as long as I remember, the world consisted of a kaleidoscope of images and other sensations which made me feel very lost, and never fitted into my ways of thinking. People were inexplicable in the things they did and what they wanted from me. Furthermore, with my sensitive nervous system, any exposure to unfamiliar situations or people would catapult me into the dark tunnel of sensory overload where I was continuously bombarded with jarringly loud sounds, intensely bright colours and other sensations that hurt me. After a while, I gradually learned to avoid or get away from things that overwhelmed me by lying on the floor, shutting my eyes and covering my ears. With more and more people who came into my life at this stage, I tried my best to make some sense of the world by working out the routines in our daily activities. In some ways, the drills I had to do were pretty predictable. When the instructor laid out things on the table and said something, I was supposed to give or point to one of those things. Because I couldn't work out the reasons behind these tasks, I did a lot of guess work or learned to read the subtle signs for the answers.

Sarah speaks

It was a positive step that Tim could start mainstream Kinder with his peers. But my heart went out to him. The fundamental and pervasive nature of his sensory difficulties became clearer to me with every obstacle that came along, and these came hard and fast. He found it extremely difficult to process incoming information and almost impossible to integrate the different sensory modes - touch, movement, balance, seeing and hearing. This made planning and implementing any actions immensely challenging. Problems of this nature are common in autism and daunting to confront. It would take me some time to come up with ways to help Tim.

I was slowly becoming aware that Tim's difference led to his early struggles with making sense of his world. Tim sees the world in bits and pieces. This fragmentation proves a huge challenge in grasping how the separate parts fit into the whole. In addition, the problems he has with retrieval of information from memory further contribute to his difficulties. From what he said, Tim has the kind of memory that is not easily accessed, a non-declarative memory. There are two kinds of memory, non-declarative and declarative.[1] The difference between these two types is how amenable they are for conscious recall. Non-declarative memory, like riding a bike, is largely preconscious. This type is not available for recall and can only be triggered. Declarative memory, such as the last time we spoke to a friend, or went to a certain event, is conscious and can be retrieved. But events that most people recall through declarative memory, such as visits to friends, are not available to Tim as his recognition of events is largely triggered by associated sensations or similarity with past experiences. This is a serious impediment and is exacerbated by the fact that retrieval of such memory is dependent on language. This posed another huge problem as he still did not grasp what language was. Getting to understand Tim's differences and how to tailor his learning to these differences began to consume my time and energy, as it was largely uncharted territory. However, I took comfort in the fact that because it is a little explored area, the only prerequisite is a readiness to put aside prior assumptions to allow new information to open up a way for the plan of action.

Tim speaks

I started Kinder at four years of age like many of my neurotypical counterparts. Any new setting is hard for me, and kinder was no exception. It was one huge jumble of overwhelming sensations. Even today, I can still remember all the busyness taking me to sensory overload. The large airy room, replete with bright posters, child-size tables and chairs, with a semi-enclosed space with books and beanbags at one end and a toilet with cubicles at the other, was perpetually busy. The Kinder day started with the 20 odd kids coming into the room, slamming their bags down, then going about different activities which were set out at the tables. Some kids would always be running around laughing with periodic screams. While most parents would be sharing activities with their child, they also made a lot of traffic congestion talking to each other. Drop off and pick up times were totally overwhelming.

After morning tea, we would line up for outside play. I tried to stand at the back of the queue because I found the shuffling, pushing and giggling at the line truly jarring; being jostled unexpectedly would send me off to a panic attack. I also stood back when it was nap time because I hated the scrambling to get our mats and the rush to a select spot or to be closer to friends for our rest in the afternoon. I liked circle time when we sat more or less quietly and the teacher would read a book or talk about different topics. Morning tea-time was also fine as we sat and ate at our table, but sometimes, it could be complete chaos. When I couldn't take it anymore, I would lie down, curled up in the corner of the room near the bookshelves and count the minutes before Mum came for me to go home.

When Mum stayed with me, it was just tolerable, but when she left, even if it was only for a short time, I would feel completely overwhelmed and lost. The other parent who used to stay with her child was Julie, and we soon got to know her and her son Laurence. I remember Laurence being very quiet, he didn't run around, talk to other kids or busy himself with different toys and activities; he stayed beside Julie. It was obvious he could be easily overwhelmed too.

Julie was always friendly and I was drawn to her from the start. Her kindness came across as genuine, without any condescension or discomfort; she didn't patronise me just because I did not talk, behave or play like other children. As time went on, Mum found out that she shared something in common with Julie, they have a child who is different. I have severe autism, but Laurence, although we both have a tendency to sensory overloading, is a highly gifted boy with prodigious talents in diverse areas including music, mathematics, the sciences and chess.

One day, I got thrown off track by some changes to the routine and became very unsettled. I couldn't wait for Mum to come for pick up time. She finally appeared, but instead of taking me home immediately, she started talking to the Aide. I had had enough, and couldn't wait any longer. I decided to make my way to the gate which I managed to slip through when some other children left with their parents. I walked down to our car and found myself at the front of the school. Without warning, commotion hit me as car doors opened and slammed shut, engines growled as cars moved in and out, plus the noise and movement of traffic on the road. It all added up to a total disarray of uncontrollable noise and movement. Mum wasn't there and I was completely overwhelmed; I just didn't know what to do. Suddenly I heard Julie beside me, her voice was very soothing and it calmed me down. I was content to just stand there with her. Pretty soon, a member of staff came and took me back to Mum who was really relieved to see me. Apparently they had been scouring the place looking for me since I went missing, but didn't realise I had gone out the gate. Both Mum and I felt it was our lucky day.

Sarah speaks

What was particularly terrifying about this incident when Tim disappeared from my side, even though it was only for 15 minutes, was how unpredictable this was. Until now he had always remained within safe distance, perhaps lying down in the quiet reading corner while I caught up with the Aide about his day – I didn't for a moment think he would have left the school grounds. He was totally lacking in the necessary skills to fend for himself; he had no speech, no understanding of the situation, and no means to look or call for help. I found it hard to understand that some of the other parents present did not lend a hand, but on thinking it through, I realised that Tim would not go to them because he didn't see anyone he was not comfortable with as a source of help. Julie was the only person at Kinder he could relate to other than the staff or myself, and it was truly fortunate that she was there at the right moment. She told me she thought

Tim looked scared and so she stayed by him until help arrived. Her empathy was a godsend, and I felt that this had come from having to deal with a child who was different. The incident was a wake-up call to be more vigilant, and one of the first which permitted a glimpse of the long and daunting road ahead.

---

1. Tulving, E. (2002). Episodic Memory: From Mind to Brain. *Annual Review of Psychology. 53*: 1–25.

5
ON THE ROAD LESS TRAVELLED

Two roads diverged in a wood, and I,
I took the one less traveled by,
And that has made all the difference.

Robert Frost

Tim speaks

From the very first meeting I have always felt a kinship with Laurence. Like me, he also seemed to find it hard to deal comfortably with the busyness of Kinder. Laurence didn't talk much to anyone, and was always by his Mum, Julie's side. Later on, when we got to know them better, we began to understand that Laurence is also hypersensitive in many ways.

Julie says she could sense Laurence was different from day one. His intense curiosity, alertness and drive to do things made him quite unsettled, but also gave him the impetus to become part of the world on his own terms. Only a few days old, on the day Laurence came home from the hospital, Julie put him on the floor to lie down, and she could see that he was already striving to master this new environment, when, in his struggles, he rolled over. Julie was amazed, but at the same time, concerned that this early mobility reflected a difference in his make-up. It was the start of her journey in understanding and supporting Laurence.

Julie could see that the young Laurence found loud noises and busy places unsettling, and she limited outings with him. As she could sense his passion for learning and mastery when something of interest came along, she also provided him with the necessary opportunities and stimulation. For instance, when Laurence was about three years old, he broke his arm at Kinder when following the example of an older boy climbing a tree. As he was learning guitar at the time, and could not play because of his broken arm, the teacher decided to teach him music theory. Julie felt that the world had opened up for Laurence, as music was a more natural way of self-expression, and his greatest joy at that time was to go to a music shop and read the sheet music. He also asked for the written music when he went to his sister's violin lessons. Laurence was entranced with written music because he could hear what he was reading, and shared with Julie (who herself did not read music) some particularly beautiful pieces. Of course, the world didn't quite understand his gift of music, as exemplified by the staff at the music shop who asked Julie whether Laurence had dirty fingers when he was flipping through the music books.

Because of his differences, Laurence has a hard time adjusting to conventional social expectations, starting with the four year-old Kinder which I also attended. Julie felt that because the staff didn't accept his differences and tried to mold him to behave like the other students, it became a largely negative experience. Attached to a prestigious K to 12 grammar school, the early learning centre had its fair share of aspiring parents and competitive children. When an assessment requested by the school indicated Laurence was highly gifted, extension programs were set up to meet his additional needs. Julie was actually surprised at the assessment results, but thought that this label of 'giftedness' might not serve Laurence's best interest. This was confirmed when the school, in trying to meet Laurence's intellectual needs, made few attempts to meet his other needs. In addition, the other parents were up in arms at the special treatment received by Laurence, and wanted their children to be included. The teacher, lacking the resources to cater for additional programs, was resentful of this extra responsibility. The aftermath of this saga was that Laurence felt pressured and unhappy, and his confidence and engagement with life sagged.

Laurence entered his first chess tournament at five years of age among notable players and has since taken part and won many tournaments, both around Australia and overseas. He was the Australian Under 10 chess champion as well as the Australian Under 12 champion. He was accepted into the Australian National Academy of Music (ANAM), a highly prestigious facility that trains gifted music students at an advanced level on their instruments, and became one of their regular performers. He plays several instruments and successfully obtained his Licenciate of Music (LMus) in piano at the age of 15. He attended high school to do his first VCE subject at the age of ten, at the same school where he did Kinder. Until the age of 14, he undertook VCE and various other subjects including university courses. With the completion of his VCE, he went on to the University of Melbourne to start an undergraduate science course at 15.

Julie felt that in her parenting of a highly gifted child, she has met more than a fair share of difficulty. Because of his differences, the trajectory of development for Laurence is unique and by no means smooth. It had been a steep learning curve for her to understand how his mind works, to make the necessary adjustments and to obtain appropriate support for his learning needs. There were many obstacles in their way, as in a world which does not value diversity, one of the major challenges has been the attitude of others. I sense that Julie is not the kind of parent who would exploit her child's giftedness for her own benefit; she has unreservedly taken on the many challenges of bringing up a gifted child with total commitment and much self-sacrifice. In addition, she has to deal with the reactions from people regarding Laurence, which can be very negative and judgmental.

Most of us see other people through our own lens, and we are always tempted to see the things we want to see and to discard those we find different or incomprehensible. I feel constantly judged because I do things others find strange. For instance, I hum incessantly when I am anxious, I find humming soothing, putting me in touch with my sense of self. It's no different from those who listen to music on their iPod or Walkman. Yet, when I do this in public places like supermarkets or restaurants, people look askance, some try to stare me into silence, some back away or give me a wide berth. I don't think they know what it is like to be bombarded with overwhelming sensations at every turn, or how I need this to tune out. On the other hand, there are some people who say they like my 'singing', I have often been told I have perfect pitch. Then again, this group don't really understand me either, they think it shows how happy I am when I hum. The other thing I do to handle overload is to sit or lie on the floor, and I sometimes need to do this in public places that have lots of unpredictable noise and movement. The range of reactions is interesting, it just freaks some people out, and yet, there have been several kind-hearted folk who would come up and ask if I was feeling okay.

Mum handles my weirdness in public by explaining to people that I have severe autism, and most of the time this works. Without this label, I can imagine that the world can be quite unforgiving. It is not surprising that there are many people who would find Laurence's brilliance disconcerting and even threatening. At Kinder and at school, there were teachers and others who thought that Laurence should fit in and behave like the other students, and they were highly critical of Julie, blaming her parenting for his differences. Closer to home, Julie's parents, siblings and in-laws also never understood Laurence, and objected to his giftedness. For example, one Christmas, Laurence's paternal grandmother was exceedingly rude to him, constantly putting him down, and Julie felt Laurence's pain. Julie has also frequently come across others who attacked her and her son. After a concert given by Laurence, one parent came up and said, "Did you tie him to the piano?" Julie has also been subject to negative comments after successful chess matches by Laurence.

At the other end of the scale, however, Laurence has been surrounded by admirers after his musical performances, whilst Julie has been ignored. She felt overlooked and brushed off, and because Laurence's achievements would not have been possible without her dedicated support, it must have been hurtful. With her encounters with the negativity expressed by family, relatives, friends and the public over the years, Julie has not only been able to examine these reactions to arrive at a better understanding, but also done groundbreaking postgraduate research into envy and giftedness.

Despite the challenges, Julie is adamant that she has been more than compensated by moments of satisfaction, pride and joy. I believe that because she has given so much of herself, she has developed a powerful mindset that enables her to see Laurence's gifts with continual wonder and gratitude. Her wonder increases with Laurence's different paths to learning, his ability to master things based almost purely on his thirst and drive to know, and his tenacity in working out the world on his own terms. Her gratitude derives from the opportunities provided as a parent to understand and know another human being whose differences pose huge challenges at comprehension, and to be intimately involved with the development and realisation of his enormous potential. Of course, to walk a different path takes immense courage, perseverance and resilience, courage to acknowledge, accept and embrace differences, perseverance in the face of difficulties and the ability to get up again from the falls and knock backs. These qualities Julie has in abundance.

Julie said the relationship between Laurence and herself can be summed up in one word: love. I know from my own experience that if I did not have the unconditional acceptance of my Mum's love for me, I would not be able to be the person that I am. I would lack the courage and persistence to explore the labyrinth of my own inner world and those of others around me, and my drive to be more self- aware, to delve into deeper and darker thoughts and emotions would suffer. I would not be able to create and tell my story and those of others with the same degree of openness and freedom. In short, I would be unable to realise my strengths, be who I want to be and live more meaningfully. It is a tribute to Julie's love in her uncompromising efforts to provide Laurence with the support and opportunities he needed in his early years, that he has been able to succeed and make significant contributions to his fields of interests and live a rewarding and satisfying life.

∼

Sarah speaks

I am also grateful that Julie helped in many other ways. Her warmth and friendship were the highlight of our time at kinder and considerably eased our involvement within the Kinder community. Julie's confirmation that she also felt out of place because of Laurence's differences was reassuring. I began to look at Tim with new eyes, and his inability to follow in the footsteps of his peers became less of a sore point, calling for understanding and not stigmatisation or modification. I could see that Laurence, too, was sensitive to the Kinder environment and did not always enjoy Kinder because of his unique development, a mind that was already way ahead of most of his age peers. In following similar but unique paths with our sons, Julie's acceptance of differences provided the impetus to use challenges as a springboard for understanding my child in order to bring out his potential.

6

IF FISHES HAD TO CLIMB TREES (DOORS TO LEARNING)

> *Everybody is a genius. But if you judge a fish by its ability to climb a tree, it will live its whole life believing that it is stupid.*
>
> Einstein

Tim speaks

I enjoyed some of the things I did at Kinder. After getting used to the barrage of unceasing sound, movement and busyness, some of the activities revolving around painting, playdough, sand and water, and eating our morning tea became more familiar and predictable. Whenever I was comfortably engaged in these activities, I saw that other people seemed happy and I could more or less blend in. The kids were also more interesting to watch than the adults around me who mostly seemed to want something out of me which I couldn't produce. Some of my Kinder classmates were nice to me, they included me in their games and showed me what to do. One of their favourite activities was in the outside sandpit where the kids would collect leaves and bark and put these into the child-sized pots and pans, adding sand and water to stir and pretend to make a meal. Whenever I was feeling less anxious, I also collected leaves with them. Because their cooking game made no sense to me, I preferred to put the ingredients into the puddles I made in the sand pit. I loved water and the feel of sand on my hands, and could spend all my time at Kinder playing this game without any fear of overload from the chatter, clatter and laughter of those around me.

But there were other gains too during this year. For as long as I was aware of people it had been a huge struggle in trying to make sense of them and the sounds they made. Their constant babble was just noise without meaning, until this year; this was when I finally got the notion that the sounds people made stood for things. This realisation followed many hours of intensive interventional sessions in ABA, speech therapy and other programs. I remember a particular drill, in which the teacher or therapist held out two toys, a dog and a ball, I had to point to the right object when she gave me the word, 'dog' or 'ball'. We did the drill many times every day. One day I suddenly realised that the word had to mean the thing held out, and also that the same label is the name attached to the object, which would always stay the same. This realisation took three months after hundreds of trials but I was able to pass the drill thereafter. I felt I had scaled a summit. It turned out to be only one of the foothills, of course. But from this insight, understanding the connection between language and the things they stood for, helped me begin to see the world in a new way. Activities, routines and people began to make more sense. It gave me the impetus to keep going.

∽

Sarah speaks

Chris, Tim's speech therapist, worked largely at this time on eliciting sounds from Tim. Chris used a method of saying the initial or end sounds of consonants, vowels or combinations, which Tim had to mimic. For better results, Chris used physical prompting by shaping his lips and parts of his jaw in conjunction with activities Tim enjoyed, including pop-up toys, to keep his momentum going. Later, visual prompts were added with pictures as cues for the sounds, a method known as Nuffield. However, despite intensive efforts, Tim never went past the stage of repeating sounds during the sessions. Speech therapy had not brought about spontaneous words or utterances in other more natural settings. In addition, the huge challenges Tim had with verbal instructions gave the impression that whatever understanding of the world he formulated, language did not play a significant part.

Chris, as well as later speech pathologists we employed during Tim's primary school years, Anna, and Susanne (who worked for some time with Rosemary Crossley[1]), also introduced us to the Picture Exchange Communication System (PECS) and 'communication temptations'. These are popular methods to help the child in understanding communication and language use. For example, the adult would hold out some treat – a jelly bean, a favourite toy or some other communication temptation – and the child has to take the pictures for 'I want' and 'jelly bean'/'toy' and give these to the adult before receiving the treat. The adult also describes to the child in words what is occurring. For some time, we used these programs diligently with Tim, carrying a communication book with all the icons of pictures or photos categorised into familiar food, activities, people and so on. Tim's progress was slow; he always needed to be prompted to use the communication book and he did not or was unable to initiate any communication on his own. His delays in all areas were further confirmed in a psychological assessment when he was approximately five. His developmental age was just over two years, with the range between one and a half to three years. It was disheartening as well as distressing for us to watch his struggles in acquiring basic concepts and life skills.

I kept thinking that there must be a way to reach Tim, but I had no idea where to start. Both at home and at other settings, Tim had not been able to keep pace with the intensive efforts helping him to learn. At the time, it did not occur to me that I should start by looking at Tim's responses to ABA drills, speech therapy as well as his day-to-day behaviour to pick up the clues on how his mind worked. It took me quite some time to see the obvious; that Tim's responses, although unsuccessful with the programs he was being put through, contained vital information on his unique learning needs and cognitive style. What I needed was a shift in perception, and this took time because we had been so focused on getting successful performance. This in turn translated into an assumption that Tim was somehow 'uneducable'.

For example, Tim had no problems with ABA drills that involved matching pictures/photos to similar sets within the same category. On the other hand, Tim had difficulty with other drills in the use of coloured blocks to form a repeating pattern. He was unable to figure out what to do when the initial blocks were laid down with the verbal instructions, "do the same". However, when the required sequence was placed in front of him, Tim could use more blocks to match the order set out by this array and pass the drill. I began to see that the primary component of the way Tim sees the world is visual. His responses also indicated that Tim did have the concepts for **same, similar** and **different**. Chris, our speech pathologist who had worked with Tim from the age of three, agreed, and said that children like Tim tended to pick up reading first before speech.

If language, somehow, appeared foreign, Tim had no trouble

with music. He would hum all day long. Tim modified songs he heard, as well as composed his own tunes with chords, and I could see that he was using music instead of language for expression. I was also able to discern that the types of tune and tone of Tim's humming gave an indication of his moods. His hummed tunes left me in no doubt that Tim was also using music to convey feelings. There were specific tunes for joy, sadness, fear, anger and even complex emotions. I did not have training in music, but was told by a music therapist at Early Intervention that Tim has perfect pitch.

When I combined all that I learned from my observations, I could see that Tim would respond best to learning material with strong visual components, an emphasis on music and stepwise expansion of familiar activities and concepts that he had mastered. I also knew that I had to act promptly, because, at the early age of five, Tim had already developed a defiant and defeatist attitude to learning. There was no time to lose, as the years of formal schooling would be fast approaching. I also needed to keep an open mind, to be aware of Tim's strengths, and what he liked doing to develop programs on what he enjoyed. Through a period of trial and error, I began to develop assorted strategies to support his unique learning style through appropriate material, to keep Tim's interest alive, and to engage him in further exploration of his world and understanding of people.

Children on the spectrum are known to have difficulty with meaning. Noam Chomsky proposes that all children have an innate Language Acquisition Device (LAD) that gives them the specific capability to understand (receptive) and the ability to speak (expressive) their mother tongue[2]. I have often wondered whether there is also an innate meaning acquisition device (MAD) in all children. My challenge, then, was to help Tim make sense of the world in terms of how most people see it, which would become the cornerstone for the pathways to reach him.

One of the most obvious ways to entice Tim to pay attention to the world was to reinforce how our daily activities fit into our lives. For example, I made books with photos of Tim to illustrate all the activities we did, especially the ones he enjoyed most, including train rides, going to the beach, rowing on the river, picnicking at the park, or eating at restaurants. After we read the books, we would do word games such as pairing up photos with words. We role-played some extra exciting activities both before and after they occurred, including meeting up with friends, going to a birthday party, visits to the musical theatre or going on holiday. It worked. Tim loved poring over the pictures in these homemade books. Invariably, after a visit to the beach, or the swimming pool, he would locate the relevant book and read this with me. Role-playing was also fun for both of us, with setting out morning tea in picnic ware and eating on the picnic rug in the lounge room.

Gradually, I was also able to see how Tim's earlier difficulties with ABA were due to challenges with understanding language. His difficulty appeared to center around following instructions which had become the major stumbling block in learning. I eventually came to the conclusion that Tim had not done well with ABA drills because he failed to see that people use language to communicate thoughts or make requests. As the instructions were all spoken, Tim failed to grasp what he was expected to do. Instead, he learned to read the subtle cues of the instructors to pick the correct answers. This was a major breakthrough in my understanding of Tim and I was encouraged to keep looking for other ways that cater to his differences in exploring the world with him.

Tim speaks

It was Mum who gave me a better method of making sense of language. Our family had always read books, and when I was about six years old, Mum started to make books about our activities. She took photos of our daily routines, including going shopping, to the library, Kinder, playground, swimming pool, preparing breakfast, lunch or dinner, or going to visit my Grandpa, her dad. I also got books on special occasions, train rides, going for a picnic at the park, or a birthday party. I loved the ones on my swimming lessons the best, and would retrieve them and go over these endlessly. When I got too jumpy, looking at these books gave me a sense of control. We not only read these books together, but Mum also made word games out of them. For instance, with the activities I loved most, train rides or swimming, she wrote the key words on cards which I then placed against the photos. My strength in visual and memory skills enabled me to pair the words people used when they spoke with the scenes they represented. Finally I began to understand what they were saying. This became my way of getting meaning out of language around the age of seven.

After I learned to grasp some preliminary ideas from stories that Mum read, I was able to see how the world was viewed from the standpoint of the characters. I then started to use these viewpoints to make sense of my family and other people. For instance, one of the earlier books was called *The 27th Annual African Hippopotamus Race* [3], about a lovable hippo who wanted to race in the swimming carnival held annually at the Zambezi River. This unlikely hero was young and inexperienced but very determined and put in lots of practice. When the big day came for the race, his measurement and weight were recorded but came nowhere near the size or weight of the race favourites. However, he surprised everyone including himself by doing his best and winning. I loved the book and really took the story to heart. In making sense of the story, I began to understand why people wanted to achieve their goals and were prepared to put in the effort to win.

These early attempts to understand people also gave me an incentive to make up my own stories with make-believe characters and plots. For a time, the stories in my head provided a commentary that I was able to compare with what I was observing in real life. The sense of control of the social world began to come as I incorporated these stories more instinctively to work out what drives people's behaviour. This was another summit, but the gulf between other people and myself would take a long time to bridge. I still felt like I was from a different planet.

---

1. Director of DEAL Communication Centre who later played a large part in Tim's communication endeavours.
2. Noam Chomsky is an Institute Professor and professor of linguistics emeritus at MIT, widely known as the father of modern linguistics, a philosopher, prolific author, and globally influential political activist. | MIT150 | Massachusetts Institute of Technology 150th anniversary". mit150.mit.edu. Archived from the original on November 16, 2015. Retrieved 2015-10-24.
3. Lurie, Morris, (1989) *The 27th Annual African Hippopotamus Race*. UK: Simon & Schuster.

7
FINDING THE WAY THROUGH THE MAZE

Sarah speaks

While I was gleaning how Tim's mind works and how he learnt, I devoured the books of other individuals on the Spectrum. I discovered that Temple Grandin[1], like Tim, is a visual thinker. She uses a process of translating words into visual information for comprehension. This method was, I discovered later, also used by Tim to finally be able to understand language. When Tim was more confident in his use of language, he began to go through the reverse process of mapping visual thinking into words for typing, the communication method which he picked up later.

Apart from her amazing visual spatial skills, I was also fascinated by Temple Grandin's memory. Neurologist Oliver Sacks, who has given the world various perspectives from minds which function differently, interviewed and wrote up her story.[2] He relates an incident which illustrates how Temple Grandin's memory works. He got lost on his way to see her at Colorado State University and phoned her to ask for directions. Temple repeated the directions in entirety, "in virtually the same words", not from the point where Sacks was lost, and he speculated that these were held in Temple's mind, in a fixed 'program' that could not be separated into component parts. I was beginning to understand a little more of how Tim's mind works, and felt that memory in autism must be a very different process. While most people organise their personal memory in terms of what is important to them, retaining key elements and discarding others, there seemed to be no such organising framework with people on the spectrum. With the latter, memory appears to be an objective visual rendering of what happened and can be recalled in minute details but without the meaning most neurotypicals give to experiences in terms of emotional significance.

Tim speaks

Afterwards, when I was able to talk to Mum using Partner Assisted Typing, I tried to explain that my process of gaining understanding of sensory data takes several steps. Initially, the world comes into my head as raw sensations which don't mean much to me. For instance, when watching other Kinder kids in the playground, I could see their activities as separate bits of raw data which blended into the rest of the sensory input I was getting, the fresh air in my face, the crunch of gravel at my feet, the chatter and laughter from kids, etc. Then, I would begin to work out these sensations in terms of a routine or sequence. Slowly, the picture emerged according to the context: who (that girl with long blond hair who lined up with me to go outside), what (she banged all the pots and pans together to look for some container), how (and put the container under the tap to fill it up). These visual images would stir up other experiences of water play, with which I could then compare. Once the whole sequence was repeated with time, I began to form a more comprehensive picture of what my classmate was doing. When we went outside during morning tea break, I would be able to see that the kids would be doing similar kinds of actions with an end goal, getting water for playing at cooking or making a moat in the sandpit. Using this method, I could attach meaning to the separate sensations and my own observations.

After working on the raw sensations and images to put them into the context of routine activities, I began, after much effort, to acquire some means for understanding the world. However, this was sometimes a hit and miss affair as I could be completely thrown off by a change in routine. For instance, when I was put into the car in the morning, I could now see that Mum used a certain route that took us to Kinder by the landmarks we progressively passed. As Kinder had become more predictable, I worked out what lay ahead and so could prepare myself for what to expect for the rest of the day. On some days, however, Mum would take a different route, maybe drop one of my sibs off to school first before the others for an early morning activity. Because of this change in routine, I would be thrown off track, failing to work out what I would be facing. Since I was not able to communicate my distress, I would end up kicking and screaming when we finally made our way to Kinder. In time, Mum figured out that the best way to keep me calm would be to take the same route no matter what.

～

Sarah speaks

Tim's learning trajectory diverged in many ways from his neurotypical peers and I had to relinquish all my preconceived ideas to be able to understand and assist him. It is quite a different process with typically developing children, who have an almost instinctive feel for the meaning of events based on personal likes or dislikes, gleaned from a personal perspective in seeing the world. In autism, in the case of Tim, the meaning of events is contextual, and personal meaning is derived from context as a second stage result. This process for meaning to emerge in context to become personally significant became the mechanism that helped Tim to arrive at an understanding of mathematical concepts. This mechanism also illustrates how the learning approaches used by ABA drills on counting with one to one correspondence as discrete and separate trials were unsuitable to Tim's learning needs as reflected in his dismal performance.

∼

Tim speaks

In the early days, to understand things, I needed to see the larger picture and with this, fit the separate pieces into the whole. For example, with an event, I had to take in each and every aspect, such as the physical details of the setting, time, place and the people involved. I formed a mental picture by laboriously combining all these elements and then using this for comparison with similar events from memory. Only then would the significance of the event gradually emerge and the different aspects fall into place within the overall scheme. Using this framework, the relationships of the various parts could then be teased out in relation to the whole picture. Neurotypicals seem to be able to do this in a blink of an eye, but for me it is a consciously driven, step-by-step process, and this difficulty made me think that somehow I always fell short of the mark.

The way things were taught in ABA was to break up the whole into separate parts and to present these parts singly and in isolation. Without the bigger picture, understanding the discrete bits split from the whole was extremely difficult. For example, with ABA maths, I was able to rote count to twenty, but I never understood the idea of numbers and so had huge trouble with the drills. When the ABA therapist asked, say, "give me five", I was supposed to give her the required counters out of a pile, but I would just keep going, counting aloud the string of numbers I rote learned. Nothing worked, even with modifications to the drills to make them more interesting like putting the counters into slots which I enjoyed, or matching the counters to the printed numbers. Once again I felt I must be stupid because these things seemed so easy and obvious to other people.

I got really discouraged with trying to learn, but luckily, Mum started to take my learning in another direction. For example, with counting, one of the things she used was a large chart, with the numbers one to ten in the first row. Underneath this row was another row with detachable matching cards of one to ten. A third row was left blank. When we counted things, she would give me the number cards to put under the first row, then she would put out the required number of treats in the third row, small pieces of chips or raisins which I was able to eat afterwards. This game was repeated many times, in combination with other number activities. I remember vividly the number songs we sang, including "Three jellyfish", "Five little speckled frogs" and my favorite, "Ten green bottles sitting on the wall". As we sang, I was allowed to blow the paper cutouts of these objects off the bannister, which I enjoyed.

All the activities helped, but I think the one that cinched my grasp of numbers was a 'staircase' made from my brother's pre-loved Lego blocks, with the number represented by its corresponding blocks. Mum showed me how to finger-walk up or down the Lego stairs, depending on whether we were counting forward or backward. In addition, we would count aloud the steps as we went up or down the stairs at home, and gradually, I began to form a picture of an imaginary staircase with numbered steps, going skyward, a stairway to heaven. Then the realisation came one day, when I was about six, of a line consisting of numbers starting from 'one' that kept going, stretching longer and longer as the numbers grew larger. This image helped me make sense of all the activities and the songs where number words were used to represent things you could count with a number line that kept track of how many. Additions and subtractions came easily because using the image of the Lego stair, for example, in adding five to seven, I mentally projected my finger to walk from step number five forward seven steps to step number twelve. Subtraction meant going the other way, down instead of up. So I could see that if we had four tickets to the movies, with our family of six, two people would miss out. Soon afterwards, with the image of a number line, I was able to grasp negative numbers stretching the other way, with zero as the point of reference.

Once I understood the concept of numbers, it was pure joy to start playing number games. Mum made more material for mastering mathematical operations. With multiplication, it was easy to visualise counting in groups, for example, four times four is counting all the legs in four tables, five by five is all the fingers in five hands with five fingers each. Division was splitting a large number into groups, say nineteen divided by three is eighteen separate clover leaves into six clusters of clover, with one left over. Because I was very visual, looking at the numbers and applying these simple rules conjured up images of the objects with the accompanying answers. In a matter of weeks, I was doing more interesting things. Fractions and percentages were like dividing up the whole into equal parts, no huge problem when I imagined cutting up cakes/pies or breaking up squares of a chocolate block. With algebra, Mum made a scale, similar to a visual aid from Montessori that allowed you to balance the weights hung on each side. With the abundance of the patterns around us, panels of buildings or bridges, I was introduced to the relationships within their forms through geometry and trigonometry. Squares, cubes and corresponding roots, pi, and other constants were also things you could work out using shapes. Pretty soon, however, we ran out of more things to do because Mum said that was the extent of the maths she knew.

Sarah speaks

Tim was around seven years old when several notable occurrences alerted me to his dawning understanding of language. Firstly, during our time spent on reading home-made and other books, singing popular songs which were also made into books with pictures for the lyrics, and miming and acting out stories, Tim started to become more engaged and to participate more in these activities. In addition, he began to show interest in family routines and outings as well as conversations. I remember that yawning or laughing, a contagious response in typically developing children, did not occur with Tim, yet more than once, he was laughing at some joke or funny event recounted by one of us which previously he had not done. There was a memorable incident during this time when Tim, his sisters and I came back from our shopping trip one day, and his sisters noted that Tim was very quiet. We soon found out why, he was sitting out of sight on the sofa steadily eating an entire chocolate bar while the rest of us were putting away the groceries. When his sisters told their Dad about Tim's latest escapade at dinner, Tim actually looked sheepish.

The breakthrough in maths was even more dramatic. When Tim was around eight, he worked with a support worker, Lauren, both at home and in school as his Aide. One day, I was excited by eager news from Lauren who told me that in the home session,

Tim had just been giving her the right answers to sums such as 54 +3 (Tim had been able to speak single word utterances including numbers). Although we had tried to move Tim from simple number games to maths operations, it was still hard to tell how much he understood. Just in case, I gave him several sums on the spot to which Tim was again able to provide the right answers. I was overjoyed that the strategies we were using had worked.

What amazed me even more in the ensuing weeks was how fast Tim picked up more advanced mathematical concepts. These included the four operations with large numbers and different bases (e.g. base 6, a Montessori maths activity), fractions, decimals, algebra, geometry, trigonometry and so on. Tim also never needed to revise learned material; once he got something, he was able to use these concepts in other applications himself. For instance, once he could multiply and divide, he was able to work out areas and volumes of shapes, distances with speed and time, or equivalent fractions to find out what was larger or smaller.

By this time, I was unsure of how to proceed, as I rote-learned a lot of maths at school, and was never confident enough to tackle more than the basics of exponential, logarithm or calculus. I began to augment my meagre store of maths knowledge by reading maths books to Tim. One of our favourite was the *Phantom Tollbooth*[3], in which word play and maths concepts are cleverly juxtaposed in an adventure story, but the contents of these were soon absorbed and surpassed. Hence we levelled out, more or less, with looking for interesting patterns around us, like the arrangements of leaves and pine cones in working out Fibonacci numbers, and in how geometric figures in buildings or bridges give shape to and form their basic structures. Later on, when Tim was in upper primary school, he sat in on the tutorials of his second sister in Year 11 maths with her tutor, a maths-science teacher. However, because I could not understand much of what was going on, it was difficult to support Tim by devising the necessary material to dovetail to his learning needs for the more challenging work.

---

1. Grandin, Temple (1995). *Thinking in Pictures*. NY: Random House.
2. Sacks, O., (1995). *An Anthropologist from Mars: Seven Paradoxical Tales*, NY: Picador.

    Oliver Sacks also claims that "people with Asperger's syndrome can tell us of their experiences, their inner feelings and states, whereas those with classical autism cannot. With classical autism, there is no "window," and we can only infer. With Asperger's syndrome there is self-consciousness and at least some power to introspect and report." (1993, A Neurologist's Notebook, *The New Yorker*, December 27 Issue). Tim's mind has always been a close door until he found a method of communication via Partner Assisted Typing (PAT) which will be the topic of chapter 10.
3. Juster Norton (1961). *The Phantom Tollbooth*. NY: Random House.

8
AGAINST THE ODDS

Tim speaks

The start of school must be daunting for all five year-olds, but despite my gains, the transition to Special School was earth-shattering for me. In addition to handling my own internal chaos, I had to deal with the external pressure to follow routines, as well as to conform by acting more or less in socially acceptable ways. Within the physical boundaries of classrooms and special purpose rooms, enclosed playgrounds, fences and gates that only opened by releasing a knob at the top, there were additionally some students who would run amok, scream, tantrum, or even hit and bite. The unpredictable and at times even threatening situations were all too real for non-speaking children like me, and all I could do was to try and block out the external world by covering my ears and lying on the floor.

On a recommendation from my speech pathologist, Chris, I started Special School three weeks before I turned six, and was put into one of the two Prep classes. There were five of us, and I was the only non-speaking kid. Educationally speaking, Special

School education was a largely nondescript experience, as I had already mastered most of the programs in my intensive home program, Kinder and other special classes. I remember thinking that I would like to talk but just could not seem to manage it.

Mum's expectation was that I would be integrated into mainstream primary school, but the staff there thought I wasn't ready and needed time at Special School first, so I didn't go into the integration program organised with the nearby primary school until later in the year in Term 3. I was confused by the bigger class with unfamiliar adults and children in addition to our Special School class, and I often lay down on the floor during floor time.

I definitely did not make the grade, and there was pressure from our Special School teacher on Mum to withdraw me from the integration program. I joined the other Prep class when my class went for integration. So there was segregation on top of being in a segregated setting, as the other class I joined didn't get to go to the local primary school for integration. I didn't really mind as I found that there were boys in the other class who didn't talk either, I didn't feel out of place.

By the time I started formal education and struggled with the school setting, the idea and practice of integration and inclusion of special needs students in mainstream classrooms had been around for some time. Integration has legal connotations, and its origins came hand in hand with the civil rights/racial desegregation movements of the 1960s in the United States. In educational terms, placing children with disability from segregated settings such as withdrawal programs, self-contained classrooms, special schools, or institutions, into regular classrooms became the benchmark for forward thinking educators. However, academic and social integration would take time in coming. Inclusion is based on the philosophy that all students with disabilities have a right to be included with their peers in mainstream settings and programs. Inclusion represents the ideal of educating each child to maximise his/her potential. Inclusion requires putting in the necessary support services for children with special needs, with the only stipulation that they will benefit from being in the class, irrespective of whether or not they can keep up with the other students.[1] My experience with primary school turned out to be a lesson on how much work still needed to be done to achieve these ideals.

Mum decided to take matters into her own hands. She found out about an integration program from the grapevine. The mother of another boy, Salil, who was a couple of years ahead of me, told Mum about D Primary School, which was known for running an innovative inclusion program. Like me, Salil is also nonverbal, and was considered poor material for the integration program run by the Special School. Salil's father is a lawyer, and after a period of negotiation with the Special School and D Primary, Salil was able to attend D Primary School.

When Mum spoke to the Special School administration about my integration at D Primary, she met with considerable resistance as they deemed that I was not ready. D Primary School was unable to proceed with my part-time enrolment because the Special School was dragging its feet. Finally, after several meetings and Mum's deliberate lobbying of the Special School teaching staff, who vouched for my good conduct, I obtained permission to join in the inclusion program for half a day per week in the final term. After a few weeks of adjustment to my new environment, I settled into mainstream primary school. This arrangement continued for another six months until Mum thought I should spend more time in mainstream school and requested another half day of inclusion. It was a repeat of her past negotiation as we again came up against enormous resistance from the Special School.

It was around this time that Mum got wind from Salil's parents that they were planning to move him from Special School into full time inclusion at D Primary School. Mum also learned that Salil's lawyer father had to use all his advocacy skills to fight tooth and nail to get their son into full time inclusion. According to Salil's parents, special schools resisted losing their students because the student's Government funding went with them when they left. Full time inclusion was always Mum's goal, but she feared that she did not have the tenacity nor the negotiation skills to fight for my right to be fully integrated. When she came to school as a volunteer helper Mum could see that I was spending a lot of time in class lying on the floor with my hands on my ears, and because of an incident when I was bitten by another classmate, Mum came up with a creative solution. She contacted a primary school in the country that was willing to take me full time, and the two of us left Melbourne and the family to spend four days of the week in the country school about 100 kilometers from home where I attended Grade 2.

It was a tough decision for Mum and of course, for the rest of the family. Mum had to organise the week in advance, get the housework and shopping done, meals prepared and other tasks. My brother was at Uni, but my elder sister was in Year 11, and taking two Year 12 subjects, and my second sister had just started high school. Mum asked people to drive my two sisters to school, but they took public transport back. My sisters really missed not having Mum around, and it was especially difficult for my elder sister to take on additional household responsibility when she already had a full plate. It was definitely not easy for me either. Like a fish out of water, I hated being away from home and my familiar routines. Because I found it difficult to take in different expectations and requirements, I failed to follow instructions or sit still. I would lie on the floor, hide in the locker room, or run out of class into the playground when it was class time. Even when it was play-time, I did not behave well outside either; I hit out at other children, took food from them, or ran off where I wasn't supposed to go. The Aide, who was relatively inexperienced with special needs children, didn't get far with me. Mum got complaints from the teachers, other staff and parents, and had to take me home early. She also found it hard to divide her time between the two homes and to organise different things for me to do in the country after school, which I attended less and less because of my errant behaviour. Luckily, after one term, Mum managed to persuade D Primary School to take me back as a full time student, so we were able to come home to family and familiar surroundings again.

When I was in primary school, changes in routine upset me because they threw my notions of anticipated events into disarray and I would be at a total loss. So if there was computer class on Wednesday in the library, and we were suddenly told that the library would be used for a talk and we would have a room change and couldn't do computer, I would get utterly confused and inexorably, panic would set in. I was most fortunate to have a fabulous Aide working mainly with me from Grade 3 to 6, who not only anticipated my anxiety about any changes but was also able to make good use of the schedule board to explain things to me, otherwise, I would get disoriented to the point of being out of action for the rest of the day.

In Grades 1 and 2 at D Primary School, we had a class called Perceptual Motor Program (PMP). We kids would form groups of about five and line up as a group in front of the equipment. There were usually about six or seven different activities including jumping on hoops on the floor, throwing beanbags into a bucket, crawling through a tunnel, skipping, climbing and throwing and catching basketballs. When the teacher gave a signal, usually by blowing a whistle, the whole group would move on to the next equipment. At first, I kept running around the gym with the Aide in tow, finding everything crazy and chaotic. The chatter and noise the kids made, the different groups on various physical activities calling for specific skills, the milling around the equipment waiting for your turn, and the piercing whistle when you had just warmed up, and then had to move off, all these things combined to make PMP classes totally incomprehensible and overwhelming.

But about three quarters of the way through the year, I found there was a method to this madness. The kids usually chose or got chosen by their own friendship groups and I would usually hang out with the same group of kids. Although the equipment might be moved to different spots, there was an order to the activities, with climbing usually to the rear near the back wall, and the beanbags and basketball games on the opposite side of the climbing frame. Gradually, I got the hang of things and started to participate with the help of the Aide and the kids in my group. Once I understood what was expected of me, I was even able to enjoy myself.

I was pleased to be in D primary but that didn't resolve my constant feelings of overwhelm and confusion. I was often overloaded by the constant hum of activities in and out of class, posters, art and other work hanging riotously from walls and ceilings demanding attention, and open playgrounds inundated with the sounds of running feet, chatter, laughter and jostling bodies. Thankfully, with the support of Aides, teachers and classmates, I was eventually able to adjust, to become part of the class, engage in group work with other kids and take part in specialist classes and activities.

The next few years brought a relatively calm and productive time at D Primary School where I attended full time. Though struggling with the inevitable overload associated with the demands of a bigger school, larger classes, diverse activities with specialist teachers and different school routines, I was supported by a great team of Aides in an inclusive milieu. I am forever grateful to Donna, my fantastic Aide, who has been absolutely professional and dedicated to the needs of her young charges with special needs. I was extremely lucky that out of a group of about 15 integration students, I won the lottery with Donna. She came to D Primary School when I was in Grade 3, just returning to Melbourne after spending years working in early intervention in Western Australia. Without her, I would not be able to participate as much as I did at school.

Donna's facilitation enabled me to access many of the school programs both in and out of the classroom. I did the same work as the rest of the grade as Donna would modify the material for me by enlarging print outs, setting out the sequences of instructions more clearly, or producing visual cues with diagrams/photos where necessary. I took part in music, dance, drama, PE, excursions and school camps. Mum came as a volunteer helper for my Arts, Chinese (Language Other Than English) and swimming classes. There was a team of support workers who took turns with our supervision in the playground. Donna understood my needs very well. In her creation of the wide range of material, I could work more independently, and with her assistance in and out of class with specialist programs, I took part in all the things that my class did. Some of the highlights included the annual camp, sleeping in a dorm with my friends, activities like boat building, archery and nature walks at night.

The school dance night was another memorable event, where we dressed up in formal gear and danced to an appreciative audience of staff and families, in the hall that was transformed into a dance floor by the ambience of disco lights and music.

Donna's approach dovetailed with what Mum did with me at home, and I was able to translate what I learned at home to school and vice versa. Although I could see a correspondence between what I was learning at home and at school, I still found the world around me extremely difficult to understand because people rely on speech almost exclusively.

Sarah speaks

Our home-based program provided Tim with the necessary resources to grasp language, number and other concepts, as well as the meaning of routines, activities and events. His world also expanded with his incremental understanding. Targeting and fine-tuning the precise ways for Tim's learning were laborious, time consuming and painstaking. However, once he had picked up the crucial concepts, he began to use these as stepping stones for further learning, and was able to make progress in leaps and bounds. For instance, when he finally understood language, around the age of seven, Tim became interested in word play, and took delight in how a sentence can have a range of meaning just by the change of a single word, for instance, give in, give up, give way, give away, give off can all be used in similarly constructed sentences to mean different things. A recent example as illustration; a lady in his wonderful support network commented on some artwork he did with my facilitation. She complimented Tim on his work and told him that one day, she could say she knew Tim before he became famous. Tim typed in response, "I don't know about being famous, but if I were infamous, you can say you knew me before you wished you didn't." Tim also took great delight in collecting idioms and metaphors, like other children collect swap cards, and spent pleasurable moments in deciphering their meaning.

We also spent enjoyable hours going through poetry and musical lyrics as I discovered that Tim loves rhythm and rhyme. Once Tim had grasped the essentials of language, he became entranced with the cadence, rhythm and vivid imagery of language, and derived much enjoyment from books such as *We're Going on a Bear Hunt*[2] as well as *Twelfth Night*[3] at Grade 5, with memorable lines such as "I hear music dying with a dying fall." (*Twelfth Night* was his first introduction to the Bard via a comic book rendition I was able to get hold of). But for all his gains, Tim remained non-vocal and still had no means of using expressive language.

∼

Tim speaks

Grade 3 was a milestone; again, we owed much to the parent grapevine. Julianna, the mother of Joshua, who was a couple of years ahead of me at Special School, told Mum that Josh had learned to type with support at the DEAL Communication Centre (DEAL stood for Dignity, Education, Advocacy and Language), run by Rosemary Crossley. Mum had heard of Rosemary at University years ago, when she read the book *Annie's Coming Out*[4] and had been inspired by the story of Anne McDonald, then in an institution for the severely disabled and deemed to be intellectually extremely low functioning. Thanks to Rosemary's assistance and advocacy, in a celebrated case, Annie was able to leave this institution and become integrated into the community.

Mum couldn't wait to meet Rosemary in person and to learn

a method of expressive dialogic communication for her son.

---

1. www.inclusionbc.org/our-priority-areas/inclusive-education/history-inclusive-education
2. Rosen, M. (1989). *We're going on a bear hunt*. UK: Walker Books.
3. Shakespeare, W. (2004). Elizabeth Story, (ed.) *Twelfth night, or, What you will* (Updated ed.). Cambridge: Cambridge University Press.
4. Crossley, R. and McDonald, A. (1980). *Annie's Coming Out*. Melbourne: Penquin Books Australia.

9
UNCOMMON COURAGE

Tim speaks

Just before we went to DEAL there was an incident that seared itself into my memory. The school psychologist came to our school to do an assessment on me. I still remember every detail in her office when she asked Mum to come in for a feedback. She was angular and thin, wore spectacles, and her eyes were pale with no hint of any emotions. She began by checking my responses on the assessment done a couple of weeks earlier, and without any preamble, told Mum that I was severely autistic and intellectually disabled.[1] What I felt then would more than make up for the psychologist's lack of emotions. It was anger. No, it was rage, but also, a huge sadness that almost suffocated me. Although I had always known that I was different, I felt my world disintegrating with her verdict, 'guilty', and the sentence, 'will never amount to anything'.

What was even worse was that the psychologist had made her pronouncement right in front of me, *as if* I was unable to understand anything she said, *as if* I did not have the capacity to understand things of importance, *as if* I was a lesser human being. Being labeled and dismissed was especially painful because of all the work that I had put into the remediation and intervention programs with the hope of getting better.

However, all dark clouds have a silver lining. Not long after the psychologist's visit, Mum and I went to our appointment at DEAL Communication Centre, our first visit which I will never forget. It was the first time we met Rosemary Crossley, the director who had made such an enormous contribution to bringing viable means of augmentative and alternative communication (AAC) to those with little or no functional speech. I was 9 years of age and despite my intensive home learning programme, years of discrete trial learning, speech therapy, occupational therapy, as well as other methods in the armamentarium of autism treatment and education, I had not been able to communicate using my own voice or other independent means. I also have dyspraxia which severely curtails my possibilities for speech and writing ability.

Sarah speaks

Rosemary Crossley occupied a special place in my mind after reading *Annie's Coming Out* approximately 20 years ago. I was deeply touched by her story of helping Anne McDonald, a client she had come to know at an institution for the severely disabled, emerge from the silence of severe cerebral palsy. Anne had huge challenges in speech and independent movement but Rosemary helped her to become an author, speaker and advocate for disability, among other achievements. In making an appointment with Rosemary, I was aware of my hopes that she could achieve for Tim something similar to the miracle she had with Anne. At the same time, after the years of interventional strategies starting when Tim was two that had not lived up to their promises, I also held my expectations in check in case it turned out to be another blind alley.

Rosemary's warmth put us at ease at once, and her down-to-earth demeanor belied the enormous commitment and skills she had in assisting children with little functional speech. In the next two hours, Rosemary took charge, and helped Tim to use his index finger to point to laminated boards, keyboard and finally a speech-generating device that gave voice to what he typed. I was surprised by the speed at which Tim was able to master typing, with the help of Rosemary's hand under his wrist. Of course, there were the inevitable stops and starts, including difficulties with starting (initiation), putting his finger onto adjacent keys, or repeatedly tapping the same key (perseveration). Rosemary explained that these difficulties could be tackled by holding the typist's hand back for a couple of seconds, raising the keyboard to an inclined angle, and asking the child to look at the keyboard while typing.

When Tim started to type the correct answers to the questions asked, and then a quaint little story using full sentences, my emotions and my cup runneth over. After all these years of silence, I finally heard him speak in his own words through the machine. It was momentous and very moving for me. Unbelievable as it seems, my every expectation would be met in Rosemary providing the right means for communication for Tim.

Tim speaks

Typing under Rosemary's facilitation and tutelage was by no means easy. My spirit to communicate was strong, but my recalcitrant body was unwilling, just like a wild horse that bucked, kicked and tried its best to throw off an inexperienced rider – me.

Rosemary's support was fine but my right arm felt like lead, and moving my index finger across the keyboard required total concentration and excruciating effort. I felt tense and overloaded, was completely drained after the session. However, the incentive for honing this exciting new skill was clear-cut. With the uncompromising face of the psychologist still fresh in my mind, I was going to bust my guts to prove that she was wrong about me.

With Rosie's hand under my wrist, I laboriously moved my index finger on the keyboard. In this two hour session, I was shown firstly, how to point to answers (Yes/No, multiple choices) to questions, and later, to type with support on a voice-output device. Thoughts I had never been able to express until that moment had finally found a way out from my mind where they had been trapped. In the space of but an hour, I answered some questions and wrote a little story. It was about Sesame Street characters with the pictures shown me. The feeling of exhilaration and power that accompanied these modest accomplishments was unbelievable. Nothing spectacular, just a short story about Big Bird and Grover, another day on Sesame Street, but it was the first time I was able to use my own words to create a story. That simple communicative act, a thing most people take for granted, was, for me, like reaching the summit of Mt. Everest, a milestone. I had found my voice – what exhilaration and power! From that first encounter with assisted typing, I knew that I would do everything to find ways to communicate, to show people what I am capable of, more importantly, to connect with others. With these initial successes, I changed from someone without a voice to someone who could connect with the world, previously totally out of my reach. Something told me my life was about to change.

Tim 24.6.04

Big Bird was not happy
because he had a row with
Grover. Grover had made a
very big mess. He had built
a house for a new girl on
Sesame Street. Sand was
everywhere. Big Bird quit.
He was mad. Sand was
even in his nest.

*First typed communication (aged 7)
Facilitated at DEAL by Rosemary
24.06.04*

Rosemary Crossley, or Rosie, to her clients and friends, cuts a giant figure in my world and has made a huge impact on me, and on the lives of others like me, those with little or no speech. I still have an unaccountable fear of her, although she has always been affable and kind. Her no nonsense approach and direct way of talking mean that we are expected to work and to do our best with her. When she tells me firmly to get off the floor, sit up or to stop scratching in unmentionable places, she means business. At the same time, you know she is not trying to put you down, but to set up the expected standards of behaviour in mainstream settings, and it is best to practice this as soon and as often as possible.

What is deeply admirable about Rosie is her capacity to believe in people who are different, those without voice, without the necessary means to communicate via the usual channels of talking and writing. Rosie is indifferent to a diagnosis of autism, cerebral palsy or motor difficulties, etc. To her, these labels do not fully define a person. She sees every person as an individual and looks for the innate intelligence behind all people in their demeanor, expression, body language and other responses. She puts this credo into practice by investing considerable energy and effort to unlock a person's potential with every available means at DEAL.

The beginnings of what was to become her life's work was a summer job at what was then called a spastic centre for children with cerebral palsy, during her study at university. Because she enjoyed what she was doing with these children, she eventually ended up working at St. Nicholas, a government institution for children with severe disabilities. There, she met Anne McDonald, and the rest is history. At that time, there was no knowing that, on their eventful journey, they would eventually take on the establishment for Anne's release from St. Nicholas and co-author a book, 'Annie's Coming Out', which was made into an award winning movie of the same name.

Anne, with severe cerebral palsy, was 12 years old when Rosie came into her life in 1974. Anne and a similar group of children, later called the 'Beanbaggers', were severely physically challenged, not even able to sit up independently, without speech, and were presumed to be severely affected intellectually as well. After getting to know her charges, Rosie, who had the job of devising programs for this group, was stunned to discover that Anne as well as the others, were intelligent and not only understood what was being said, but could learn to express themselves. From that moment of realisation, Rosie was determined to find ways for them to communicate. Eventually, after teaching the children to use Yes/No signals and to choose between multiple items, she taught Anne to read and spell by hitting letters on an alphabet board with her upper arm supported so she could raise her hand.

Rosie was able to convince some of the professionals who worked with her that Anne and the others were communicating. However, it was only after a prolonged battle with the institution and the authorities plus a Supreme Court case that Anne was finally deemed to be able to communicate and manage her own affairs. At 18, Anne was allowed to leave St. Nicholas and move in with Rosie and her partner Chris, where she lived a full and interesting life which included graduating from University, travelling, writing, speaking at Conferences and working with Rosie as an advocate, until her death in 2010.

From these turbulent beginnings, the DEAL Communication Centre, directed and run by Rosie with the help of a handful of staff, was established in 1986, specifically to provide methods of communication to people with little or no functional speech. At first, the Centre was funded by the government, and worked under an atmosphere favourable to inclusion set up by the Cain and Kirner governments in the 1980s. As the Centre charges no fees for its services, economic hardship came in the loss of government funding in 1993 under the Kennett Government, a blow which they fortunately survived, relying on private donations and fundraising. On a positive note, this setback has meant that DEAL gained the freedom to do what they needed, without having to justify their philosophy or ways of doing things to the bureaucracy.

The obstacles that came her way were numerous and unrelenting, yet Rosie set about overcoming these with great tenacity. Her clients come from a variety of backgrounds and a variety of disorders with the common denominator of having little or no speech. Most of us are severely challenged, and with sensory overload, high anxiety, not to mention an outlook of self-defeat and self-doubt that has been inculcated after years of failure in mastering rudimentary life skills and literacy and numeracy tasks independently. It is enormously difficult to get us to do anything academic, let alone change our limiting beliefs about ourselves. When faced with pressure to perform, some of us would withdraw and stay paralysed and noncommunicado whereas others may run off or hit out. I have great respect for Rosie who has to deal with the resistance that goes with making us work, to figure out lesson plans to cater for our individual needs and interests, as well as to motivate us to keep slogging away at something which demands all our willpower and concentration to stay on-task, and to move our recalcitrant bodies to type out our thoughts and feelings.

∼

Sarah speaks

Resistance does not end with the clients themselves. With the acquisition of communication via PAT/FC, many parents, still struggling with their disabled children with enormous challenges, also find it extremely hard to accept that their children are capable of thinking and feeling like 'normal' people. I must admit that, after Tim was able to type, I had to work on revising many of my preconceived notions of disability before I could welcome this new identity of Tim as someone who is intelligent, aware and very articulate. Time and time again, I have come across parents who are unable to do this and therefore, reluctant to accept their children as intelligent, capable people. For these parents, it must be very difficult to let go of their protective role, and give their children the freedom of decision making once they have found their voices. On the other hand, there are also parents who, unable to get the results from their children that Rosie was achieving, attack her out of their own sense of inadequacy and guilt.

Of course, such resistance from the parents was often mirrored many times over in the mindsets of the professionals who work in the field, and the authorities. We have encountered many professionals who have entrenched notions that people with little or no speech are intellectually disabled, and their approaches to intervention or remediation reflected this belief, that not much can be done for this group who would not be able to keep pace with their typically developing peers. According to Rosie, this type of thinking is most evident in the education department's approach to psychological assessment of students with disability. School psychologists *are trained to be familiar with the two major instruments for assessment, the Wechsler Scale of Intelligence for Children (WISC), or the Stanford Binet for IQ testing.*

The problems with these tests soon become very obvious because they were designed for and standardised using typically developing children. With students with little or no speech and associated motor difficulties, these instruments largely confirm their differences, and inevitably give results with performances that fall well below average intelligence. Or, when unable to be assessed, psychologists are told to guess the IQ range that these children function at, which would again necessarily be well below average. Although assessment can be done with other instruments that place less demands on verbal output or physical manipulation of tests material, such as the *Ravens Progressive Matrices*, the *WISC IV* and *Stanford Binet* (4th Edition) are still routinely used for children with disability, as exemplified by the cognitive assessment of Tim at D Primary School.

However, Rosie strongly believes that given the appropriate instruments, such as the *Peabody Picture Vocabulary Test* (PPVT), a test of receptive vocabulary or other instruments that are non-language based, as well as the right support in the use of Yes/No strips or multiple choice strips, and/or typing on voice output devices, this group of nonverbal children could perform better than expected. More recently, Rosie has been doing more systematic research with her students with complex communication needs. Using the *Peabody* (PPVT-R), where the student gives the answer by pointing to the right picture for the word, her participants consistently achieved results within or above their age appropriate range.[2]

Tim speaks

It is inevitable that Rosie's work would meet with enormous backlash because her clients have begun to challenge the cherished and established beliefs and attitudes about people with severe disability with little or no speech. This is when Rosie's uncommon courage and ability to stand up for what she believes in comes into play. She has battled for the right to communicate using Alternative and Augmentative Communication (AAC) for all individuals with complex communication needs and other difficulties in many arenas, including speaking out, petitions, lobbying and protest marches.

Despite the continuing attacks against her work, and the negative publicity that regularly spews out of the academia, professional associations and peak bodies, Rosie perseveres with her vision to give voice to the voiceless with great courage. She does not give up easily. In giving voice and empowerment to those with little or no speech, she is acting out of her conviction that this vulnerable group "can't speak but have plenty to say", the motto of DEAL. Furthermore, she has not become embittered by the prejudice and antagonism directed not only against her work, but also against her personal integrity. To repel these attacks, she has channeled her energy into a variety of ways to establish that non-verbal people do have the capacity to think and understand, for example, using non-verbal test instruments which can be undertaken by anyone who can point.

The point is (no pun intended), most people can learn to independently point to the answers. Rosie also uses other tests with multiple choice formats in her own assessment armamentarium such as the Australian Government's Naplan tests. She is further exploring research to prove that given the right test instruments, people without speech can do tasks well within the normal range of intelligence.

What keeps Rosie going? She derives enormous satisfaction from seeing her clients be able to speak out, to participate in the community and to succeed at school and university. Many of us, her clients, will attest to the differences her work has made to our lives. By imparting to us an invaluable skill, widening our options and changing our limiting beliefs, we have been able to live fuller and more meaningful lives. Once thought to be incapable of thinking and expressing ourselves, her clients have emerged from special institutions to enter mainstream schools, go on to university and do many things their 'normal' peers do.

One of her success stories, US client Sue Rubin, has shown what differences a means of communication can make. Sue became an independent typist after learning to type with support at aged 13. Sue and her mother were first introduced to supported typing by a psychologist using Rosie's methods, who believed that Sue had potential to communicate, despite being diagnosed from an early age of having intellectual disability with the mental age of approximately two years old. Rosie had been invited to continue working with Sue and their sessions on supported typing took place for some years. Through the use of partner assisted typing, Sue has since successfully graduated from university and not only work as an advocate for people without speech, but also publicised her viewpoints in speeches, articles and an award-winning documentary.[3]

Throughout Rosie's tireless efforts, her social network including family, friends, and the committee of the Anne McDonald Communication Centre (DEAL was renamed after Anne's passing in 2010), have provided staunch support to keep her going. Rosie's work continues, including traveling to other countries to work with children of diverse language and cultural backgrounds. Armed with her skills, her faith in the innate ability of her clients and a variety of communication devices, Rosie is sometimes able to get children from non-English speaking backgrounds, including China and Indonesia, and who have never spoken, to communicate by spelling or pointing to symbols on the iPad at first go. For many of us, her work provides the hope that people with little or no speech can be accepted and included in the community. I am looking forward to the day when her critics will be silenced. Perhaps this day will come when the writing on the wall and on speech generating devices are so obvious that the expressions of our intelligence can no longer be ignored or written off. Thanks to Rosie's unstinting efforts, courage, ingenuity and belief in us, this day is becoming a reality.

Sarah speaks

One of the highlights of my day would be to talk to Tim via assisted typing. It gave me the longed for but never before achievable opportunity to ask each other questions. I was amazed at how much Tim noticed the world around him and I was often surprised by some unexpected information. For example, he typed that his hearing was so acute that he could hear the traffic from the main road several blocks away, and when the garbage trucks came around every week, it was like the Grand Prix. He could also make out what the neighbours' were watching on TV when he was in bed and supposed to be sleeping. He said he would make a good secret agent.

Tim was also able to explain to me about the gulf in thinking that marked his differences from other people. How he saw the world depended very much on his feelings at the time rather than what he wanted to achieve. Tim said that people who think in language are able to go from A to B along a straight line, but others like him who think in pictures work in a different way. Scenes of the situation at hand would be uploaded onto his mind, and it is hard for him to separate the parts to work out its meaning until he could see the total picture. Because of this delay, things do not always go forward towards a goal because it is not always simple to link the means to their ends. Tim also thought that his need for things to be predictable was part and parcel of this inability to see the natural progression of events. I was astounded at Tim's perceptiveness, and gratified that he was able to differentiate these differences to show how his mind worked.

Another incident, soon after Tim learned to type with support at nine, gave me some insight into how far his mind, silent to the world before his ability to communicate, was able to stretch. The acquisition of assisted typing was a watershed in the work Tim and I did together. In the weeks following our visit to DEAL, he started to talk to me about his thoughts and feelings. This time was an emotional roller coaster ride for me as well, as I had to revise many of my previous evaluations of Tim's capability when I began to learn more about how his mind worked and to grasp the implication of his uniqueness. I felt immense gratitude and not a little awe that my child with autism was far from severely intellectually disabled or developmentally delayed as assessed by the professionals we previously consulted. Very much to the contrary, Tim's typed communication revealed a mind that reached further and deeper than the majority of his peers, with every indication of strong ability and skills that most would envy. For example, in response to my question how much did he understand time, meaning, could he tell time using the clock? Tim typed, "Time is not linear, that's just the way people see it. Time to me is spiral."[4]

I was reminded of an anecdote related by an autism researcher and academic, Gernsbacher[5], with a nonverbal son on the spectrum, slightly younger in age (aged eight) to Tim (aged nine), who typed in response to her question of "What is imitation?", (expecting for his answer, 'to copy' or 'mimic'), that "Imitation is the highest form of flattery".

An occasion around this time reinforced how crucial it was for Tim in acquiring a reliable means to communicate. When Tim was ten years old, he had to take a blood test in Sydney. We had been consulting with Dr. Annabel Stuckey, a Sydney based GP who specialised in the Pffeifer treatment of metallothionein supplementation and in order to proceed, she needed to check Tim's zinc and copper levels, which necessitated a blood test. The experience of his first blood test at age six was horrendous, having to be held down by two adults with much resistance and screaming. At ten, with the ability to communicate using Partner Assisted Communication (PAT)/FC, we discussed the procedure involved, his own fears, and also practiced with a pointy pencil. Even with a plane trip which he found uncomfortable because of the pressure on his ears, Tim was able to go through the procedure this time smoothly without any incident. The pathology staff actually commented on how calmly he handled the whole procedure, something they found amazing even in typically developing ten year olds. It has been the usual practice to give general anesthesia in blood tests with children on the spectrum, including all within our circle of Tim's friends.

This is one more incident in a history of many that gave unqualified evidence that Tim was actively communicating, and that PAT/FC has enabled him to give voice to his own thoughts and feelings, and receive information about coming events to help him manage his own fears. About a year later, under Dr. Stuckey's supervision, Tim went on the Methyl-B12 regime, which involved an injection twice a week. I was able to administer this at home after watching a video from Dr. Stuckey. Once again, there were no issues after Tim and I discussed the procedure and went through some practice. I was gratified and moved that Tim consistently showed his characteristic determination to do his best by cooperating with all aspects of this treatment.

1. Sarah recalls that the psychologist had said that Tim was "severely autistic", but in Tim's mind, this was equivalent to intellectually missing the mark. As of writing this footnote, Oct. 2018, Department of Education, Victoria, has initiated a policy for programs for students with disability and additional needs based on students' functional needs, bypassing formal cognitive assessment for allocation of funding. A pilot program has been undertaken with the aim of shifting the focus from clinical diagnosis to functional needs for ascertaining the necessary resources for meeting those needs.
   https://www.education.vic.gov.au/about/programs/Pages/inclusive-education-for-students-with-disabilities.aspx
2. Personal communication. Jan. 2017. Since mid-2018, Rosemary's research has been completed with the finding that using test instruments appropriate to the cognitive styles of students with little or no speech, a significant number of these students have been found to be functioning within or above the normal range of intelligence. Paper presented at the ISAAC Conference, July 2018, Gold Coast, Australia.
3. Rubin, S. (2004). *Autism is a world*. Documentary produced by Geraldine Wurzburg and CNN.
4. Because of Sarah's curiosity about Tim's description of time, she later looked up some explanations from physics. (e.g. John Gribbin, 1998, *Q is for Quantum*. London: Wiedenfeld & Nicolson). Time has been defined as the fourth dimension, on a similar footing as the three dimensions of space. Apparently there is no suggestion that time flows in a linear fashion from the past, to the present, and on to the future. All times have equal status, being a reference point in which events can be sequenced. Tim often uses analogy, metaphors and visual imagery to understand and explain things, and it is possible that the spiral may be an analogy for time as he saw it. Sarah was unable to find any references to this concept from her layman understanding of the reading explored, although there are references to the 'cycles of time' in the Vedic texts. It is intriguing that the worldview of particle physics is looking more and more like the cosmology as expounded in the Rig Veda (see Gary Zukav, 1979, *The Dancing Wu Li Masters : An Overview of the New Physics* . NY: Harper & Collins.)
5. Morton Ann Gernsbacher is research and psychology Professor at University of Wisconsin-Madison. After her son was diagnosed with autism, Gernsbacher devoted her research to the examination of cognitive and neurological processes of individuals on the spectrum, and has claimed that speech difficulties in autism are associated with motor planning challenges and not from intellectual or social impairment, and has given examples of her son's typing as demonstration of competence, that may also apply to other autistic children who are non-verbal. The anecdote referred to was in one of her papers. Morris, E. K. (2009). A Case Study in the Misrepresentation of Applied behaviour Analysis in Autism: The Gernsbacher Lectures. *The Behavior Analyst*, *32*(1), 205–240. http://www.ncbi.nlm.nih.gov/pmc/articles/PMC2686987/

10

INTO THE ARENA

Tim speaks

I remained on a high for weeks after learning how to communicate. I had finally discovered that words could bridge this great divide between me and other people! I started to make good use of language to talk to others even if it was just a trivial comment about what I did. When I typed to talk to my indispensable Aide, other students or teachers, they responded to the things I was saying. It made me feel that I was a person in my own right. I felt I had joined an elite group of people who talked to each other as equals and showed how much they cared. For instance, when I told another school Aide that assembly was really loud when everyone clapped and stamped whenever there was an announcement, she said, "Sorry that was too noisy, it's like that sometimes, but you handled that so well." I felt ten feet tall.

Mum and I caught up every day, well, several times a day depending on whether I had things to talk about. When I was with Mum, words would gush out of me, like a bubbly drink when the lid was finally unsealed. It was fantastic to be able to tell someone about my thoughts and feelings after being confined to the isolation and silence enforced by my recalcitrant voice apparatus.

∼

Sarah speaks

I looked forward with the greatest pleasure to catching up with Tim on a daily basis via assisted typing, and continued to be entranced with how Tim saw the world using his unique lenses afforded by autism. I was also bowled over by his sense of humour evidenced in many of his communication, not only with me, but also with other typing supporters which confirmed that it was Tim who was in charge of his communication. For instance, his Aide, Donna, often showed me his typed output with her. On one occasion, the Grade 3 class was looking at future careers, and I read with amusement how Tim continually tried to 'play up' by steering the conversation to this end. When asked what people look for in choosing a career, Tim typed 'money', adding that Donna "must be raking in the money."

She replied that, unfortunately, teacher aides were not high income earners, and that money was the last thing that attracted her to her career. When asked about his career aspirations, Tim typed 'pilot'. At this time, Donna was not aware that he did not like airplanes as the pressure on his eardrums hurt. When asked the qualifications for a pilot, Tim typed, "he needs to speak Hindi." I could certainly see that a sense of humour is an essential ingredient for living under conditions of enormous challenges as Tim had to do.

From his communication, I was also beginning to see how Tim's mind works. One of the prevailing fallacies surrounding autism pertains to the difficulty people on the spectrum have in working out metaphors and figures of speech. I think this tendency towards literal-mindedness comes from challenges in awareness of different levels of meaning in language. Humour is usually found when two or more of these levels intersect. For example, Tim had difficulty with a neighbor referring to our dog, a Chihuahua, as a "hell-hound". Tim said that "hell-hounds" reminded him of huge black Alsatians with tongue lolling and a mean stance. Our tiny dog, in contrast, could fit into a shoebox, even the cat next door was bigger. Then, it dawned on him that the neighbor was being funny. After that incident, Tim became interested in wordplay and enjoyed challenging himself in working out puns, punch-lines and the layers of meaning found in language use.

Tim speaks

But eventually reality reasserted itself and I could see that despite this mammoth breakthrough I still had many obstacles to confront. The process of typing via facilitated communication itself was not a simple process, as my body often refused to follow the instructions I gave it. I also realised that I had to be familiar and comfortable with my facilitator before I could produce typing that made any sense. Typing is a slower and more deliberate means of communicating. Spelling out the words as I type means I have time to decide what to say and how to say it. Just as the mechanics of speech were too difficult for me to coordinate; going through and grasping each thought, and then trying my best to tell my recalcitrant body to type out these ideas, at the same time as translating the visual mode in which they occur into words was also hard to configure. In order to achieve best results, my focus had to be maintained at all times which proved almost impossible when I had an unfamiliar person who couldn't anticipate my needs.

At first, I could only type with several people, but with time and lots of practice, I began to feel more confident about typing, and gradually, my circle of facilitators expanded. Nevertheless, I still do my best typing with Mum who is one person I can always rely on to know my moods and needs thoroughly.

∼

Sarah speaks

In addition to movement difficulties, performance anxiety and sensory overload, Tim's typing can be affected by another important factor, the kind of facilitator supporting him. I find that people who have been trained and have experience in giving support or facilitating can quickly pick up the typist's style and needs, and so make the necessary adaptation. On the other hand, those who lack training and/or experience need more time to do as good a job. The mindset of the facilitator also makes a difference. For example, Donna, Tim's fantastic Aide at D Primary, became a firm believer that Tim was typing his own thoughts when he answered "bullion" to the question, "What was in the treasure chest?" Donna said that the answers from the Grade 3 class consisted of gold, jewels or coins, and she had not expected "bullion." In fact, she was unsure whether the word Tim typed was spelled correctly. I subsequently checked and saw that it was.

However, later in the year, Donna talked to the school psychologist who suggested that Tim's ability to communicate was based on Donna's need to succeed. Thereafter, Tim's typed communication with Donna suffered, and although he was still able to give simple answers, he never produced responses in the more complex and well-expressed forms as he had done prior to Donna's encounter with the psychologist. My understanding of what occurred was that Donna's confidence in her support of Tim was undermined when she subsequently questioned whether what Tim did was influenced by her. In thinking herself responsible for Tim's answers, Tim himself was affected adversely by the way she saw him, that is, incapable of communicating on his own steam. As for the psychologist, because Tim had huge difficulty in the tasks that comprised the cognitive assessment done earlier, she drew the conclusion that Tim was severely intellectually disabled, based on her professional interpretation in a report as a prerequisite for funding. It was evident that she was unable to accept that Tim was intelligent and could communicate. There is a range of perceptions among the professionals we come across, and some of them are marvelous in their respect for and acceptance of Tim. However, that psychologist's attitude was also reflected in a considerable number of the consultants we met.

I also went through a stage of uncertainty wondering whether my physical support of Tim's arm 'caused' him to type what I subconsciously wished him to say. However, over time, and over many hours of assisting him, I gradually came to realise that the common assumption, that lack of speech and other autistic challenges mean lack of ability, was erroneous There were many times that I was able to see that the information Tim provided had not come from me, a notable example being the incident with the blood test in Sydney. After this self-scrutiny, I was ready to cultivate an open mind, and there were no further issues with my facilitation. In addition, I saw that Tim's progress in typing was predicated by his determination to communicate in the face of enormous hurdles, that whatever support I was providing was merely used to drive his own immense desire to use this means to talk to people.

Tim speaks

The last term at D Primary School went too fast for my liking. Everyone was excited about going on to high school and the class buzzed. I too was caught up in the anticipation of stepping onto a bigger stage, but anxious at the same time at the transition to a new setting. Mum had looked around for the school most suited to my needs, and told me that the high school I was bound for provided a smorgasbord of opportunities, including well organised classes where students looked engaged, a language other than English (LOTE) program with Chinese, which would continue my interest in this subject done at Primary school, good student initiatives where a couple of student leaders actually took prospective parents for a tour of the school, and a middle school head who was very much on the ball. This head of middle school would also be supervising the integration of students with disability. Mum and I also went to an interview where we met the school administration and gave a demonstration of my mode of communication.

Arrangements were made for a couple of sessions at the school for orientation and Donna, my Aide, came along to support me. She spoke to Mum afterwards and said I did a great job in meeting some of the Integration team, sitting in on a class and having morning tea in the Student Well-Being House.

Then, reality crashed around us. From day one, my autistic differences singled me out. The high school was huge, with over 2000 students and 400 staff members, and the movement, noise, jostling from people jarred my nerves and decimated my information processing ability. I was unable to understand instructions as my hypersensitivities propelled me into constant overload. However, when I tried to ameliorate sensory overload by covering my ears, by humming or lying on the floor to tune out the sensory onslaught, people would tell me to stop. It came as no surprise that the school saw me as lacking in capacity.

Needing to rely on typing with the support of a facilitator, I was at a distinct disadvantage. Because of my sky-high anxiety, it was next to impossible to produce any coherent typing with my new Aide, Rebecca. Mum asked for permission to help train Rebecca, and also arranged for her to go to DEAL to train under Rosemary. However, this method of communication was deemed by the new Head of Integration (his predecessor, who spoke to us earlier, had left) to be unsuitable, and he refused permission for the Aide to train with Rosie. Pretty soon I was told that Rebecca would not be able to support my communication at school either, and my Litewriter, which I had only received at the commencement of high school, sat in Rebecca's desk drawer during school hours. I guess it's no secret that the Integration Head didn't think I should stay on. Since I wasn't able to type, I couldn't do any of the work. It was humiliating as it put me completely out of step with the rest the class, in addition to feeling utterly isolated and excluded as a result. I was relegated to nonentity status, denied my voice and my personhood the moment I stepped into the school grounds.

I have in mind a photo of a black student who was bused to a desegregated school during the 1960s in one of the southern states of the US. She is wearing sunglasses, so you can't see her face well, but her posture is resolute. Around her are white students and parents or people from the school community whose faces and body language show frenzied emotions from outrage to hatred. When I stepped past the school gates during my years at high school, I felt like that black student running the gauntlet of people's rejection and repudiation. Mostly I was met with indifference, but I could still sense the underlying message that I did not belong, as the position from the head of integration was clear, that I shouldn't be there.

The integration head tried both directly and indirectly to make it difficult for me to remain at school. His strategies included withdrawing my mode of communication via typing with support ("unfortunately, we have no resources to train staff to facilitate Tim's typing"), suggesting as politely as possible to divert me to other learning institutions such as special school ("dual enrolment, perhaps"), and another mainstream school ["not talking about Ferntree Gully (25km away), but a school somewhere in the vicinity"], as well as showing that I was completely unable to handle school activities. For instance, assemblies, classes like Wood/Textiles and PE lessons were very noisy and overwhelming for me, but when my overload caused behaviour such as humming, lying on the floor or running off, I was withdrawn from such classes and put in the library where Rebecca would spend time colouring or going through first readers with me. To be fair, I liked Art because the room was relatively quiet, and as Rebecca used to be an Arts teacher, she enjoyed working with me, but I felt that colouring instead of year level work was another message that I did not have the ability to handle the high school curriculum.

Because I felt increasingly alienated and deeply unhappy at school, Mum went to work to find ways to make things better. She spoke to Rosemary who recommended Emmy Elbaum from STAR Victoria, a parent advocacy organisation, to come on board. We were informed by Rosie that Emmy had worked for many years as a teacher, special educator, and advocate as well as in policy and advisory roles.

Emmy's appearance was incredibly deceptive. Softly spoken, always respectful and sensitive to my needs, Emmy's mild manners are at odds with an impassioned belief for the rights of the individual, and fierce determination to utilise her considerable experience, knowledge and skills to achieve the best possible outcomes for a vulnerable group of young people.

Emmy never doubted my ability; I think she has learned to see all individuals using a second sight that bypasses their exterior to perceive their core potential. When I typed that I wanted to study law and work as an advocate, she never questioned my aspirations. Instead, she made every effort to enable me to participate more fully at school so that I could better achieve my goals. We met regularly with our team (Mum, Emmy, and Eden Parris, our other advocate from *Communication Rights Australia, CRA*) to discuss and plan how to get the necessary support at school so that I could have access to school programs, do the subjects I liked; English, Legal Studies and History or take part in co-curricular activities. They would also brainstorm how I could best complete the required assessments. In every one of these sessions, Emmy would ask me what I needed to achieve my goals, as well as how I wanted to achieve them. My answers were always treated with complete respect, as the team planned to take my responses into consideration for the next Student Support Group (SSG) meeting at school. Emmy's support of me extended beyond school, as she would often send me information about seminars on advocacy, social justice, law courses and things of interest to me.

Student Support Groups (SSG) were the vehicle in which the school, student, family and other support workers come together to work out suitable programs for the student with special needs in an individual education plan as well as to iron out any problems. As the only student, I felt intimidated by SSGs with its full complement of integration staff (Deputy Principal, Year level Coordinator, Student Welfare Director), my aide and some of my teachers. These meetings appeared to be solely concerned with examining and tearing apart my competence, and deeming me completely inadequate to deal with mainstream high school. However, there were no doubts in Emmy's mind of my rights to a mainstream education, which was in fact our entitlement under Education Department policy. Over time, as she continued to reassure us and to offer advice and strategies on how our goal could be achieved, I felt more confident to tackle the insurmountable roadblocks that kept pushing me towards the brink. At the same time, she would guide us in negotiating for the necessary support for fuller participation in school, my rights to use my preferred mode of typing to communicate, and how to achieve social inclusion with friendship as a priority. Without Emmy and my *CRAustralia* advocate, Eden, my high school education would have remained an unattainable dream.

To those who don't know her, Emmy remains an even-tempered and thoughtful person, but she was incensed at the veiled discrimination, and what she saw as a violation of my rights to an inclusive education. I invariably needed to do my work at home, with Mum as the facilitator, because not only is she by far the best facilitator, but I do my best work in a familiar and conducive environment. However, the work I produced at home was constantly called into question and never taken into consideration in assessment. In one instance, Emmy was aghast by the lack of respect shown by the same chair of the SSG when he thumbed through and queried the authenticity of my Year 8 English book review, stating that no Year 8 student could possibly write like that! With this and other dismissive gestures, I felt condemned as a lesser being, denied my full personhood. In the eyes of this administrator and others like him, I would never be granted the right to be a human being with legitimate entitlement to my own thoughts, feelings and dreams.

As time went on, the SSG meetings gradually became more and more focused on behavioural issues as I began to play up against the intolerable situation. I wanted to take my revenge against the system that did everything to disempower and dehumanise students with special needs. Sometimes, without warning, I was overwhelmed by feelings of utter powerlessness and despair, and had this urge to do something to regain a sense of control. I hated school, and in protest, did anti-social things to find an escape route through suspension. I felt like a prisoner at the dock as the battle lines were drawn, with the school against me and my team. As the prosecution read out the charges against me - throwing tanbark, books and other objects at people, endangering people using the toilet with my obsessive splashing of water, refusing to sit quietly at the desk, hitting and running away from my aide, and so on - I desperately prayed to be swallowed up by a hole in the floor. If not for the help of Emmy and my team, I would never have been able to face another SSG meeting.

Emmy excelled in her role as an advocate. Not that she would ruffle any feathers, that was not her style. In her characteristic calm and reasonable manner, she would examine the school's presenting arguments and deliver just the right solution to counterbalance their case. If, as they said, there were no resources to deal with my complex needs, she suggested that we needed to look for other sources of funding. With concerns on union regulations with regards to staff well-being, she said that my frustration as a result of not being able to communicate would decrease once I started to type; and when I began to be given opportunities to socialise with and get to know other students, the issue of student safety would be resolved. Of course, my errant behaviour and reluctance to be at school needed to be seen in the light of high levels of anxiety which would be addressed by getting the right support so I could be productive and happy at school.

On the other hand, the erosion of my self-esteem and confidence through ostracism and alienation, intentional and otherwise, was nothing short of devastating. Without anyone to relate to at school on a personal level, I found myself sinking ever lower into the depths of depression and despair, with intermittent thoughts of putting myself in harm's way.

11

WARRIOR FOR JUSTICE

Tim speaks

It was only through the unremitting efforts of my social support network, whose belief in me never wavered; Mum, my family, friends and especially my advocates, Emmy and Eden, that I was able to continue with my daily routines. Fortunately, child psychiatrist Dr. Michael Gordon came in at this stage to help me. He is head of child and adolescent psychiatry unit at Monash Medical Centre and took me on as a private patient, becoming an integral part of my recovery process.

In addition, with the strenuous negotiations of Emmy and our team, the school finally began instigating more inclusive practices. I started to type with my new Aide who came in second term in Year 9. But even as I tried to do my best to live up to expectations as a good student, I found that the experience of the past two years had sapped much of my confidence and belief in myself. At this stage, I was still struggling with my identity and found it hard to come to terms with the negative appraisal of people around me with regards to my autistic challenges.

As I gradually began the onerous task of getting back on my feet, I realised just how lucky I have been with all the support I received. In particular, Emmy has made an enormous difference to my life. However, it was not until I got to know her better on a personal level that I began to see the forces that shaped her commitment to fight for social justice. She was a child Holocaust survivor, and this harrowing experience had led to a well-developed sense of justice and a keen sensitivity to the suffering of fellow human beings. After surviving Bergen-Belsen in the final months before Allied liberation, she was sent to Switzerland to stay at a clinic run by the Lendli Order of nuns while her brother went into foster care. They were only reunited with their parents on migrating to Australia after four years when she was six years old. According to Emmy, her mother wanted to get as far away as possible from Budapest where they lived during the war.

Her school years were uneventful but marked by regular nonattendance as she stayed home to care for her mother who was sick and to help out at her father's shop. What she recounted as memorable about school were events that seared her heart with a sense of injustice. For instance, her best friend with better marks was denied entry into the 'professional' stream while a boy whose parents were wealthy was admitted. Similarly, the wealthy students never got the strap when they broke the rules. On one occasion, when students who came from an orphanage had to report to the office, they were announced collectively and not individually by name. This upset Emmy who complained to the principal about the blatant disrespect for the same students. From these less than promising school experiences, Emmy went on to become a teacher, I think, because she wanted to make a difference for the better treatment of all students.

It seems natural that Emmy would eventually be drawn to special needs students whose vulnerability as well as complex needs attracted her attention. What she found unacceptable about the special school system, here, as she had previously, were the practices that routinely denied students their rights to be fully included as human beings. For instance, when talking to a special school student, Emmy was struck by his perceptiveness in response to a question about what he disliked about school. He told her that the students had to travel by a blue bus which made the passengers feel that they were singled out and different, adding, "It's alright with you, you can leave any time." Another instance which Emmy found incomprehensible, was when a teacher told the students that if they behaved, they would be allowed to read their readers. She felt this should be the right of every student, regardless of behaviour. Neither could she understand learning programs which set out everyday tasks in minute detail, focusing all attention on the sequences to do something obvious such as putting on a jumper, but not on the individual students themselves. Having myself gone through discrete trial behavioural programs in early childhood, I also found it degrading to be repetitively performing basic or simple self-care tasks accompanied by a constant barrage of meaningless reinforcement, "very good, great job, well done."

Emmy does things differently. With an intuitive ability to look at the young person under her charge as a human being capable of thinking and feeling, she refuses to see students as robots with merely the ability to mimic the simplest tasks. Her insistence on the acknowledgement of and respect for the individual helped me come through a significant and prolonged personal crisis and re-emerge as a human being.

I feel immensely privileged to have Emmy as my advocate, mentor and friend. One of the things I value most is her innate capability not only to rise above personal suffering and negative experiences but also to use such experiences as a springboard for change. Her family had suffered much during and in the aftermath of the Holocaust, however, Emmy steadfastly refuses to be mired by the deep anger and obsession with personal grievances expressed by child Holocaust survivors of her acquaintance.

Emmy feels strongly that rather than holding on to our own grievances, we should redirect our energy into acknowledging the suffering of all groups, and to be open to redressing the wrongs committed against those who have been discriminated against, maltreated or stigmatised unjustly. With all the wonderful things she has brought into my life, this willingness to transform traumatic experiences into a positive and enduring legacy to achieve social justice for vulnerable people has been the greatest gift.

Despite Emmy's help I continued to struggle. At recess and lunchtime, I was taken to the Student Well-Being House, again at the fringe of the school, and had my food in a small room on my own with an Aide. At times, the school assigned a few boys from my class to join me, but all they did was talk and laugh among themselves, and were not really able to take the necessary initiative to get to know me. When I lay on the floor to deal with the overload caused by their voices and laughter, another boy would mimic me and lie down next to me, to more hilarity. Because I was feeling so defensive, I thought that their laughter was directed at me, and I hated their lack of understanding of what I was going through with their thoughtless remarks. It was at these times that I thought of myself as an apology of a human being and that I should never have come into this life. As no one at school appeared interested in me or my welfare, with no means of communication, I felt utterly alienated and powerless.

My feelings of being an abject failure had intensified during the years of enforced silence in Years 7 and 8 when I felt cut off from the rest of the world. Denied my method to communicate via typing with support by the first SSG chair/Integration Head, I was left without a means of letting people know that I was a thinking feeling person. I wasn't able to show that I was capable of doing the subjects I liked: English, History, Science and Social

Studies. Instead, I was coloring with my Aide, and reading basic readers. Heck, if they only knew, I was doing calculus and reading Shakespeare with Mum in primary school. All interactions at school were completely one-sided, them talking to me, and very likely thinking "what a waste of time, he probably didn't get a thing I said". To be denied a voice also meant the denial of me as a person with an identity. I felt like the living dead, going through the motions of existence without any means to make the vital human connections that made life worth living.

There is an infamous experiment, the Stanford Prison Experiment (SPE), dreamed up by a crazy psychology professor, Zimbardo,[1] which was diabolically clever in coming up with how people responded to their life situations. Zimbardo recruited 24 students who were randomly divided into two groups, 'guards' and 'prisoners', and both groups spent time in a simulation prison at the basement of the psychology faculty at Stanford University. The experiment was meant to run for two weeks but was terminated after six days because a post graduate researcher protested that this was having huge adverse effects on the mental well-being of the 'prisoners'. This group of volunteer students was suffering from apathy, withdrawal, occasional bursts of anger and hostility, and other symptoms of clinically depressive states. Although they could leave anytime, only one of them did because it got too much for him. Apparently the utter powerlessness they felt in their situation rendered them unable to make choices for their own welfare. These effects were still felt years later when some of the 'prisoners' were interviewed. The 'guards' didn't do too well either. With the mandate to run the 'prison' as well as all the associated status and privilege, there was deliberate denial of human rights and denigration of the 'prisoners'. Abuse of power was even more extreme in response to challenges to their authority by the 'prisoners' who were really students like themselves.

A recent paper on inclusion gives this definition:

"Inclusive education requires recognising impairment as one of many forms of human diversity, and welcoming and viewing diversity as a resource rather than a problem. Inclusive education, therefore, creates a situation where all children can be valued and experience a sense of belonging and where all children are encouraged to reach their full potential in all areas of development."[2]

Wonderful from a theoretical point of view, but I don't know if this works in terms of day to day reality in schools. Schools are establishments for learning, with set standards and assessment procedures for achieving those standards, and the competition that inevitably follows will mean that some students will not be doing so well. Let's face it, there will always be judgment we make about people in terms of success. What intrinsic value could people see in this kid who lies on the floor and covers his ears in Assembly, and what contributions was this kid making in English with coloring at his own table, and even then, with the Aide alongside? Would I be asked to address the school on Speech Night as an outstanding alumnus and their first Rhodes scholar, as my elder sister was? Not in my lifetime. Or would I be flown to Sydney, after submitting a winning essay on the issues of privacy in a world that relied increasingly on information technology, as a presenter to the privacy commissioners, the attorney general and other luminaries, as my second sister did at 15? In my dreams perhaps.

This is not an indictment of inclusion, an ideal that we should keep striving towards, but a statement about the typical mindset, mine included, of what achievement looks like. It is next to impossible to achieve full inclusion in educational institutions where contributions that are valued are defined basically in terms of excellence in academic, sports, music and similar areas. Hence, my experience at the bottom of the food chain in an institution that valued such excellence was devastatingly similar to those of the SPE 'prisoners', and my sentence lasted six years, not six days.

∽

Sarah speaks

Tim's nickname for the first SSG chair/Head of Integration was 'The Iceman'. I thought, at first, that this referred to a male version of the Snow Queen, who put children under her spell such that everything they saw and touched was warped and tainted by their feelings of dehumanisation and despair. "No", Tim said, "it's the one from Eugene O'Neil's play". I did a double take, completely unprepared for Tim's identification with the desperate characters and dark themes of the play. We had read the storyline of *The Iceman Cometh*[3] from another book on addiction, but I had refrained from going into it in greater length as I was worried that it might affect Tim unduly.

The play is set in a bar, where a group of alcoholics is waiting for the arrival of a charismatic salesman, Hickey, to start the party. The people who made up this group are out of touch with reality, preferring to live in the delusion that one day, their goals will be achieved. In the meantime, they drift through life aimlessly and bicker among themselves. The arrival of Hickey brings a surprising revelation, he tells the group that he has stopped drinking and urges them to see the lies they are living in. When one of the characters comes face to face with the cover-up story of his mother's death, he is no longer able to live with this realisation and commits suicide. The core theme centers around people's need to live in self-deception as these 'pipe dreams' allow them to keep going with their lives.

After pondering on the implications of Tim's situation, I began to realise that being an integral part of our family, he had imbibed our intrinsic values of working hard to achieve success. Our Chinese background which places undue emphasis on academic achievement as well as the successful experiences of his siblings in and out of school had formed Tim's 'pipe dreams.' At the start of high school, he had high hopes of doing well in his favorite school subjects, participating in social activities, being accepted as part of the student body, and having rewarding social connections with staff and students. However, these goals had become largely unattainable in the face of the insurmountable obstacles that came his way.

Because of his challenges, lack of speech, movement difficulties, hypersensitivities and autistic behaviour, he was out of place in a mainstream high school that valued conformity, and he deemed himself a 'write-off'. In addition, coming face-to-face with this cruel twist of fate, he saw himself as a total failure, fit for nothing but the scrap heap. His subsequent slide into self-rejection and depression was inevitable. The 'Iceman' had come and taken away Tim's sole means of proving himself intelligent, capable of doing high school work as well as socialising with people, and Tim could no longer face that implication that the goals he had set, realistic and achievable by most people's standards, remained a pipe dream.

∼

Tim speaks

After all the work I had put in over the years, making sense of my world, understanding language, learning how to communicate and overcoming sensory and movement difficulties to persist in my typing, I was stumped in the last round by a school administrator who refused to see me as anything but disabled and a misfit. Because I felt unacceptable with him and other people who agreed with him, I also figured that it would be hard to find acceptance elsewhere.

I still didn't have anyone to talk to at school. Things which I could previously take in my stride began to wear me down. For instance, when some classmate who usually smiled and said hello walked past without acknowledging me, I would feel physically sick and emotionally drained, rendering me unable to function for the rest of the day. I also felt deeply depersonalised, despairing, with a slow but steady slide into depression, accompanied by intermittent thoughts of self-harm. Part of me no longer cared. With nothing to engage me at school, I vented my frustration and took revenge by throwing tanbark, books and things at people. I created havoc with my obsessive splashing of water which was not always intentional, and even hitting and running away from my Aide. Of course, these behaviours were just what the school needed to back up their position. We were told to consider looking for special educational settings more suited to my complex needs. The school also resorted to disciplinary measures and suspended me for these infractions. It suited me fine. I had now worked out a way to avoid school by deliberately doing things that would get me suspended, and gladly took the time off. But that didn't resolve the problem, I was still desperately unhappy, and couldn't see any light at the end of the tunnel.

---

1. Zimbardo, P. (2007). *The Lucifer Effect*. NY : Random House.
2. Cologon, K. (2013). *Inclusion in Education: Towards Equality for Students with Disability*, Issues Paper, Australian Department of Education, Children and Families Research Center, Institute of Early Childhood, Macquarie University.
3. O'Neill, E. (1967). *The Iceman Cometh* in B. Cerf, B. (ed.) *Plays of Our Time*. NY: Random House.

12

SPEAKING LOUDER THAN WORDS

Sarah speaks

I watched in dismay and acute powerlessness as Tim spiraled down. Without the means to communicate at school, his sense of himself as a worthwhile person took a huge battering. The benefits that assisted typing had brought over the past four years as well as his growing skills and confidence in connecting to people, vanished like the morning mist. He withdrew into himself, and often, was not even willing to talk with me. However, his mental agitation and emotional turmoil were consistently revealed through meltdowns. Tim was not handling things well and at home, in a more supportive environment, he became obsessed with soil and water, taking hour-long showers several times a day, muddying and flooding the bathrooms. There were also occasions when his intense emotions became unmanageable even with these rituals, and he would punch doors and walls as well as smash windows. Luckily, he did not hurt himself seriously until a time (an only time in Year 11, of which more later) when his hand went right through a window and he ended up with a partially severed ligament that necessitated plastic surgery.

It was a very trying time for me as well. Tim's difficulties made him very challenging to live with. At the same time, I faced huge pressure from the school in different ways. Firstly, whenever Tim 'played up' at school, including splashing water in the toilet, throwing tanbark or running off, the administration would ring up and ask that he be taken home. I feared that escalation of behavioural issues would provide ammunition for the school to remove him for good, so I invariably dropped everything to pick him up. I also felt he would not be able to learn much in his heightened state of anxiety and agitation. Home would be a safe and supportive place for him to calm down and talk over his issues with me if he felt like it.

When I dropped Tim off at school in the morning, I often had to plan so things could be put aside whenever the call came from the school to pick Tim up. Of course, I dreaded the times when things could not be dropped at an instant's notice. For example, I had commenced further studies in a PhD program with the Olga Tennison Autism Research Centre at the start of Tim's Year 7, and a couple of years down the track, I began the data collection phase of my studies. One morning, I was at a neighbour's house testing her nine-year old child. The mother had gone out on a brief errand when the inevitable call from school came. I told the Head of Middle School that it was impossible for me to collect Tim until the mother of the boy came back because I could not leave him on his own. Fortunately the school understood, and I was able to finish the testing session by which time the mother had returned. But I remembered being torn between my own needs and grave concern for Tim's well-being on this occasion, and empathised with Tim that he had to deal with situations where he was placed at a distinct disadvantage every school day.

Many times, the school administration would give an explicit reminder that Tim's behaviour continued to pose a safety issue for other students, for example, in throwing tanbark at people, or flooding the toilets. Several of these occasions would bring about disciplinary action in the form of suspension, which Tim actually reveled in because it gave him a legitimate excuse to skip school. At this time, the school stepped up the pressure for Tim to undertake cognitive assessment, presumably to get hard evidence that he did not have the wherewithal to do high school work. As our advocate Emmy had said, cognitive assessments were not a prerequisite for school attendance, I was initially reluctant to follow up, but finally took steps in contacting the Academic and Child Psychiatric Unit (ACPU) at the Royal Children's Hospital in Year 8, as nominated by the school for an assessment.

With the assent of Professor Alastair Vance, head of the ACPU, I was able to be present as well as facilitate Tim during the sessions. The results were beyond expectations. Tim's scores placed him in the 99th percentile in verbal comprehension skills; and in light of his motor difficulties, a score just below average in the performance/perceptual tasks with an IQ well within the normal range. Tim also indicated the features of dysthymic disorder with associated anxiety and hyperactive/impulsive symptoms, in other words, clinical depression. In Professor Vance's report, Tim's condition was likened to the 'locked in' syndrome where individuals with intact cognitive and mental capabilities are unable to express these due to accompanying severe physical disabilities. No one, including the school personnel, could now doubt Tim's ability to access the secondary curriculum.

∽

Tim speaks

Things started to heat up in the second half of Year 7 when we were put in touch with *Communication Rights Australia*, an advocacy organisation for people with little or no speech, recommended by both Rosemary and Emmy. Adele Braun, one of their advocates, came to school to represent me in negotiating for the right to use PAT/FC, my preferred method of communication.

One of the first things our advocates instilled was the awareness of my rights. The Victorian Education Department has in place a policy of inclusion. According to departmental guidelines, every parent or legal guardian has the right to choose the manner of school for their child to be educated. Just knowing that I had a right to be at mainstream school made an enormous difference to how I felt. It relieved me of the feeling that I was an interloper who did not deserve to be there. But the functional difficulties remained, as I was still not allowed to type.

I began to realise how much we – people with special needs – needed the skills of advocates, the expertise of other consultants, the support of our parents, family and social network whose faith in us meant so much, alongside our belief in ourselves. In my case, the latter had taken a damaging blow with the sabotage of my confidence and self-worth by my experiences at school.

My advocates repeatedly emphasised that the school needed to provide reasonable adjustments to ensure that I could access their programs, including the right to type with assistance. They pressed for Rosemary Crossley to come in and train the Aide in facilitating me. However, the Integration Head refused this request and insisted that the school would seek its own consultants. Their consultants were drawn from special schools staff without expertise in PAT/FC, which no special schools had endorsed. The message was clear – the school did not consider my method of communication, PAT/FC, appropriate for use. After much effort from my team, Rosemary was finally able to come and facilitate me in giving a demonstration of my communication method towards the end of Year 8. The occasion reminded me of a circus; Rosie and I were in the ring, and the Head of Integration was the Ringmaster, with my teachers and other support staff members, our audience. I had no trouble with Rosie supporting me, though, and enjoyed the one and a half hour session which Rosie and I gave – a performance that drew positive responses from the audience. My teachers actually laughed when I typed that I had an 'exit strategy'; playing up so that the school would call Mum to pick me up. Rosie said, "You are a toad." There was more laughter when I typed, "No, just a small fish in a very big pond."

The upshot of this demonstration, our first triumph, was, I would be allowed to type with the support of an Aide who would be trained by Rosie. However, with this victory, Adele told us that *Communication Rights Australia*, would be terminating their service with us because we had reached our objective – being able to train up an Aide to support my typing at school, which had now recognised my method of communication. It was a relief that Year 8 was drawing to a close, as I looked forward to the approaching summer holidays. My Aide Rebecca was leaving too, to be replaced by a new person. The drain on Rebecca had begun to show over the past few months. With the escalation of the battle between the school administration and our team, she must have felt caught between her loyalty to the school and her role in supporting me. She had lost much of her original enthusiasm at the start of Year 7, and she had spoken of going to the Union after several disagreements with the Head of Integration. Given my propensity to play up, I supposed it must not have been an easy task to support me at school, a responsibility in which she had the lion's share. Emmy had remarked on how fragile she seemed at the end of term SSG meeting. I guessed Rebecca would be looking forward to a new start at another high school with a reputation for their music program.

Sarah speaks

It was a great relief that the demonstration of Tim's typing with Rosemary's facilitation went well. I was not allowed to attend, but on picking up Tim at the end, I caught sight of the Middle School Head and the Student Welfare Coordinator in earnest conversation with Rosemary. Both these teachers had not been sympathetic nor supportive of Tim in the past, and it was a welcome sight to see them actually seeking information regarding the demonstration. Speaking with Rosie as we all drove back, his teachers were quite convinced that Tim had the intelligence to do work at the high school level. Rosie recounted with delight Tim's throwaway line that he was "a small fish in a very big pond", an impromptu demonstration of his wit.

I kept comparing what had occurred at this session with the debacle of a recent SSG meeting which Rosie was allowed to attend after strenuous and lengthy negotiation. But it was to no avail, she was constantly interrupted whenever she spoke by the Integration Head who told her, contrary to SSG guidelines, that it was not her position to give her opinion. Actually, after the typing demonstration, the Head of Integration reported to me that Tim had performed and behaved poorly, and appeared hyperactive. I checked with Rosie afterwards. Contrary to the viewpoint of the Integration Head, Tim was in good spirits and worked well with her, but became so excited with the laughter from the audience that he stood up and jumped on the spot before returning to his seat where he remained for the rest of the session.

Tim speaks

Without a means to connect with anyone at school, I had been floundering in a sea of self-rejection and despair. There was no time to indulge in pessimistic thinking, however, as Mum was diagnosed with breast cancer around the beginning of Term 4 in Year 8 and scheduled for immediate surgery. She had worked round the clock to support me and look after the family, as well as embarking on a Doctor of Philosophy (PhD) program on autism research when I started high school, thinking that she would have more time. However, the stress of dealing with my high anxiety levels, depression and behaviour both at school and at home, as well as the uphill battle for inclusive schooling had taken its toll. She had to take time off for treatment. Throughout her operation, chemotherapy and radiotherapy, Mum remained optimistic about her recovery and her resilience was infectious. I took heart from her example and tried to pull myself together again, with the support and encouragement of those who believe in me.

Sarah speaks

It was a hectic and tumultuous time during the summer break with the treatment for my illness in full swing, but I felt supported by the family as well as our circle of friends and pulled through without mishap. On the resumption of school in the new year, I was pleasantly surprised to discover that Tim's new Aide, Jenny, was an excellent and friendly special education teacher with extensive experience in working with students on the spectrum. However, she would be temporary, working for one term before her transfer to another teaching post. On the other hand, her position on PAT/FC was clear, she would not facilitate Tim's typing, but would be happy to train the next person, who would take over in second term, in all other aspects of her work. Under the experienced guidance of Jenny, Tim had no issues during this time, and it was a welcome change at the next SSG meeting that the Head of Integration actually took pains to instigate inclusive practices such as allocating the necessary resources for Tim to take part in the Year 9 Urban Exploration Program (Xplore) which students spent a week around the city to familiarise and report on various landmarks and institutions.

The next Aide, Nicole, was a lovely young woman. Tim got on well with her, and furthermore was able to type under her facilitation after I demonstrated what she should do. She also saw Rosemary for a session. Although young and relatively inexperienced, Nicole was able to do a creditable job in supporting Tim both in class and in other activities. The factors which enabled her to achieve this relationship with Tim were her firm belief in Tim's ability and her commitment to helping him with his communication and doing well at school. It was heartening to see the long and arduous process of ensuring Tim's successful inclusion yielding fruit at long last. Then, much too soon after the calm before the storm, all hell broke loose.

13

STORMING THE CITADEL

 What does not destroy me makes me stronger.

Nietzche

Tim speaks

With our advocates' help, the school, bound by law to uphold inclusion and provide equal access to the curriculum, finally implemented the use of supported typing as the method for my communication in Year 9, 2010, after more than two years of negotiation. It is strange, really, but I felt deflated, empty of all feelings. There was a time when I wanted so much to be able to talk to people, to show them I had the ability to think and feel, to participate and be included. But in reality, after facing the long and trying years of being without a voice and the opportunity to be heard and acknowledged, I had become pessimistic about my condition as well as my future. I was young and didn't know what I could offer to the world, which had left me behind. I still felt angry and alienated, but tried my best to work with my new Aide Nicole. She also did her best to support my communication and to attend classes and do work. But even with her help, I felt isolated without anyone else I could reach out to. After putting all my efforts to try and work at being a good student, I could no longer keep up this pretense. Because Nicole was the only person I could talk to at school, I began to direct much of my angst and frustration at her.

Sarah speaks

For a short period it had seemed like a honeymoon in Term 2 (Year 9). Things had gone smoothly with Tim doing everything right with Nicole's support. He took part in the Xplore program without incident, attended classes and worked on the year level material, and even completed assessment tasks. One of the highlights was Nicole reading out one of his presentations in English, which was received positively. Then on returning to school in Term 3, Tim became very obsessive, for example, saying what sounded like 'shower' nonstop, or touching objects, pens, rulers or doorknobs, compulsively. Although he still typed with Nicole to talk to her at every opportunity, he refused to do any school work. On one occasion, with a History test, Nicole recounted that Tim knew the answers because she had revised the material with him, but he did not type in response to the questions she read out. Nicole finally had to ask the Integration Head to come in to read out the questions while she concentrated on facilitating, but Tim just typed the answers willy-nilly, and got most of them wrong. According to Nicole, the Integration Head did not encourage Tim to do better, but went through the test perfunctorily and seemed happy when it was finished.

Then, without warning it seemed, Tim started to type things

with suggestive and explicit sexual overtones to Nicole. As the term progressed, Tim also interlaced his communications with rude and aggressive comments. Nicole became extremely uneasy and alarmed. Her boss, the Integration Head, had to intervene by calling Tim to his office for talks and warnings on the seriousness of the offences, and finally instigated suspension proceedings when none of these measures produced the desired results. I was also called up to meet with him and the Head of middle school to discuss this turn of events. Tim's latest misdemeanor also formed the topic of concern in the agenda of SSG meetings, but very little was achieved because of the way the school viewed the current behaviour problem, putting the onus on Tim to toe the line without investigating the underlying issues that caused such negative behaviour, or making systemic changes to help Tim feel more accepted and understood. We once again contacted *Communication Rights Australia* for their help. Adele Braun had left, but Eden Parris, an experienced human rights lawyer, came to advocate for Tim.

Tim speaks

It was fortunate for me that Eden had just increased his work hours from one day to three days per week not long before I was assigned to his case-load in 2010. These extra hours were put to good use working with this intransigent situation. Under Eden's experienced guidance and tutelage, I began to learn about advocating for myself. Firstly, I started by paying more attention to the basic framework and strategies Eden used in negotiation. I learned that *Communication Rights* is the only advocacy organisation for people with little or no functional speech in Australia. The organisation grew in the 1970s from a self-help group of people with speech-impairment who used alphabet boards to communicate, to a state-wide body with government funding today. It was fortuitous that I received their advocacy at this time because the human rights model had not long been adopted to direct their work. In 2003, Jan Ashford, the CEO, had begun a process of developing the human rights model as the basis of advocacy. She went to the US, Canada and the UK, on a scholarship, to investigate an audit tool for assessment. With no ready-made audit tools available overseas, *Communication Rights* developed their own training kit on human rights as well as an assessment instrument for evaluation of clients' situation, as a springboard for advocacy.

I further learned that the essential framework for their advocacy work comprises the right to 'freedom of expression' stated in both the *United Nation Convention of the Rights of Persons with Disabilities* (UNCRPD, which the Australian Federal Government has ratified) and the *Victorian Charter of Human Rights and Responsibilities* (VCHRR). Further work was done by Frank Hall Bentick who took the issue of communication to the UN, and in moving from an advocate to a position in the Minister's office, was effective in including augmentative and alternative communication (AAC) as a valid mode of communication within the VCHRR. The freedom of expression provision means that it is the right of every person to self-expression using a medium of choice. This includes other modes and formats, which typing with support would fall under. The UNCRPD also gives explicit support to the use of AAC to provide an effective and inclusive education. But the Victorian Education Department neither endorsed nor prohibited the use of supported typing.

With my new-found knowledge, I was more prepared for Student Support Group (SSG) meetings, the arena in which all issues relating to integration were addressed. SSG meetings were supposed to occur once a term, but in the face of my recalcitrance, were called by the Integration Head as the chair of the SSG, with the need arising to look at urgent concerns. These extraordinary meetings usually put me on high alert, as I knew by then how they would be conducted. In addition to the Integration Head, the Head of middle school, Student Welfare director and my subject teachers and support staff also attended. My team, consisting of my two advocates, Mum and myself, was definitely outnumbered. With the Integration Head as chair, the tone of these meetings was largely negative and accusatory, as he wasted no time in describing all my infractions. On these occasions, I would be completely unable to function as I invariably felt like a condemned man in the dock waiting to hear my sentence. My anxiety, already sky-high, would go through the stratosphere and grip me in its stranglehold.

In coming to my rescue by crossing swords with the school administration at SSG meetings, Eden became my hero and role model, and taught me lessons vital to my survival. A trained lawyer, his example inspired me to pursue further studies in law and work in advocacy. I still remember one particularly heated SSG meeting at which the school produced a long list of grievances caused by my waywardness including throwing things, flooding the toilets, running off and especially in typing hurtful and demeaning communication aimed at Nicole. The Integration Head said that because of the danger posed by my behaviour to Nicole's wellbeing, as well as the safety of other students and staff, he would be getting complaints from the union as well as the school community. Since their preventative measures failed to stop me, I would not be allowed to type whenever I caused Nicole distress. Without any hesitation, Eden took up the gauntlet. He did not mince words, but countered the school's attacks with a firm reminder that they were required, under Departmental policy guidelines of inclusion, to provide the necessary support for me to be at school. Moreover, he emphasised that I was entitled to my right to use the method of communication of my choice, by principle and by law, and the school had the obligation to train Nicole, not only to support my typing but in the skills and strategies in behavioural management. Without letting up, he passed around a statement I typed in advance to explain why I behaved as I did.

Our team had encouraged me to write a statement to explain my viewpoint, and I started by saying how I felt like a condemned man speaking out in his own defence, and that I was sorry for what I did. Because I had not been able to do the things I wanted or talk with people at school, my deep frustration and despair sometimes got out of hand, but I never meant to hurt anyone. Facing my challenges required all my focus so that sometimes I was unable to find the energy nor will to keep afloat. I concluded by saying that I felt like 'flotsam and jetsam' (a phrase borrowed from *The Lord of the Rings*[1]). Tolkien's epic of good versus evil had resonated with me. I saw Frodo's journey to the stronghold of the Dark Lord Sauron, to destroy the One Ring, the source of Sauron's great power, as similar to mine. I felt that in attempting to do the near impossible, I had been set test after test that destroyed all but the strongest. The comparison between myself and the accumulated waste after the storming of Isengard in *The Lord of the Rings* described my school situation precisely, as I found myself of no use to anyone and completely dispensable.

In this and other SSG meetings, Eden demonstrated exceptional negotiation skills that were used to great effect. Time and again, he defused the school's complaints about my behaviour by putting the problems in a different light. It was the school's job to ensure my access to the curriculum, and they had been derelict in their duty by not making reasonable adjustment or allocating the necessary resources for me to do this. My behaviour was the result of frustration and isolation due to lack of engagement and denial of opportunities to learn. He also warned that if the current situation was not addressed, our team would take this further and make a formal application for arbitration to the

Department of Education. By lobbing the ball back to the school's court, telling them to do their job rather than put the blame on my shoulders, I had a strong champion who took up my cause, giving me legitimacy and a return of my rights as a person. It was also empowering for me to know that since the school had not been doing the right thing, there were higher authorities to appeal to. Eden had extended me a lifeline and my hope was restored in achieving a more tolerable outcome. Eden, together with Emmy, proposed additional strategies for reducing my frustration and increasing my participation. Their suggestions included putting in place training of staff and arrangement of times for other students to talk to me, co-curricular activities I could be involved in, and additional adjustment in order for me to do my work. My advocates also pushed for action to remedy the situation within a reasonable time frame. I came away feeling like I had been given a reprieve.

At the conclusion of the meeting, after the administration and school staff had left, Eden took me aside and earnestly told me that I needed to lift my game. If I wanted to study law and become an advocate, he cautioned that I would have to do better to stay on at school. This incident made a deep impression on me, because I could see that Eden was not only doing a great job as my advocate, but that he really cared about me as a person as well.

∼

Sarah speaks

I felt nothing but relief when Eden came to our rescue. He did a wonderful job in leveling the playing field for Tim, and had taken the wind out of the school's sail by reasserting our rights for Tim to seek an education at the school. It was an additional source of comfort to know that Tim was inspired by Eden's example and aspired to follow in his footsteps to become an advocate for people with disability. Eden was moved by Tim's strength of mind and purpose and flattered to find himself as Tim's ideal and role model. I saw, with great delight, that both of them had taken a personal interest in each other. However, despite our advocates' representation, the Integration Head still dragged his feet in augmenting the strategies for inclusion and another year was coming to its close without resolution of the situation. Tim persisted in typing rude and at times abusive comments which derailed his progress, and I was called to pick him up when his behaviour became an issue which was a frequent occurrence. Although Eden had reassured us that the school should meet its obligation to provide the necessary support and resources for Tim's participation, and that it was not my job to take him home, at such times, I felt that rather than leave him at school where his frustration and anger would lead to more negative behaviour, it was in Tim's best interest to be in a safe and supportive environment as his mental well-being continued to be a problem.

With the end of middle school (Year 9) looming close, there was additional pressure from the school for us to leave. I was reminded both in person and in writing that Tim had not been able to do the work at his year level, despite typing with Nicole's support and the school would not be the right setting for Tim as evidenced by his behaviour. By this time, Tim had typed with Nicole that he did not want to go to school. This was not without reason, but was used regardless to reinforce the school's message that he should leave. After one incident when Tim had once again lost control and lashed out, in attempting an assessment, an emergency meeting was called. I was basically told that Tim faced prolonged suspension as his behaviour was causing great concern and had become a serious safety issue for Nicole, and with no further options in sight, Tim should look for a school elsewhere. I said I would consider their suggestion, but had to consult with our advocates first. It was the end of year, and I informed them we would see them in the New Year, as Tim needed a respite in face of the constant overload and turmoil. The holidays would give us a breather and on our return to school, the necessary energy to iron out Tim's untenable situation.

---

1. Tolkien, J.R.R. (1954-1955). *Lord of the Rings*. UK: Allen and Unwin.

14

HIGH SCHOOL SHAMBLES

Tim speaks

Among my circle of friends are two other guys like me, with autism and without speech who went through similar rough patches to the ones I was going through at high school. Being nonverbal and relying on typing with support as our main method of communication, we challenged the outmoded mindset of our educational administrators. Although these pedagogues paid lip service to the Education Department policy of inclusion, they ran integration programs for students with special needs according to the motto that all students should fit into the same mold, despite the fact that most of us come in different shapes, sizes, physiology and ways of thinking.

Joshua was about two years above me at Special School, and Mum and his mother Julianna became friends. It was Joshua's mother who told us about Rosemary Crossley under whom Joshua had started to learn PAT/FC. Although I left special school in Grade 2, our families still kept in touch. It was around Year 8 that Emmy, our advocate, introduced Mum and me to another boy with a similar condition, in a similar situation. Cameron was in Year 7 at another mainstream high school, and was also facing the same difficulties at school as I did. From questioning his capability, to presuming incompetence, to recommending the Special school down the road, his challenges were a mirror image of mine. His mother Lorraine was very helpful in sharing her experiences and strategies for successful inclusion. Lorraine was pursuing a Master's Degree in Inclusive and Special Education, and therefore, well versed in the workings of the system. She also generously assisted with valuable advice to help Mum and me negotiate for the necessary support to get into the programs I wanted at school.

Cameron has an engaging grin. No doubt, his sense of humour, mental and emotional strength and social support network enabled him to succeed in getting on top of his atrocious treatment at high school. In addition to relying on Augmentative and Alternative Communication (AAC) and typing with support for communication, Cameron had seizures and was on anti-epileptic medication, which affected his mental alertness, motor coordination and social engagement. It was, again, an uphill battle to get the school to agree to the adequate training of staff to support his typing. Like me, he was without a voice at school, and completely at the power of his school administration. There was a range of exclusionary and divisive tactics the school used to persuade the family to remove Cameron from the school. These included restricting Lorraine from speaking directly to his Aides to find out about Cameron's school day, withdrawing Cameron from class to learn in the 'Program for Students with a Disability Room' (PSD Room), requesting his parents pick him up from school early or not bring him to school on days when they had the swimming carnival or sports day as there was no activity planned for him to participate in. Cameron was allocated as many as five different Aides in the school week.

He also hated the process of transitioning from class to class in a wheelchair and developed postural and other problems as the wheelchair was not designed to be used for lengthy periods. Meanwhile, it was not helpful for him to adjust to the personal styles and work approaches of five different Aides who might not be informed of his condition from earlier in the day. He was then blamed for not being able to perform at his best in class or in communication, while the school made few if any attempts to provide the necessary environment for reasonable adjustment for his special needs. For example, despite the size of the school, it took months for them to provide a quiet room in which Cameron could rest when he had seizures. Lorraine was particularly incensed when she was cornered in the car park by the integration coordinator and told that Cameron should be looking for another school more suitable to his needs. The coordinator must have been taken aback when Lorraine basically said that she would move Cameron from where he was 'over her dead body'. The camaraderie and determination of Lorraine was a great morale booster for us as well. She was prepared to pull out the heavy artillery in taking the case to the Education Department Regional Office, to the Minister, and pursue other avenues including the Anti-Discrimination Commissioner and the Ombudsman, if necessary.

In the end, fed up with what Cameron was subject to at school, Lorraine actually did take the case to the Department of Education and an investigator from the Conduct and Ethics Committee was involved. The school was found to be negligent and in contempt, in view of the constant harassment, intimidation and discrimination faced by Cameron and the family. The school gave a written apology and the Principal was moved to another school. A new Program for Students with a Disability Coordinator was appointed and the Leadership Team changed for the better. However, by this time Cameron had developed a very defiant, rebellious and aggressive attitude towards the school and anyone at the school who tried working with him in a collaborative manner. He did his school work well with support workers at home but refused to do the same at school. All his class work was sent home, and Lorraine had to make any modifications and submit it as she saw fit. As expected, the grind of having to deal with the issues of concern faced by Cameron on a daily basis had been costly for the family. Lorraine often had to stay up late into the night to plan and work on the appropriate course of action in response to the school and the documentation of evidence for augmenting the case to the Department of Education in addition to her other commitments and responsibilities. We knew how she felt!

I take my hat off to Cameron, who graduated from high school with his VCE through sheer persistence and hard work. Lorraine and his team had organised a school-based assessment program through which Cameron was successful in fulfilling the requirements by passing all his Year 12 subjects. He was only able to achieve this with the excellent support staff at home; the people who believed in him. Emmy, Rosemary, and Jai Phillips (*Communication Rights Australia*) fought hard to keep his determination going. His seizures went on a roller coaster ride but the family refused to increase his dosage or add other medications. With such a tough time, Cameron still managed to be listed as one of the 100 Leaders on the 100 leaders Project [1]. This achievement is a testament to his courage and tenacity as well as to the dedication of his parents and social support network. Cameron is currently at Deakin University doing an Associate Arts Degree, hoping to branch into Journalism. Lorraine also did well. With her Master's under her belt, she currently works as a Teacher in the Education Support Program at Royal Melbourne Institute of Technology (RMIT), teaching students who are going to be teachers and Education Support Staff, to always presume competence and challenge students' learning irrespective of their disability. She has begun her own consultancy business in Inclusive Education, Care & Support called InclusivED.

Joshua was initially unsuccessful in trying to get a place in mainstream high school in Melbourne. The family decided to move to Brisbane, where, with the help of his consultant, a psychologist with a reputation for treating Asperger's Syndrome, he was admitted to a special school for high functioning students. The family was torn apart as Josh's elder sister, Maria, remained in Melbourne to stay with her uncle and aunt to continue with her studies. Maria was in the final years of high school and the move to another state was considered to have detrimental effects. However, the separation was hard for the entire family as Joshua and Maria were close. Maria had been his primary facilitator for typing when Josh first started with Rosemary Crossley. After one year, Maria joined the family in Brisbane and finished the last year of high school with flying colours. She went on to University, graduating in speech pathology with high distinction, and has been working in the field for people with language impairment.

In Year 9, Joshua started to develop a bad case of eating disorder, often taking nearly the whole of his waking hours to eat and had to be spoon fed at times. He lost weight and his health was seriously affected. Finally, he typed that he wanted to go to mainstream secondary school and to study at Uni. When his request was met with an enrolment at a small completely sympathetic and inclusive mainstream high school, Josh started to turn the corner and recover. He graduated from the final two years of high school to go on to University where he undertook a degree in journalism. In a recent conversation with his mother, Mum was gratified to hear that Josh has become more independent in typing, and his speech is also emerging.

Our collective story, Cameron, Joshua and mine, attests to the support and love of our families, their faith in our abilities and the enormous efforts and sacrifices they made for a mainstream education, to gain for their children the opportunities the majority of students take for granted. It is also a story about the indispensable contribution of advocates and other professionals who passionately believe in the rights of families to choose mainstream education for their children with disability. It is essentially the story of overcoming the barriers through sheer bloody mindedness, of coming to terms with who we are and of affirmation of who we want to be.

I kept thinking about the Freedom Writers[2], those hugely disadvantaged students with long histories of failure, who through their own efforts, encouraged by their inspiring English teacher, came back from the brink to achieve success. As published authors of their stories, with high school graduation and college attendance, these young people were able to reclaim their power and self-belief, and to stay in the drivers' seat to take themselves where they wanted to go. This courageous group of students had redefined achievement, from a life on the streets, replete with violence, gang warfare, substance abuse and addiction, to claw back a life worth living, going from the status of victims and losers to those of heroes. Their moniker came from the Freedom Riders, the movement against segregation and racial discrimination in the 1960s in the heartlands of the American Deep South. The Freedom Riders were vilified and brutally attacked, some even lost their lives, but in their heroic efforts for desegregation and equality, they were able to jumpstart the process of empowerment for African-Americans and narrow the gap of racial divide and disadvantage. I am glad that we too, that is, Cameron, Josh and others like us, have been part of a similar attempt to focus attention on discrimination and inequality, and to be able to take a stance against institutionalised practices that confer the rewards and power only to a select group of achievers. At its core, inclusion is an ideal we should all work towards, the process just needs to keep going in order to bring about a more tolerant and equal society.

According to Jan Ashford, CEO of *Communication Rights Australia*, people like us, with little or no speech are one of the most marginalised, vulnerable and excluded groups within the community. Without a means to communicate, we have no access to decision-making, nor voice for protest against punitive or abusive treatment, as well as lacking effective control over our own lives. Furthermore, for us, to be able to communicate remains the only way to connect with the world. Without this vital social connection and the recognition by others as human beings, we are like the living dead, existing under sufferance. I can only say from first-hand experience that if severe autism is like being sentenced to life imprisonment, trapped in a body that won't cooperate, then to be denied the means of communication is like perpetual solitary confinement without any avenue of appeal.

Communication Rights Australia and Eden, its representative, as the champion for human rights for those without a voice, have made a huge difference to my fight for inclusion. For people with little or no speech, a receptive and sympathetic platform for the resolution of our problems can provide us with the necessary resilience to face our challenges and to pursue a better life. As we regain our voice, our dignity and self-worth, it will finally become possible to emerge from solitary confinement and re-engage with our human family as full-fledged members. My dedicated team of advocates, represented by Eden and Emmy, have my total respect for their passion and commitment to promoting not only the right to communicate, but the physical, mental and social well-being of the voiceless, by empowering them with a voice, an essential means to be included as part of the community.

Sarah speaks

The start of the school year (Year 10) saw a repeat of the same types of challenges Tim and I faced in the previous year. Tim continued to type communication that threatened Nicole's peace of mind and sense of wellbeing, as well as used other means to ameliorate his overload, like the obsessions with tanbark and water that could be potentially dangerous. The Head of Integration continued to pursue his hard line in terms of warnings and suspension whenever Tim stepped out of line without instigating the strategies that had been discussed to help him feel less alienated. We were again stymied in our negotiation for the necessary support. The Integration Head also stepped up the pressure on me to take Tim out of school. Eden proposed that I should investigate another school with a reputation for inclusion because we were getting nowhere. I had run out of ideas but as the date for our first SSG approached, I took our case to the Principal, Deborah, and received her permission to replace the Head of Integration as SSG Chair with another Deputy Principal, Karen, who was also Head of Senior School. There was a welcome change in the tone of the SSG meeting with Karen as chair, and she did what she could to work with our team to bring practices for fuller and more successful inclusion.

By this time, however, Tim's oppositional attitude to school was entrenched and his outbursts continued, despite Karen's attempts to make Tim's school experience more positive, including personally taking an interest in him both in and out of class, and making plans to explore his options for matriculation. I had to take action to prevent further escalation of Tim's feud with the school. Our second daughter would be spending a term at the University campus in Florence, and I decided that it was in Tim's best interest to take a break from school, and travel. I informed Karen that we would be away for a term, and she replied she would explore strategies for increasing Tim's participation when we come back.

After spending Term 2 in several places, including Beijing en route to Europe, we came back with renewed energy and cautious optimism for the second half of the school year. At the previous SSG meetings, there was discussion around the employment of a male Aide to assist Nicole and defuse Tim's aggression. On our return, we were informed that Nicole had left, but the school had started negotiation to employ a Martial Arts Therapist (MAT) Aide, and would also be looking for another aide as Nicole's replacement to support Tim. Although there were stories of MAT staff using unacceptable methods to restrain students, Damien was the 'dream' Aide, young, intelligent and friendly, the outdoor type. Damien was unfailingly empathic in his supervision and support of Tim, even when Tim reverted at times to his negative behaviour. On the occasions when Tim went ballistic and was intent on throwing tanbark, or creating havoc, Damien would run after him and enfold him in a bear hug until he calmed down. When Tim was doing well, Damien would take steps to give him turns at basketball or playing table tennis. Damien even brought in his guitar and strummed and sang with Tim. Tim was impressed with Damien's charisma and wide-ranging interests, and thought he was 'real cool'.

Gordana, a mature mother of three, outgoing with a ready laugh, and more importantly, with years of experience in student support as well as counselling, came two weeks later. Gordana readily picked up the facilitation of Tim's communication after a couple of demonstrations from me. Better still, Gordana not only took her job seriously, but cared about Tim's welfare in a more personal way. After an initial period of testing her, Tim got on with her like a house on fire. There was change in the air with Tim trying his best to resume his studies.

Tim speaks

In Year 10, after our return from overseas, I resolved to direct my energy into more positive channels and use my means of communication to make connections with my Aides, teachers and other students. With my team's support, I had slowly regained the necessary confidence in speaking out, and I was determined to be heard. Eden had explained to me that under the rights model, people with disability like me are entitled to the rights as set out by the VCHRR and UNCRPD, and the focus has been redirected to making resources available to achieve these rights. Hence the battle has shifted from getting an entry ticket to having a seat at the table but we are still a long way from inclusion and living the life we want. Finally, with the unremitting efforts of Mum and my advocates, the tide began to turn in our favour.

Gordana, who replaced Nicole, was not fazed by my antics. She knew how to deal with my negative behaviour, putting it down to adolescent angst. She also has a good sense of humour, and when we got to know each other better, I would get a laugh whenever I tried to be witty. "Everybody has problems, it's just that yours are more obvious." The statement has become Gordana's refrain. I know she was telling me that I was the same as most other people, but I couldn't help but think that I had more in common with those freaks who used to make a living from parading their deformity in the circus, the ones that people paid to stare in shock and poke fun at. But then, with Damien and Gordana's support, school became a bit more tolerable, and Damien was what I wanted to be, 'cool' and charismatic, a great guy all round. Gordana was funny, lively and great to talk to, and as the year progressed, she and I became friends. Because I didn't want to let anyone down, I decided to do my best to follow the routine and do the things expected of a Year 10 student.

Things got even better, when the first SSG Chair/Head of Integration was replaced by Karen, Deputy Principal/Head of Senior School. She was fair-minded and worked cooperatively with our team. Karen listened attentively to me at SSG meetings, and was always respectful of what I typed. As the school began instigating more inclusive practices, I started to participate more fully, with my Aides, Damien and Gordana, who were completely sympathetic. Gradually, I began to turn the corner.

---

1. http://100leaders.org.au/themes/getting-an-education/cameron-rodrigues/
2. The Freedom Writers with E. Gruwell (1999). *The Freedom Writers' Diary*. NY: Random House.

15
THE VCE SHUFFLE

Tim speaks

From the time that Karen took up the position of SSG chair, the issue of concern became my capacity to do VCE (Victorian Certificate of Education or matriculation) under the prescribed conditions. Because of my complex communication needs (CCN) and high anxiety, assignments and assessments done at school were not up to scratch, and it was essential to think of methods for me to achieve the best possible outcome. The school applied for special consideration, including increased time allowance to accommodate movement difficulties, factoring in necessary breaks, and a secluded examination room. However, under VCE guidelines, no family member was allowed to be present or facilitate me during SACs or school based assessment tasks. The problem was, because Mum was the most experienced of my facilitators, the level of work I produced with Mum's support far exceeded what I was achieving at school.

Sarah speaks

Tim's refusal to do work at school had started to cause problems in Year 9 under Nicole's support. Things had looked up when the team of Damien and Gordana was helping him in Year 10. But although he found their company convivial and enjoyable, it was difficult for Tim to do extended work at school such as assignments or assessment tasks with Gordana's support. There were several reasons for this, firstly, although Gordana had picked up facilitation quickly, she was by no means an experienced communication partner in comparison to myself. Moreover, the school environment, with people, movement and noise, was prohibitive in the face of Tim's hypersensitivity. The tutorial room where they worked was located in a busy area. When students walked to and from class, lockers would open and slam shut when they put away or got out their books. Some students even tried to look in at what Tim and his Aides were doing which was pretty distracting, until Gordana put up cardboard on the window to block the view. Later in Years 11 and 12, the school allocated the old office of the first SSG Chair/Integration Head for Tim to do SACs (school based assessments). Tim is very sensitive and became agitated, not only because of exam anxiety, but the association of the office with the times he was summoned there by the first SSG Chair/Integration Head for the reprimand and disciplinary action that followed any misdemeanor.

Tim speaks

Together, my MAT Aide Damien and Gordana made school bearable, but it was still impossible for me to do work at a similar level to what I was doing with Mum's facilitation at home. I always felt decidedly inferior when I couldn't do assignments or tests/assessment as well at school. Because I had studied the subject with Mum's support at home, what I had revised was inaccessible because the environmental conditions were different. As my exam anxiety mounted, the triggers that prompted recall went out the window in the face of my plummeting confidence.

~

Sarah speaks

Back in Year 9, after a prescribed waiting period, we finally had a consultation with Professor Ingrid Scheffer, neurologist, geneticist and autism expert of international standing at Austin Health where Tim was first diagnosed. No problems were found in Tim's genetic make-up or metabolic health, and referrals were obtained for a neuropsychological assessment with Dr. Sylvana Micallef, senior neuropsychologist, and for child psychiatrist, Dr. Michael Gordon. Dr. Micallef's assessment provided ample ground for Tim's capacity to complete secondary schooling. With the adult version of the instrument[1] used in the previous cognitive assessment at ACPU in Year 8, and although Tim again came in at the marginally below average for perceptual reasoning, he achieved a whopping Verbal Comprehension Index that placed him in the 99.9th percentile of his age peers. In her report, Dr. Micallef also affirmed that using minimal shoulder support from me, Tim was able to type all his responses which she strongly believed came solely from Tim. On our follow up visit to Ingrid, she also wrote to confirm that she saw evidence of Tim's independence in producing his communication with shoulder/back facilitation. Michael said jokingly to Tim that he was off the scale in IQ.

I proceeded to apply to be Tim's facilitator for his academic assessment. I felt I was in a good position, armed with the results of Tim's latest cognitive assessment, as well as further supporting letters from our consultants, Matthew Wilson, speech pathologist with extensive experience on FC^2, Dr. Michael Gordon, Dr. Sylvana Micallef, and Eden Parris. All were unanimous that I was the best facilitator for Tim. Matthew wrote that for assessment purposes, students with CCN would achieve optimal results with the most experienced facilitator because 'cognitive load' for the management of movement difficulties is minimised, the candidate can therefore give more focus to the task at hand. Dr. Micallef also stated that in her professional opinion, Tim's typed output came from him alone, with minimal facilitation. But all to no avail, the Victorian Curriculum and Assessment Authority (VCAA) would not budge, even with the additional stipulation of an examiner in the room to ensure exam guidelines and rules would be followed. Gordana was also unhappy with the implication that she was not as able a facilitator with Tim's school work and became decidedly cool towards me. VCE assessment was just around the corner, yet the crucial factor for Tim's success, the best facilitator, was not allowed to support him for assessment tasks.

~

Tim speaks

As my difficulties were examined at each and every SSG meeting for the expressed purpose of applying for special consideration for assessment, I became increasingly discouraged. True, the focus at this stage was not to put me down, but for leveling the playfield so that I could complete SACs. Nevertheless, I felt that I was being dissected and declared completely inadequate. Things got even more complicated because Gordana was angry that her facilitation was found wanting. What was worse, she was not included in these discussions on special consideration and felt her position was threatened as they went through the arguments for best facilitator, which Mum won hands down. Although Mum did her best to point out that the time she spent in facilitating me exceeded 5,000 hours whereas Gordana clocked up only about 100 hours, Gordana felt that her competence was called into question. I hated being the cause of Gordana's distress. She had been my lifeline when I needed it most, and has been my friend. I typed to her that I didn't even feel like doing VCE, and that it was just to please Mum who made me do it. This text was shown in the SSG meetings and Mum questioned whether I typed this because of Gordana's influence or whether I had made the decision on my own. In reality, I was feeling hugely conflicted. On the one hand, I wanted to be able to pass VCE and go on to University, but on the other hand, I felt I was being gripped in a vice; the stress of doing assessment invariably brought on something akin to panic attacks. The fear would start as pressure on my chest, so intense that I found breathing difficult. With heart pumping like it would burst, and cold sweat drenching my clothes, I would feel a blackness pass over me, obliterating me and all that I was, like a candle flame snuffed out by lack of air.

Sarah speaks

An outburst of Tim's occurred at home around this time. It was after dinner, when again, without warning, Tim smashed a window, and seemed unable to control his intense agitation. His brother and I had to pull him away as he was intent on breaking another window. I assessed the situation and decided to go out with Tim for a walk to calm down. I literally dragged him out the door. His agitation was so great that it took an hour of brisk walking before he showed visible signs of equanimity. Afterwards, he apologised and told me he felt so trapped. The breaking of windows was to him akin to breaking out of the trap. At this stage, Tim had also absconded several times, requiring the intervention of the police who located him hours later and brought him home. These episodes were immensely distressing and hugely stressful to me and the rest of the family as his safety could not be guaranteed. Without speech or independent living skills, he was exceedingly vulnerable. I tried to come to terms with the fact that in running away, he was again making the attempt to break out of an intolerable situation.

During term breaks in high school, Tim usually went to a supervised program for students with disability for two to three days per week because it gave me the uninterrupted hours between 10 am to 4pm in addition to the early morning hours before Tim got up to spend on my studies. Although I always picked the days that provided the activities he liked, Tim did not enjoy these outings because of the noise and busyness that invariably accompanied the activities.

As the pressure at school mounted in VCE, one holiday in Year 11, Tim was having breakfast before attending the holiday program when, without warning, he got up, punched through the glass in a window, and ended up with a deep gash to his wrist. With severe overload in the past, Tim had pushed his hand through windows before, but never incurred such a serious injury. I rushed him to the local doctor who said, on examination of the hand, that I better take him to hospital. The attendant physician in emergency also refrained from treating the injury because Tim had partially severed a ligament and required plastic surgery. This was scheduled for the following day, and luckily, the procedure went smoothly without complication. After Tim recovered, he told me that he hated the holiday program days because the students who attended them had severe disability and most of them were non-speaking. He disliked being herded en masse from one place to another, with the unending demands to follow the scheduled activities no matter how overloaded or pushed he felt. Furthermore, Tim had no means of communication, and although the program staff did their best to make their charges safe and happy, they were unable to facilitate Tim's typing. Tim took out his frustration on the other kids, there were a couple of incidents when the staff reported that Tim threw tanbark and soil at them. Once again, I decided that my studies could wait, as I needed to defuse the pressure during school term and make the holidays more enjoyable for Tim. We made our own plans for entertainment.

∽

Tim speaks

Mum and I love to read books or watch movies which give us a window into how people deal with real life challenges. One book which made a huge impact was *The Diving Bell and the Butterfly*;[3] the story of Jean Dominique Bauby, a successful journalist and editor prior to his brain injury. Bauby's autobiography was written by blinking his left eye when suffering from the locked-in syndrome after a massive stroke. This method of communication was instigated by a speech specialist who found that the only part of Bauby's body under voluntary control was his left eye. She taught him to communicate by blinking once or twice to indicate 'yes' or 'no' as she went through every letter of the alphabet. The book was brought to life by a film of the same name, and because I am a visual thinker, the film affected me deeply.

I strongly identified with his comparison of his paralysed body to a deep sea diving suit, that is, a cumbersome body which did not obey his intentions. This kind of suit is used to withstand the pressure of the ocean depths and is made of steel, weighing over 120 kilograms. Even after intensive training and supreme effort, moving in the diving suit under water is extremely slow and laborious. The butterfly referred to Bauby's spirit which was able roam free. But as his condition did not improve, he tended to spend most of his waking hours reminiscing about memorable and beautiful experiences, while his disabled body continued to decline. After watching the film, I began to have nightmares where instead of Bauby, I found myself encased in a diving bell, suspended in the deep. My cries for help were muffled by the steel cage, and there were no ways to emerge from it. No matter how desperately I raged and fought, I was engulfed by the darkness around me, a watery grave in which I would be forever entombed. On waking up, shaken and disoriented, the fears I faced in my ordeal in the abyss which swallowed me were still vivid. I was reminded again and again by this recurring nightmare that I too suffered from the lock-in syndrome, as reported in the ACPU assessment in Year 8.

Sarah speaks

A positive turn of events came in Year 11 when the Legal Studies teacher, Jesse, took a special interest in Tim and made sure that he was included in the class. Jesse even invited me to observe how Gordana worked with Tim during his classes, and it was heartening to see Tim, with Gordana's support, listened to the teacher, did work sheets and answered questions during class. Jesse also bent the rules with Tim's assignments done with my facilitation at home and assessed them accordingly. Both Tim and I were thrilled that these came back with high scores and Jesse's positive comments. With the first SAC in this subject, in multiple choice and short answers format under exam conditions with Gordana's support, Tim achieved 49%, a borderline pass. I was happy, as Tim had minimal experiences with exams.

Going through Tim's answers in this SAC, I noticed that he actually knew all the material for the questions in his revision with me. But because of his overload and anxiety, much of this material was not accessible. Whenever Tim could not recall the relevant answers, he would make up something on the spot. For instance, on a question on the procedures in which legislation were passed in Parliament, Tim wrote something about "the present government, which is the Gillard government", a response which did not score any mark. However, his success in Legal Studies was short-lived.

In Year 10, Tim was encouraged to take subjects offered by Distance Education Council Victoria (DECV) because he missed quite a number of classes. He was doing Australian History, Units 3 and 4 (Year 12) in Year 11 with DECV, and did all his assignments at home with my facilitation. With his first SAC under exam conditions, Tim's exam anxiety and overload got on top, and because he was unable to recall what he had revised at home, typed something he had made up at the spur of the moment, and failed. The teacher also called into question the discrepancy between the SAC and the assignments from home, and DECV stipulated that in future, all assignments in the subject had to be done with Gordana's facilitation at school. I organised material for practice sessions in the subjects for future assignments and the upcoming SAC with Gordana, but after the first practice, Tim refused to do any further work at school. When the second SAC was undertaken, Tim became increasingly agitated during the trip to school, and I could see that a meltdown was looming. Gordana asked me to leave him in the exam room (the first SSG Chair/Integration Head's old office) with her to sort things out with Tim. I felt very uneasy, but did not want to make things difficult and left the school grounds for a walk. After five minutes, I got an urgent call from the school to come and collect Tim, he was in strife.

As expected, after I left, Tim rapidly descended into meltdown mode, lashing out at Gordana, who had to call the Integration Head for help. In the scuffle that followed, as he was trying to restrain Tim, Tim kicked him. Karen was alerted by the noise and also came in to help. Tim was still extremely tense and in danger of another outburst when I arrived to take him home. We were told that Tim should not come back to school in the next two days, as once again, suspension was instigated.

∼

Tim speaks

As Mum and I got in the car to go to school for my Australian History SAC, I could feel a buzz in my head. Taking deep breaths and our customary morning walk did not help, neither did talking with Mum about the exam. There was no time for further discussion and we made our way to school. I kept thinking about the dismal results from the first SAC, and with this one, because I didn't want to practice with Gordana, I could tell it was going to be abysmal. My whole body was tense when I got out of the car, and my head felt like it was going to explode with the build-up of pressure. When I walked into the room, it was like the movie, *The Green Mile*[4] where condemned prisoners went to their execution to be strapped to the electric chair and killed. Mum was asked to leave. Suddenly I couldn't take it anymore, and lost my grip completely, hitting Gordana. When the Integration Head, the 'Iceman', came in to ask me to stop, I went berserk, flailing out and kicking him in the process. Karen then came, and I was beginning to become aware of what I had done. Still on the floor when Mum came a few minutes later, I reacted to her urgency. Karen walked with us to the front entrance where Mum told her she would make sure I'd be okay. I was glad to take the rest of the day off, as well as another two days from school.

∼

Sarah speaks

After this incident, Tim no longer wanted to continue with Australian History. Moreover, he seemed to have regressed in his ability for other school subjects. Karen and Deborah, the Principal, called a meeting to discuss Tim's future, and with reluctance, I agreed that it would not be conducive to his mental health to continue with VCE. However, Tim would still attend classes and work with Gordana although these would not count towards assessment. In the face of Tim's high anxiety and propensity for overload, class attendance in Year 12 became sporadic. Although he still wanted to spend time talking to Gordana, the school made this increasingly difficult with another ruling. When Tim did not attend class after an initial settling in period of 15 minutes, he was required to go home with me. By that time, I had neither the energy nor will to fight for Tim's right to attend and participate at school on a more reasonable basis and as the year progressed, Tim went to school less and less, and my day was spent in caring for him. I reasoned that, this arrangement could be used to our advantage, we now had the time to deal with Tim's issues, without the distraction and without heightened sensitivity and overload from school attendance which would create further problems.

Tim speaks

I continued with Gordana's support in Years 11 and 12, and did my best to attend classes in English and Legal Studies but was again hampered by my constant overload. Because I had missed some classes, I also became discouraged with class work, which was based on things I had missed. Despite much discussion around the kinds of additional support to enable me to undertake assessment, I was unable to do any assessment tasks within the strict requirements of the Victorian Certificate of Education (VCE). I found that my lack of exam savvy as well as my unrealistic expectations for success, coupled with sky high anxiety levels meant I invariably failed to produce the standard of work I was able to do under Mum's facilitation at home. But then, the work done with Mum's facilitation was not allowed to be taken into account under the VCE guidelines, and time and again, I became extremely agitated whenever I had to do an assessment task. In the end, the school administration, with Karen at the helm, decided that VCE would not be the right pathway for me, and so I was excused from formal assessment altogether. Nevertheless, I managed to remain till the end of Year 12, when I 'graduated' with the rest of my class.

I came away from my high school ordeal bloodied and torn. I had felt like a bottom-feeder in an entrenched education system geared towards achievement and success. My spirit to continue on my journey, to find meaning in my condition, remained strong, but my ego begged to throw in the towel, to withdraw to a safe place, a refuge where I could deal with the sting of my defeat. I still suffered from a terrible sense of inadequacy, but with time to think back on my years at mainstream high school, I am at liberty to make my own assessment on my achievements or lack of. I am proud that I have made the attempt to step into the arena, and stay long enough to make a point. It had not been easy but I did my part to confront discriminatory practices and pitched my meager resources to challenge an establishment that benchmarked student success in terms of test scores and exam results. I felt that I had accomplished something in just staying afloat. At the very least, I was able to show the powers that be that I had what it took to do the work of a high school student.

---

1. Due to the recency of Tim's last assessment less than 2 years ago with ACPU,

Sylvana had used the adult version of the instrument to negate the practice effect, as there were no parallel forms for any versions of the Wechsler. Tim had reached the minimum age of 16 to be able to be tested with the *Wechsler Adult Intelligence Scale*.

2. We saw Matthew Wilson when we visited Joshua and his family in Brisbane in December 2011. Matthew had trained in FC under Rosemary, and with her recommendation, had taken up Joshua's facilitation. Tim spent around an hour working with him on that occasion.
3. Bauby, J-D. (1997). *The diving bell and the butterfly.* France: Editions Robert Laffont books.
4. Darabont, F. (Director) (1999). *The Green Mile* (Motion picture). United States: Warner Bros.

16
BACK FROM THE BRINK - ONE QUOTATION AT A TIME

Tim speaks

At the end of Year 12, the school took the trouble to give me a send-off. They called it a graduation party, just for me. I was skeptical. Of course, I didn't really 'graduate', that was impossible because I couldn't and didn't do any assessment, thus, I had not earned the official status of a graduate. Because I hadn't completed my course, I took it that they didn't want me to attend the Year 12 Graduation ceremony, just as they didn't give me a place at the Year 12 formal which I had wanted to attend, out of curiosity.

The times spent with Gordana in the tutorial room F13, was the highlight of the whole of Year 12. But that too was coming to a close, and although I felt like a non-entity at school, it was still relatively predictable, especially with Gordana's support. It was immensely difficult to face the transition now that high school was about to finish, but I knew I wasn't ready to continue with studies in any form. I felt trapped in a nether world, without any sense of belonging. On the one hand, I was able to communicate and make connection with some people who had been sympathetic, and that spurred my dream that I might be able to take part and make some contribution to the majority world. On the other hand, I was rebuffed and hamstrung, time after time, stumped by my many autistic challenges.

∼

Sarah speaks

In the Disney movie, *Frozen*, Elsa, the Queen has the power to freeze everything. Elsa also has a tendency to use this power unintentionally when she becomes defensive, and is distraught when her action puts a frozen spell on the kingdom and hurts people, especially her beloved sister Anna. Autism researcher Helen Tager-Flusberg has this to say about Elsa, who she believes represents the prototypical female autistic:

> "Around the time that she accidentally injures [Anna], her little sister, Elsa virtually stops communicating and playing altogether. Elsa's social impairments [were evident] where she remains distant from people. As her responsibilities as queen and Anna's guardian mount, Elsa **experiences so much anxiety** and **sensory overload** that she brings on a severe winter in the kingdom with her magical powers. That's when she [had to run away] to create a castle of ice on the distant cliffs. Elsa's symptoms in the behavioural and sensory domains are also obvious. She has magical powers [akin to savant skills] that are sparked by her touch, which turns everything to ice. She wears gloves to ease her **sensory hypersensitivity**, just as some people with autism wear certain fabrics that are less

likely to irritate them. We also see hints of Elsa's **anxiety**, so common in autism: her **fears** about her magical powers, her reluctance to be in the limelight as queen and her desire to 'let it go.' Toward the end, we also see her anxiety as Anna falls into a deep coma."[1]

There are parallels between Elsa's and Tim's predicament. In the grip of intolerable levels of anxiety, Tim would go into the meltdown mode and unintentionally damage things and hurt people. His fears of causing damage and hurt resemble those of Elsa's. However, I believe this sensitivity is a two edged sword. On the one hand, it leads to overload and avoidance of everyday activities that can be over-stimulating. On the other hand, it sharpens Tim's ability to read people's mental and emotional states including his own, as well as intuitive skills in attuning to the situation.

It is this sensitivity coupled with extreme anxiety which led to his disastrous outburst at the SAC in Year 11, and he had felt huge guilt in hitting Gordana. His decision to withdraw from VCE, again, similar to Elsa's withdrawal from social contact from deep anxiety, was brought about by the fear of another meltdown in the face of exam pressures. The extreme stress associated with assessment was therefore something he could sidestep when he no longer had to face these situations. Gordana, as Tim's friend, was understanding and had not judged Tim. However, it led to the school's recommendation for Tim to attempt no further assessment. In hindsight, the administration's ruling for Tim to go home if he could not go to class after a 15 minute catch-up with Gordana, was most likely set up to ease Gordana's peace of mind. As she had been face-to-face with Tim in a situation where he lost control, she would understandably be reluctant to manage any further panic attacks when Tim was having a bad day.

∼

Tim wanted to go to the Year 12 formal. The students made their own arrangements for a table with their group of friends and Tim was not invited to join a table, as he hadn't been given opportunities to make friends among his peers. He would be sitting with the teachers. Gordana didn't feel like going, although we offered to pay for her, and Karen thought it might be too overwhelming for Tim to attend. I could see his disappointment, but tried to put things in perspective.

S: "Look, you wouldn't want to be sitting across the table from the 'Iceman' all evening, would you?"

T: "You know, I've always wanted to do something for him before I leave. It would work if I accidentally spilt orange juice on his shirt, or ketchup on his dinner jacket. It's not like he can suspend me now, I'm hardly at school anyway."

S: "I doubt if Karen would be asking you to dance."

T: "I could ask her. I won't be graded on how well I dance. It's not an assessment, right?"

In the end, Tim decided he didn't want to go without Gordana, but I could see his longing to join the party which all Year 12 students were looking forward to. Later in the following year, he had his wish to party, nothing extraordinary by everyday standards, but for Tim it was "such a rare treat". The daughter of some family friends was getting married. Our children were not invited, but after speaking to the bride's mother, Tim was able to join us. It was heart-warming to see him taking part in the celebration, enjoying the wedding feast, dancing with his Dad, and talking to relatives and friends, as well as people we met for the first time, who all commented on how clever he was with his typing, and how well he communicated.

As Year 12 drew to a close, the school initiated contact with the Department of Human Services for funding for transition programs for students with disability, and we, Tim's team, Emmy,

Eden and myself, were also invited to a special end of year celebration in his honour. Tim was advised not to attend the Year 12 Graduation ceremony and celebration, due presumably, to his propensity for overload. Gordana compiled a DVD of the school experience, rooms at school where Tim spent time, together with his teachers' well-wishes. Karen said it was a pleasure to know Tim, that he was a "worthwhile person" and wished him future success. Tim was, again, very tense throughout the whole affair, but managed to rise to the occasion, literally from lying on the floor, by giving a short speech of thanks, after de-stressing with soil and water. I could see that his agitation was brought about not just by being the honoured guest who had to meet expectations, but also because this was the last time he would be at school as a student. One stage of the journey had been completed, and another was about to begin.

∼

Tim speaks

I felt nothing but relief as I stepped out of the Student Well-Being House to make our way back home after my 'graduation' party which I sullied by putting soil and water on my head and my uniform. I had been made to feel I did something disgraceful with this act many times in the past, and although unacceptable, it was the best way to manage my extreme anxiety. However, all things come to an end, good and bad, and it was now time to reflect back on the past six years of high school and what lay in store for the future. In the time that followed, I would be able to sift through the debacle of my high school experience, pick the bones of my disillusionment and perhaps come up with a few choice morsels of insight for my pains.

∼

Sarah speaks

It was with mixed feelings that I reviewed Tim's high school years. On the one hand, there was enormous stress associated with the lack of understanding and acceptance of Tim's differences and challenges, yet I could also see that Tim had made much progress in various ways, which would not have been possible except for the many difficult circumstances encountered during these years. I was also immensely grateful that we had been given the commitment and support of dedicated and skilled advocates as well as sympathetic school personnel who remained our friends and part of our social network. With their help, Tim had at least been able to undertake an education that opened up further options for fulfilling his dreams.

We had applied for and been accepted into the transition program at Kevin Heinze Garden Centre, an award winning program based on horticultural training to equip trainees for employment. In the meantime, I would also continue to explore ways of helping him come to terms with his issues. I had little idea of the inevitable obstacles that lay ahead, but I was aware that another phase of my work with Tim had commenced and I must once again put aside my assumptions, open myself to walk alongside Tim and be led by him.

Tim speaks

It was my naïve assumption, based on the strong belief that I could achieve anything if I worked hard enough, that I could be performing at least on a par with my classmates at high school. I was going to invest my all; physical and mental resources, skills, and will power, to follow the examples of my siblings to graduate from high school and go on to tertiary studies. My dreams were severely tested and this created the perfect storm, bringing on the depression which lasted many months. If this condition has a name, then it is my huge difficulty in accepting who I am, and my over-dependence on the opinion and judgment of the people in charge, those who overlooked my strengths and focused only on the external manifestation and challenges associated with autism. My high school experiences precipitated a crisis of identity and confidence from which I am still recovering. However, seen in a positive light, the same situation also fueled a relentless drive to discover the kind of person I am, and to explore who I want to be.

~

Sarah speaks

I remembered a time when I was invited to the wedding of our neighbor, Pippa, who had migrated to Australia from England. After the formal ceremony and speeches, the bride came up and introduced me to her sister, who had been living in Hong Kong for some time with her husband, as Pippa thought we would have something in common. Hong Kong was my birthplace where I had spent my childhood and teenage years before coming to Australia as an overseas student. The husband struck up a conversation and told me that he worked in the civil service in Hong Kong. The time was just before the 1997 hand-over by the British colonial government back to China. The wife, however, said not a single word, and kept looking at me with disdain bordering on contempt.

In my thirty-five years in Australia, although I had come across racial prejudice periodically, I had never before encountered such blatant and overt intolerance. During the rest of the wedding, I kept ruminating whether there was something wrong with my appearance or my manner of speech that had caused such strong negative reaction, but I had dressed appropriately for the occasion and could only say that my English has always been up to scratch. I ransacked my brain for some obvious fault or misconduct, but could not come up with anything other than my Chinese features and background. It was difficult to believe that this woman, whom I just met and would never meet again, had caused me such mental agitation and distress, but then I had forgotten that in Hong Kong, racial prejudice was commonplace when I grew up, as some of the British expatriates thought themselves many rungs above and a race apart from the local Chinese populace whom they lorded over.

This incident, and the intense feelings it engendered, bore a resemblance to Tim's experiences with discrimination especially in high school. However, mine was short-lived while Tim had to endure these on a daily basis. Although I knew that prejudice was based on ignorance and misinformation garnered from negative stereotypes from a small deviant section of the group, discrimination is very real and its effects can be devastating. Anyone open to listening to Tim would be able to tell after a quarter of an hour in his company that he is a competent and eloquent communicator. His typing also reveals undisputed intelligence, a unique sense of humour and an unerring ability to capture the essence of people's message. Tim has been further informed by a number of people in his social network that he is an excellent communicator. Penny Robinson (*I Can Network* "enabler", whom we met in 2014), statistician and lecturer at Monash University, herself on the Asperger's end of the spectrum, once said that Tim summed up a situation with one sentence after a thirty minute group discussion. Stephanie Gotlib, CEO of *Children and Young People with Disability Australia,* an advocacy organisation to which Tim has made some contributions, has also given similar feedback that not only is Tim succinct and to the point, but expresses himself beautifully. However, all his strengths, skills and positive personal qualities count for nothing in the face of people who are bent on seeing only his obvious autistic mannerisms, lack of speech, vocalisations, hand flaps, or the odd misdemeanor of lying on the floor. This latter group can only see Tim as the autistic at the severe end of the spectrum, but also one who challenges their rigid ways of thinking on disability. They have steadfastly refused to look deeper and to acknowledge Tim as an individual with a unique personality and gifts, and their attitude has brought him immense anguish and despair.

Tim speaks

As the years go by, however, my isolation has given me the space to stand aside to observe my world, and gain some perspective on how I dealt with my differences. I come from a far from usual family, you might even say, an atypical family. Every one of us is fiercely individualistic, but we all have the same credo, we work hard and push ourselves way more than necessary. Mum said this comes from my Dad, a classic example of an extreme work ethic, continuously pushing his limits, physical and mental, but I think Mum does the same, only she does it differently. It was Mum who, almost single-handedly, took up the daunting task of bringing her four children up. She stopped work as an educational psychologist when her third child, my second sister, was born, and poured her energy into the family, especially on me when I came along four years later. As a Chinese mother, Mum instinctively subscribed to the high achievement ethic, but she was no tiger mother, who set impossibly high standards for her children in order to compete with her peers. What Mum did was even more devious, she instilled from an early age the belief that we can all succeed if we persevere, and she imparted to us her love of learning and of books. She also devised ways to give her children a leading edge. In this she was especially inspired by

Maria Montessori and her methods. Mum scoured book-shops, toy shops and other places to secure games, puzzles and gadgets to interest us and provide the hands-on material we could use. She spent hours making many of these supplementary learning tools herself. Mum never pushed, but the children got early exposure to plenty of things to do, from debating to maths and science tournaments, from literacy competitions to music.

Mum read to all of us, and my second sister got some light bedtime reading of *Lord of the Rings* by Tolkein. Because she couldn't wait to get the end of this gargantuan book, and as Mum only read a chapter at a time, she finished the book by herself at eight years of age. Mum also shared her psycho babble from the time when we could understand language; it was part of how she explained things, as routine as tea with biscuits or milk with cereal. However, the Jungian stuff, archetypes, symbols, synchronicity, the Shadow and other concepts, I got initial acquaintance from my second sister, who was into Jung in a big way, midway through high school. Later on, Jung's work helped me understand much about the *Lord of the Rings* trilogy, especially what I went through.

Being last in line of four children is a mixed blessing. I was loved and pampered by all at an early age, but I also had hard acts to follow. I guess I also imbibed or internalised, in psychological parlance, the performance-at-our-best ethic, and high achievement naturally came along with it. All my siblings got scholarships to top tier high schools after going through the programs Mum devised, and they all did exceptionally well at school and beyond.

I still remember Mum and Dad's joy on the day my elder sister got her VCE results, perfect scores in two of her six subjects, and an ENTER rank that placed her well within the top 100 students across the state. Our parents were thrilled when she got into medicine on a full academic scholarship, and continued her outstanding performance in graduating with honours. At 25, the icing on the cake came when she was awarded a Rhodes scholarship and went to Oxford to complete two Master's degrees, her second in half the allotted time. If my second sister ever needed someone to compete with, there is one in the family, but then again my second sister also blazed a dazzling trail herself. She won an academic scholarship for high school when she was in Grade 5, skipped Grade 6, and did extraordinarily well with tons of prizes and awards throughout her high school years. In Year 12 with a higher ATAR rank than our elder sister, my second sister, ever the perfectionist, cried when she received a call from the Principal to personally announce her results and congratulate her as one of three duce of the school. She was disappointed because she had aimed to attain the top tier rank but just fell short. Again, our parents' pride and joy overflowed on this occasion and on her entrance into law on an academic scholarship. She also managed to achieve a high distinction average as well as faculty prizes in the years that followed. My brother certainly felt the pressure to do well as the eldest son in a Chinese family, and he didn't do too badly either, graduating in physiotherapy, and doing three years of medicine before moving on to other things. My sibs also got into heaps of things including taking part in school concerts and plays, debating, chess clubs, tournaments of mind, captaining the social service team and co-captaining the gymnastics team (elder sister), or winning poetry and other prizes (second sister).

I suppose that as a family, we are not your average Joe or Josie. Among such high flyers as my sibs, I am the proverbial black sheep. For Mum, parent-teacher interviews for my brother and especially my sisters were welcome events, with glowing reports for their achievement. As for me, I hung my head in shame as Mum got earfuls of my failings at SSG meetings. It didn't stop there either, together with the dismal feedbacks not only about my errant behaviour, but also that I was miles behind fulfilling the expected academic standard, Mum was put under enormous pressure to take me elsewhere. Since I also wanted to have the full and fulfilling lives my sibs were able to lead. I couldn't help but compare my abysmal performance with my siblings and realize that I was never going to make the grade. On the other hand, Mum has always given all of us this idea that we could be anything we wanted if we tried hard enough, and she certainly had high hopes for me.

Mum has often been told that my second sister is highly gifted, but Mum informed me that I have the best mind out of all my siblings. Who was I to question her judgment? Mum may come across as a pushover, but beneath that demure exterior is an intellect second to none, and totally hard-core when it comes to her tenacity. Let's just say it would be easier to deflect a guided missile than Mum once she sets her heart on a course. After my diagnosis of autistic disorder, Mum resolved to do everything in her power to put me on the road to an independent and fulfilling life. What made my high school failure even more galling was that from as early as two years of age, Mum had poured her love and energy into making good this resolution. But with a family of four children, and just Mum, my siblings had to miss out on her attention in many ways. Some of these occasions actually made my sibs, especially my sisters, angry with Mum. For instance, she couldn't attend a lot of my sibs' school engagements with me on her hands. My brother had won the Year 11 Biology prize, and Dad was the only one who went to Speech Night to see my brother receive his prize. At least, my brother had one parent there to witness his triumph. My sisters got prizes every year, and Mum, in most cases, just dropped them off and picked them up at the end of the prize giving ceremony. I know for a fact that autism is something of a millstone around my neck but whenever we faced the backlash from school, and Mum got the explicit message to remove me for good, I felt that I had failed to live up to expectations despite all of Mum's devoted attention and everything she had done for me at the expense of my siblings. No matter what, I would never turn out to be the son she made so much sacrifice for.

To cut a long story short, the feeling of being a misfit and a total failure wove its way into the core of my being at high school, and did not let up under the constant barrage of negative feedback and judgmental attitudes that came my way. But after a while, with difficult circumstances for which there are no real resolution, a person needs to acclimatise. Without the pressure cooker of having to face school, I stepped back and began to take another look at things. My mentor, psychiatrist Michael Gordon, has told me that to know ourselves, said by Confucius as well as Plato, is a precept for a worthwhile life. I started to see that I had been naïve and unrealistic in thinking that I would be able to live the life that my siblings lead. After all, success can be relative. There is a Chinese saying, 'It's better to be the head of a chicken than the tail of an ox'. Using my siblings as my yardstick, I would never make the grade, but looking at my friends who went through Special School, I am actually a high achiever. As an outlier, I was foolhardy to compare myself to those people I admired, but, because of my autistic challenges, what they accomplished may be unachievable, just as a paraplegic need not blame himself if he can't run, or do any number of physical things as well as the able bodied.

One of my former classmates from Special School had also just finished special school and was heading to a supervised day program. He also does partner assisted typing and told me, matter-of-factly, that school had enabled him to learn daily living skills. He was able to accept this with good grace, and did not tie himself into knots over the fact that he had never done an essay, or sat for an assessment. When I thought about it, Mum and my family had never put pressure on me to be a star academically. It was me who beat myself up when I wasn't able to do well in my subjects or shine at school. But being an academic high flyer does not mean automatic acceptance either. There were people who did well at school, but still never got the kind of things they were looking for. My siblings certainly didn't have a trouble free existence with work life and the wider world after school. I remember a saying that 'No one is a failure when s/he has friends' and count myself lucky to have not only a great family, but also friends who actually like me for who I am, autistic warts and all, including Gordana, Emmy, Eden and others.

There were other things that gave me food for thought. Towards the end of Year 12, I was asked to present at a forum for inclusion run by STAR Victoria, the advocacy organisation of Emmy Elbaum, my wonderful advocate and mentor. With Mum's facilitation, I talked about my high school experiences and answered questions from the audience. To my surprise, I got some really good feedback, and it opened my eyes to the fact that there are other students with complex communication needs and their families out there who also faced the same obstacles, and who may be even worse off. Some months later, one of these families got in touch with Mum. This parent actually said that she finally plucked up the courage to approach us as she was full of respect for what I had gone through and that her son was struggling at school. I was flattered and moved, and readily agreed to speak with her son's integration team at P Primary School which turned out to be a very rewarding experience. The class teacher said that seeing how well I communicated changed her view of students with CCN and she could now better understand their challenges. The head of integration/deputy principal also commented on the potential of students without speech when a mode of communication could be used to bridge the gap. I offered some suggestions for strategies that would work for students like us, which were all taken on board. *Communication Rights Australia*, which also advocated for this student, told us later that this meeting had led to positive changes and increased acceptance for the child.

I learned from this experience that no matter how insignificant we may be, we can all make some contribution on our own rights and in our own ways. The negative things that we go through may just be the kind of things we need to 'know ourselves' and to keep striving to reach our goals. There is a Japanese saying, 'Fall seven times, get up on the eighth.' I think that I may need more than falling seven times to learn how to get up, but when I fall, I should remind myself of the Chinese proverb that 'Failure is the mother of success', and keep at it.

---

1. Helen Tager-Flusberg is professor of psychology and director of Center for Autism Research Excellence at Boston University. https://spectrumnews.org/opinion/columnists/frozen-offers-glimpse-of-autism-in-girls/

17

MAN WITH HEART

There is no difficulty in the world that cannot be overcome by the man with heart

Chinese Proverb

Tim speaks

I had no idea that meeting Chris Varney in a café, in October 2013, was going to be such a milestone in my life. He had just done an inspiring TEDxTalk on how he learned to overcome his autistic challenges, and my second sister, his classmate in law at Monash University, wanted to introduce us. I have always found meeting new people difficult, as my social anxiety grips me and I lose the confidence to say anything worthwhile. Chris has earned a reputation as a well-regarded autism expert but with a difference as he is on the spectrum himself. I had expected that meeting someone like Chris would be like walking up to a celebrity, completely at a loss, without any ability to engage his attention or interest.

In some respects, my expectations were met, I was at a loss. I was overwhelmed; utterly captivated by Chris' charisma and thoroughly charmed by his overflowing warmth, vitality and enthusiasm. On the other hand, I didn't need to work hard to make a good impression as talking to Chris was easy – he was so receptive and encouraging. I gave Chris a copy of my poem on autism, and said something about wanting to persevere and to help bring out the best in people, which apparently made an impact on him. Chris has a habit of writing things down. Later, he told us that writing notes helps him make sense of things. Not that he needed to consult his notes, with his prodigious memory, he was able to repeat verbatim what I said at that time on numerous occasions afterwards, to my astonished embarrassment. Thus began my adventure with the man who is passionate about changing the negative preconceptions of autism.

I have begun to see Chris as the mythic hero, and what he does as the hero's quest. Small wonder his TEDxTalk, 'Autism: How my Unstoppable Mother Proved the Experts Wrong', has been watched by over 300,000 viewers to date (April 2017). Its contents comprise the timeless stuff of legend, not to mention Chris's superb delivery. There are many universal elements in his story; how the hero sets out on his journey, allies who come to his aid and adversaries who hinder, powerful spells and mighty weapons, the tests, trials and obstacles on the path, the battle to confront and defeat the ogre/dragon, the transformation, and the return with the rewards of the heroic journey.

Every hero starts out as an ordinary person in the everyday world. Chris is no exception; he was the eldest of four children, born in middle class suburbia to professional parents and with an extended family of grandparents, uncles, aunts and cousins. Chris must have been every family's dream child, intelligent, good looking and warm-hearted with a big love for the special people in his life. However, it soon became apparent that there were problems. From an early age, Chris found certain things difficult. These challenges would lead to behavioural manifestations including inflexibility, anxieties, obsessiveness, fixations with tactile, odorous, and other sensations, as well as meltdowns. In kindergarten, Chris would not take part in any of the activities at certain times, and even run screaming from the room. These challenges became more obvious, especially in social gatherings, unavoidable within the close circle of extended family and friends. Over time, problems with socialising with other children persisted and professionals were eventually consulted. The diagnosis of high functioning autism must have been a shock to everyone, but at least the problem had a name and a definition.

Chris' diagnosis was a wake- up call to the family, especially to his mother, Lisa, who came to his rescue as Chris' first ally. With the foresight and courage to trust herself and to ignore the prognosis of autism experts, Lisa continued determinedly and assiduously to give Chris the necessary resources for harnessing his considerable strengths. She set up a network of social support, from the circle of family, friends and teachers, to help Chris navigate his challenges. Everyone in this network was able to give Chris the means to foster self-belief and confidence and to focus on what he could do well or come up with strategies to overcome his challenges. This 'I can' mindset, as Chris calls it, was also propagated by surrounding the young Chris with a range of material including movies and books on resilience and success. With the encouragement and support of his network, Chris was able to find his own inner resources to deal with his challenges. Whenever he found things too intense or worrying, or had meltdowns, Lisa kept her head, and this calmness and strength flowed on to Chris and gave him the prerequisites needed to cope with his anxiety.

There were other significant people in Chris's 'I can' network including his kindergarten teacher who helped Lisa with strategies to work with Chris, and his Grade 4 teacher who gave Chris the experience of winning. By far the most important mentors, however, were his grandfather, Bob, and his high school teacher, Christine Horvath. A serious stroke had immobilised the left side of Bob's body. With slurred speech and movement difficulties, he was totally dependent on carers to help him with daily living. However, far from giving up or withdrawing from life, Bob took a keen interest in everything that went on around him. From the beginning, Bob was able to see past Chris's challenging behaviour into the strength of heart and mind beneath. By giving Chris much needed additional tuition in certain areas such as sports and social niceties, Bob demonstrated profound understanding and acceptance of Chris' differences. With Bob's strategies, Chris gradually became more involved in these challenging arenas with some degree of competence and comfort. The pair were drawn even closer as special trust and intimacy developed when Chris, as early as ten years of age, spent time as Bob's personal carer. By helping his wheelchair- bound grandfather, Chris also learned to see past the external façade into the real person underneath. He could see that Bob's sharp mind, sense of humour and lively concern for the welfare of others were intact. Moved by Bob's gutsy approach to adversity and unfailing concern for others, Chris began to understand that with the right mental outlook, in meeting hardship with courage and strength, we have the potential to inspire others.

Christine Horvath, his high school teacher, was also very perceptive in noting the different ways that Chris's mind works, and showed remarkable insight into his unusual talents in language, attention to details, creativity and retentive memory. Christine gave Chris the encouragement and platform to showcase his natural gift as a story-teller, and so earned Chris a well-respected niche in high school. A circle of close friends also contributed in many ways, helping Chris focus on the task at hand in primary school, interpret social cues in high school, and avoid the pitfalls at university.

It was inevitable that the challenges of high functioning

autism continued to hobble his endeavours to overcome the many trials and obstacles that tested our hero on his journey. There would always be some people who judged Chris as different and who excluded him from play dates and parties as a child. There were the school-yard bullies who made vulnerable students' life an ordeal, and invariably, school administration personnel and teachers who lacked empathy and created additional problems by strict adherence to rules and regulation. Trials of a more personal nature came in the death of Chris' grandfather Bob and Christine Horvath's battle with cancer which she lost, when Chris was 16 and 18 years of age respectively. With both of these sad events, Chris went through a sorely tested time of grief. Again, Chris's mettle sustained him. At their funerals, in thinking about what these two special mentors had meant to and done for him, Chris was even more determined to find ways to encapsulate what they had taught him and to bring that message of empowerment to others.

For myself, growing up with my lack of speech, and other telltale autistic traits, I have always felt a deep sense of inadequacy, bordering on self-loathing. The lack of self-worth condemns those of us on the spectrum to a life in which we would never dare to take initiative, never expose ourselves to risks or ridicule by going out of our comfort zones. We hesitate to do anything that is exciting or fulfilling, already feeling defeated by an 'I can't' mentality. At the same time, to shift our core beliefs can be profoundly difficult with autism. This process requires superhuman effort for people on the spectrum who tend to resist changes and cling tenaciously to the known and the familiar. With the call to do battle with his inner demon, exemplified by defeatist attitudes, Chris became committed to tackling his own limiting beliefs. He worked tirelessly and persistently to confront this ogre with the help of his 'I can' network. In the process, his transformation, from the old 'I can't' self to a new, reborn 'I Can' self, becomes a reality.

The return journey can also be demanding for the hero who must make choices that determines whether s/he is going to recoup the aspects of his/her humanity to fully be his/her ideal self, or fall back into the old patterns. There was never any doubt in Chris's mind what he wanted to do, and this stage of the journey saw Chris go from strength to strength. Among his many achievements, Chris did some amazing work with World Vision and at sixteen went to New York as a youth ambassador to the UN. He has studied and graduated from one of the most prestigious law schools in Australia. He has put his considerable skills in working at various organisations aimed at making the world a better place, such as World Vision from age ten onwards, and later, Foundation for Young Australians. Through his advocacy for just causes, Chris is a sought after speaker and continues to be involved in many functions to achieve a better quality of life for young people.

Chris's journey has seen him harness his potential to transcend fear and doubt and develop amazing insights and gifts. Chris believes that others on the spectrum should be able to taste the same empowering freedom to access the ability and confidence to live more meaningful lives. His vision: to create a 'rethink' of autism. Drawing from his own experiences, Chris uses his personal philosophy of 'I Can' to help others set up support networks of family, friends and teachers to achieve their goals through mentoring, advocacy and education of the wider community. This process of self-transformation, from the 'I can't' to 'I can' mentality, is deemed 'quiet magic' by Chris, in his work as a gifted mentor to many young people both with and without autism.

Chris' vision of self-transformation for young people on the spectrum came to fruition with the founding of the 'I Can Network', which was officially launched on 23rd November, 2015. Two years from its inception at Monash University in 2013, the 'I Can Network' is the first autism-specific social enterprise to be run by people with autism engaged with the work of empowerment, changing mindsets and limiting beliefs. Its scope includes addressing issues such as bullying, further education, employment, inclusion and participation in the wider community, and its strategies comprise mentoring, advocacy, education and fundraising.

At the heart of the hero's journey is self-discovery and self-awakening to the truth of who one is. It comes as no surprise that Chris regards being true to himself, the person he has become with the support of his 'I can' network, as what he values the most. For Chris, this involves responding to a higher calling to fulfill his vision of bringing the 'I Can' message and 'quiet magic' to help others on the autism spectrum. In devoting all his time and effort to the 'I Can Network', his brainchild, Chris has given up his high salaried job, and eschewed working for lucrative pay, as well as other more immediate rewards. However, Chris is adamant that he is reaping many rewards from this enterprise. He says he is provided with numerous opportunities in working with people's strengths and the strategies to bring about positive changes. In addition, Chris finds huge satisfaction in the cascading effect of self-transformation in those he works with. 'AWEtism', a neologism created by the *I Can Network*, is already focusing on the many awesome gifts of autism.

Chris's 'I Can' credo, exemplified by his story, is a wake-up call to those still groping in the dark night of self-doubt and defeat, living a life circumscribed by an emphasis on the deficits associated with a label of autism. Like Chris, we have to summon our courage to follow our passions and focus on our strengths to confound the experts' gloomy predictions of a future based on difficulties and limitations. By taking the example of Chris and others like him to heart, we will be able to embark on our own hero's journey of self-transformation from apathy and disengagement to self-esteem and confidence to live a life worth living.

18

WONDER IN A WATER DROPLET

Sarah speaks

As high school drew to a close, Tim was getting increasingly anxious about what lay ahead. I was grateful that Gordana would tell me things from Tim's perspective. She had from time to time specifically mentioned Tim's reluctance to work towards matriculation or VCE (Victorian Certificate of Education). Since primary school I had always thought that Tim was keen to pursue higher studies, in line with his aspiration of becoming an advocate for people with disability, but the years at high school had left scars. Although I've always felt that Tim's level of intelligence and resilience would eventually win the day, through Gordana's intercession, I gradually came to terms with his decision not to do any more formal studies. It was ironic that Gordana had advocated for Tim in this case. He did not want to disappoint me, nor put any strain on our relationship by not following in his siblings' footsteps into university after high school, but it was becoming clearer to me that Tim's path into the future would be as individual as he is.

In October of that year, we met Chris Varney, and that momentous meeting became a turning point in Tim's pursuit of his goals. At that stage, Chris was on the cusp of his career, launching a social enterprise, *I Can Network*, which sought to redefine autism, working on its underlying strengths and potential, in contravention to the deficit model of ASD, still held by many in the field. In Chris, Tim saw many of the qualities he himself aspired to; in particular, a keen empathy and perceptiveness, culminating in an ability to see past the surface into the enduring positive qualities of the individual behind the disability, as well as the passion to defend the rights of this vulnerable group.

We got a call from Chris not long after our first meeting, when he tentatively asked whether Tim would be interested in presenting at the TEDxMelbourne event on 3 December, 2013. It was in approximately three weeks' time. It turned out that Chris had been talking to Jon Yeo, the licensee and curator of TEDxMelbourne, about his meeting with Tim and Jon was impressed with Tim's poem on autism that was gifted to Chris, particularly with the last line:

> *Autism reduced my understanding of the world as others see it,*
> *but taught me to appreciate the wonder in a water droplet.*

Tim was happy to assent, appreciating the honour of being asked.

We set to work at a furious pace. Tim completed an initial draft of the speech in days and forwarded this to Chris and Jon. We also arranged to meet Jon and to have a look at the venue, the Melbourne Recital Centre. The meeting was speedily organised. Parking the car near the Botanic Gardens, we walked down the wide leafy boulevard flanking the Gardens towards the city. The late spring weather was balmy, and the ambience of the backdrop of well-tended greenery was not lost on us.

However, as we walked on, I saw that Tim's anxiety was

increasing with every step. Tension seemed to soak through and then seep out from his clothes. As the avante garde outline of the Melbourne Recital Centre came into view, I could sense that Tim was battling his fears and almost losing, but willing himself to keep going. This was not the time to retreat, so I tried to steady him and keep his mind focused on the practicalities ahead. I also had to prepare myself for anything that might happen. In this state of high tension, Tim's behaviour could be quite unpredictable.

We walked into the cool interior of the spacious entrance/reception hall, looking for the stage door where we were to meet Jon. After asking for directions, we walked out again to make our way to the Stage Door to the left. It was then that we saw a youthful looking, trim man with Eurasian features and a welcoming smile. Jon was waiting for us. Whatever fear Tim had felt before was put to rest by Jon's gentle unassuming manners, his effortless, almost instinctive acceptance of Tim's differences and his ability to put people at ease almost immediately. Tim was sufficiently recovered to handle this momentous introduction by typing a greeting and talking a little about his reservations about the upcoming talk. Jon was reassuring, and said that Tim was not the only one to feel anxious; in his experience, all TEDTalk candidates felt the same way. The rest of our time was occupied with Jon giving us a feedback of Tim's draft, and taking us upstairs to have a look at the stage where Tim would be giving his talk. The meeting ended with a practice session on stage. As Tim went through the draft talk, Jon listened attentively, an audience of one. After Tim finished, Jon again made some excellent suggestions with regard to audience engagement. With immense relief at how well the meeting had turned out, I made a mental note to keep these in mind in preparing Tim for what lay ahead.

∼

Tim speaks

My world seemed to consist of endless challenges stretching bumper to bumper into the distance, and as soon as I finished tackling one, another two or three would be waiting round the corner. With the experience of being very much the outsider who had to justify his presence at mainstream school, I was not prepared to put myself in the spotlight again in situations where I would be singled out for being different. However, when Chris asked me to present a TEDTalk, I couldn't resist the lure of such an offer. It would mean exposing myself to possible failure and judgement, but it would also be a heaven-sent opportunity to tell my story on a prestigious platform, viewed by audiences worldwide. Finding my voice through the harrowing journey of severe autism has been one of my most rewarding experiences so far but using that hard-earned voice would be the culmination of all my hard work. I was not going to pass up this chance to make the most of speaking out from my position as one of the voiceless, a disfranchised group relegated to the fringes because most people feel that those who can't talk can't think either. Besides, another such opening would probably never come again.

After meeting Jon Yeo, the curator, I no longer had the excuse that he asked me to speak as a favour to Chris, who had done such an amazing job with his TEDTalk earlier in the year. I was also left in no doubt that both Jon and Chris had enough faith in me to deliver something worth listening to. With the return of a semblance of confidence, I geared up to tackle another summit. The title of the talk was 'Seeing the Unseen'. Jon had given us a sheet on tips on how to present a TEDTalk, and also the example of an outstanding TEDTalk. After watching the video and feeling overwhelmed by the excellent presentation, I thought it preferable to do a good job in putting my message across rather than a bad job in emulating better speakers than I would ever be. Feeling more in control with this resolve, I mulled around for a possible theme, hoping to conjure up something authentic as well as attention-grabbing within the time frame of just three weeks.

In an aside, Chris had hinted that I should perhaps include in the speech something about being touched by the wonder in a water droplet. This line in my poem was what caught Jon's interest, the ability to see some intangible elusive property in one of the most common elements most people take for granted. After about three attempts to cobble together something about my early struggles with severe autism, the challenge of finding my voice and of swimming against the current at mainstream high school, the light bulb suddenly switched on. In an instance I could see that living my life the way I would like depended on the ability of those people walking in tandem with me to see my potential. Based on their love for and belief in me, my wonderful support network, especially Mum, worked to bring out the best in me, assisting me to become the person I am today. Their second sight in seeing my hidden potential was what enabled me to keep pushing the boundaries of severe autism, to engage in life and all it offered in unprecedented ways and to appreciate the wonder of a water droplet through my unique perspective as an autistic.

With renewed drive from this insight, I set about fleshing out this notion of seeing the unseen potential in a child with no speech and a mountain of debilitating autistic traits. Mum, Chris and my second sister helped me work on revising the draft speech. It was a race against time, and it took another ten revisions from version number four to version number fourteen before everyone was happy. The speech, a joint effort, was ready with approximately another week remaining before the actual event. The work of practicing then began in earnest. I rehearsed my speech in front of the family, extended family including my uncle and Mum's cousin, a teacher, and over and over in my head. Chris was at our house after work every other night to hear my trial runs, and give constructive feedback. On the night before the big day, Chris came to our house at 10pm to hand me a card and a large Cadbury chocolate block, with a warm smile saying that eating chocolate always worked to make him feel better. Seeing Chris pulling out all stops to help me do a good job, and with his final words of encouragement in my ears, I felt that no matter how much performance anxiety I faced, I'd do my best to see this through. I couldn't possibly forgive myself if I stuffed this up by letting my fears get the upper hand, as I would hate to let anyone, especially Chris, down.

The day dawned bright and sunny, with a hint of warmth, foreshadowing the summer to come. We would not be leaving until 11.30am – my talk was the event's first at 1.15pm. Mum had asked Jon that I be excused from the 9.30am start for all other speakers because she didn't want me to get overloaded during the interim. As the morning dragged on, I mentally went through the venue. I'd had two practice sessions there and could visualise all the steps I would be taking, from the stage door, the stairs leading up to the passage which opened onto the backstage, the backstage with all the sound and lighting equipment, finally to the stage where a full orchestra could be easily accommodated. I also visualised the empty auditorium, filled with an audience today, but I would go no further than to imagine a group of nameless people whose faces and eyes I would not be able to meet.

On our way at last, and when we got there we were met by Chris. We made our way through to the backstage, the hustle and bustle of activities was in full swing as technicians and other staff swarmed about making things ready. Jon was busy with last minute details but seemed very glad we've arrived. He introduced us to the technicians who were keen to sound test my Litewriter and iPad. The stage had been set up with the TEDxMelbourne signage and the signature circular red carpet on which rested a small table and two chairs. This was it, the event which I worked so hard on in the past weeks, the test and the opportunity of a lifetime. There was no backing out now. I mentally switched gears, focusing on the carpet and visualising myself sitting on the chair, giving my talk. I tried to block out the extraneous surrounds to imagine how I would type out my words and successfully finish my speech.

With another half hour to spare, Mum steered me to a quiet alcove where I lay down on the couch to try and settle my palpitating heart and jangling nerves. I breathed deeply and thought about the tall trees with splendid foliage we passed on our walk through the Botanic Gardens to make our way there. Somewhat calmer to tackle the task ahead, I rose on Mum's bidding to make our way to the backstage. Chris met us again, and spoke words of wisdom and encouragement, before entering the stage to introduce me.

The rest of the event was a blur. I vaguely remembered thinking that Chris' glowing introduction couldn't possibly apply to me, and also his request that the audience refrain from applause until after I left the stage. Willing my legs, stiff with tightness, to walk the ten steps or so to the red carpet, I sank down onto the chair and tried hard to focus on the Litewriter. My peripheral vision took in Mum who sat beside me, and the movement and soft background noises from the audience, stretching out in the rows of seats in front of us, numbering in the hundreds. I wanted to beat a quick exit, but gave myself a stern reminder; having huge trouble with eye contact already, it would be impossible to face Chris if I failed to go through with this.

Feeling the gentle touch of Mum's hand on my shoulder, I typed the opening sentences. The voice speaking in the play-back sounded hollow, but I was fueled by the solemnity of the occasion. The realisation that I was talking to hundreds in the audience and possibly many more who would be watching the talk later on gave me the drive to keep going. I just had to make it to the finish line. I could feel sweat and goose-pimples on my arms, and an irresistible urge to take off my shirt and scratch. I stopped, pulled up the shirt sleeve, and tried to scratch the tension away. The inevitable feeling of sensory overload was forcing itself into my awareness. I needed to do something quickly to ward this off in order to continue typing. I acted on the next thought that popped into my head. When the iPad was speaking the recorded parts of my speech, I took my shoe then my sock off and scratched my left foot. Mum was laughing silently, but somehow, we were able to gamely keep going to the finish line. When I finally finished there was a sudden release of pent up energy, like a cork popping from the bottle, I bolted towards the exit.

Chris was at the door of the speakers' common room to meet us. What he is fond of telling people, is that the first thing I typed afterwards was, "thank goodness it's over. I can relax now!" Chris also said he felt bad about putting us through this ordeal. My thinking was I would probably not be willing to go through, let alone be able to survive this experience, if not for all the support Chris and others gave me. At the same time, I felt elation at what I managed to pull through.

∽

Sarah speaks

Tim's TEDTalk was well received, and we continued to get positive feedback and sometimes from the most unlikely places. For instance, we would be walking in the park where Tim often indulges in his obsession of whacking trees or bushes with a stick. A stranger would approach us, and I am often wary that s/he might be telling us off for damaging the bushes. However on several occasions we got a smile of recognition and a question whether Tim was the person doing the TEDTalk – what a pleasant and welcome change! Chris also told us that at eighteen,

Tim was most likely the youngest person to do a TEDTalk, and certainly the first with severe autism to do so. Tim said he had the dubious distinction of the first TEDTalk speaker to take off his shoe on stage, which Jon confirmed.

The success of the TEDTalk gave Tim more opportunities as a speaker. Chris invited him to give talks at some *I Can Network* events. Tim was also asked to participate in several instructional videos and university courses on disability. In October 2014, Tim received the 'Right to Communicate Award' from *Communication Rights Australia*. As his recognition as a spokesperson for disability grew, Tim found himself acting as an advocate for people with little or no speech. For example, he was asked to attend school meetings for inclusion for a young student with complex communication needs, and to mentor another student in a similar situation, both of which were largely positive and rewarding experiences.

I personally feel that the single most important gain of the TEDTalk was to boost Tim's self-esteem, and especially the awareness that he is able to use what he has learned to provide others with similar challenges to tackle and overcome their difficulties. The TEDTalk success restored the confidence his school experiences of 'being an outcast', had depleted. I was buoyed by his determination and willpower in the face of crippling anxiety to complete the talk, and my faith in his ability to rise to the occasion was renewed. This success heralded the beginning of his transformation from the mindset of a 'loser' to that of a 'winner', and I vowed that I would give him the necessary support to continue on his journey in fulfilling his dreams.

Link to Tim's TED Talk
www.youtube.com/watch?v=Woy-XzC-UVs

19

EARTH MAGICK

Transitions can be mind-bogglingly tough for people on the Spectrum. With recalcitrant bodies that we can't control, hyper-sensory overload and communication difficulties, transitions often mean that we struggle with making sense of the tasks at hand, as well as to understand people and help them understand us.

Upon completing Year 12, I was again faced with transition, this time to the *Kevin Heinze* Gardening Program. Set up in 1979, the KH Garden Centre has evolved as a gathering place for people from all walks of life, including special needs students transitioning from school to the workplace, people with disability from various schools and organisations, lovers of gardening, volunteers, and high school and tertiary students on placement. A rebranding occurred in 2014, with *KH GROW* replacing KH Garden Centre, signifying a change to emphasise the therapeutic features of gardening, with the acronym standing for Gardening for Recreation, Occupation and Well-Being. I had no expectations beyond the feeling that once again, I would be required to adapt to a regime where independence, skills in daily routines and time management, social competence, and occupational training would be the goals. In other words, I would find myself floundering all over again as my ineptitude showed up against all these criteria. To my surprise and wonder, I was wrong. Over the months since I started in January 2014, the Centre has become less of a transition program and more of a welcoming community where I can find a sense of belonging, and *GROW* may well stand for Get Ready to Open up to Wonders.

Resilience is defined as the ability to recover from injury, trauma and setbacks. To paraphrase Nietzche, what doesn't kill us actually makes us stronger. At *KHG*, resilience can be seen, felt and touched on a daily basis. With Mum as my facilitator, we found out that although on the surface people appeared to be doing well, all those we talked to have some kind of challenge. I was astonished and gratified to know that I was not the only one with problems; most people at *KH GROW* or others in their family have various medical issues, physical disabilities, learning disabilities, dyslexia, ADHD, or autism like myself.

On any given day, all manner of people come to *KHG* exhibiting all manner of difficulties; a young man with visual impairment with a cane being led to water the plants or transport pots from the greenhouse to the nursery, people in wheelchairs navigating between the garden beds, teachers or support workers directing their charges to weed, dig, plant and water, with many of these people needing help, like myself, to do these everyday tasks. While difficulties are commonplace, discontent is rarely seen, as people, young and old, pick up a watering can, trowel, gloves or shovel, and head off to work on their gardening projects. This is always accompanied by a feeling of conviviality, as people till the soil and reap the benefits. You can almost see the chthonic gods and goddesses smiling upon our endeavors to nurture the earth and bless us with their abundance. And what abundance, gathered from the vegetable plots and chook house. Under the direction of Georgia, one of our instructors, we wash and cut up kale, silver beet and herbs, grate cheese and beat eggs.

With generous helpings of cream, the ingredients go into bakeware and turn into the most delicious quiches and goodies that we sample with delight.

The trainees are the group I identify with. Although I appear to be the most disabled, non-verbal, prompt-dependent, not to mention constantly overloaded, every one of us is affected to some degree by autism which has a pervasive impact on our lives. On my first day of attendance, we talked to Karen (the trainees' names have been changed to ensure privacy) who we mistook for an instructor as she appeared so neurotypical. Over time, as we get to know her better, we learned that she has mild autism and attended special schools from Prep till Year 12. I sensed that Karen also struggled with self-confidence and social acceptance, especially in situations she found unfamiliar or incomprehensible. For instance, when the tea-room conversation zeroed in on our favorite destination overseas, Karen looked pained. As she had never been on an aeroplane before, she tried to steer the topic back to something she could contribute to.

Something similar is apparent in Hanson too. He is crazy about football, he plays footy on weekends, reads up on footy in the Sports page, and has encyclopedic knowledge of every team and player. However, if I talk about something besides footy, you can almost see a film coming over his eyes, accompanied by the feeling that Hanson feels out of his depth. I was a little scared of Benjy at first because of his bigness, as I assume that all big people tend to be loud and upfront. As I gradually came to know this gentle giant, I developed the sneaking suspicion that his self-effacing manner and diffidence, together with a wry sense of humor all point to difficulty with finding his own place in the world amidst different social expectations.

Marcus, on the other hand, is quite the opposite, commanding your attention at all times. Marcus does everything; talking, eating, or doing the gardening, forcefully. We all know a lot about Marcus because he never tires of telling you about what book he is reading, programs or movies he is watching, computer games he is playing, what he is doing on the weekend, and last but not least, his special interests. Yet as we talk, I come to realise that Marcus finds emotions hard to understand, and his ways of dealing with this conundrum is to collect as many facts as possible with his photographic memory and catalogue this vast store of factual knowledge into categories within a historical timeframe. Samuel laughs with abandon and loves jokes. His specialty is the weather, meticulously writing down all the details for the week on a weather chart on the display board for all to see. Samuel's a hard nut to crack, because he doesn't say much and often seems wrapped up in his own world, but it's hard not to notice his unusual gait with his feet turned inwards when walking.

I would not say that everything is peachy and perfect, but I can see that I am not the only one with problems, although mine are more obvious. As I get to know the people at *KHG* better, their behaviour indicates that they are also trying to find ways to cope with everyday stress. Karen tells us she loves art, and often does her drawing into the wee small hours, painstakingly bringing the characters of her favorite shows to life. We were impressed with her sketch book of the Manga drawings in which the personalities of her subjects could be plainly seen. Benjy has his favorite music, which he downloads on his mobile for relaxation. For Hanson it is footy. Marcus shows me how he cuts up pieces of fishing wire and twirls it with his hands to watch visual patterns which he finds very soothing.

For me, I am somehow drawn to water and sand. I have always loved the beach as the ultimate experience, getting an absolute thrill from the sights and sounds of waves breaking along the shore. Losing myself in the mesmerising rhythm of the water with its ebb and flow upon the sand, I meld into the elements awash around me. The heaviness of my mind is soothed when I run my hand through sand or soil, feeling its textures, and reveling in the touch of water tingling on my skin. Whenever overload and anxiety mount to dangerous levels, water and soil will calm me down most effectively.

Because sensory overload and panic attacks are constant, with my body and mind crying out for surcease, I invariably find myself making my way towards the nearest tap. At high school, this was completely unacceptable and I would be asked to go home or be suspended. Initially people at *KHG* were taken aback whenever I gave myself an impromptu shower, but I was given support and understanding. A towel was handed to me to dry myself by a concerned Tracy, one of the instructors, with the gentle admonition that I might catch a cold. I could also hear Amanda, the manager, telling the other trainees that this was my way of dealing with unfamiliar environments, and we needed to respect each other. In practice as well as principle, each and everyone at *KHG* are treated with similar respect, and this attitude is reinforced time and time again.

I am lucky to find myself at *KHG*, with its magic and wonder working on all and sundry. I am working to remind myself of their credo of respect for each and every individual. Whenever my mental Nazis wreak havoc by brandishing their weapons of poisoned thoughts of rejection and hatred, I will do my best to give myself that symbolic towel of support and understanding. With *KHG* ethics to see us through life, we will be able to overcome the difficulties and obstacles in our path by finding and acknowledging our inherent self-worth and get back on our feet again.

20

CONNECTIONS ALONG THE WAY

Books are an indispensable part of my life. Although I am trapped in a body I can't control, books have liberated my mind and enabled me to touch the minds of writers in all fields of endeavour and open doors to people's lives through their stories. I have riches surpassing my wildest imagination attained through the writings of others sharing what they know or experienced.

One of my friends is Eran who loves books too, and with the help of his mother, Elisheva, has set up an online bookshop. Mum and I met Eran and Elisheva through our mutual friend, my advocate Emmy. Eran is 27, diagnosed with autism at the age of 18 months. He speaks very fast, his speech a staccato of words without pause. He also types independently. He has completed secondary education at a mainstream high school and is now doing a TAFE course in photo-imaging part-time at Melbourne Polytechnic. His mother, Elisheva recited a litany of difficulties with their experience of the educational system; Eran went through special school, mainstream primary schools and mainstream high schools, and special education units within mainstream establishments. Elisheva had to approach as many as eleven schools before a mainstream high school accepted Eran. Even so, his years at this school were fraught as no one seemed to know what to do or how to support Eran's learning. Thankfully, this year, Eran's third year in TAFE, has been the best year so far according to Elisheva, because he has a support worker whom he trusts and works well with.

When scrutinised, Eran looks away, and you can sense his vulnerability and reluctance to share his inner life. I can identify with Eran, a fellow traveler, wrapping ourselves in our mannerisms and obsessions, preferring to stay invisible, hiding our thoughts and feelings, our light, from an uncomprehending world. But perhaps it is we who refuse to acknowledge ourselves, to see ourselves as we truly are – surely this must be terrifying. Do we really want to confront our greatest fears, our deepest pain or our most primitive emotions? Or do we just let our outer behaviour cloak these desperate attempts of instinctual self-preservation, and mask the darker recesses of our internal landscape?

One of Eran's favourite activities is to forage in all and any bookshop, and he is often seen with an armful of books to stock his already well-stocked online library. While the love of books is a characteristic we have in common, there is an area where we diverge; the bond between Eran and his service dog, Spot, who came into his life seven years ago. Elisheva said that with the help of Spot, Eran is becoming much more independent, he starts to sleep on his own with Spot close by, in the unit at the back of the family home. With Spot in tow, he goes out, he studies at TAFE. He even has his own flat nearby where he spends most of the day. I have always been mortally afraid of dogs, irrespective of their temperament and breed, and I find it hard to understand how an autistic person with overwhelming anxiety and a hypersensitive nervous system can have a close relationship with a dog no matter how friendly. We have been told that service dogs are specially trained to dovetail to the needs of the individual owners, and respond at a gut level to their unique requirements. The unconditional love and devotion of these dogs for their owners touch them in an unprecedented way so that they can learn to relate to others. According to Elisheva, Spot just knows when Eran is anxious, and she goes up to him and as Eran holds her close, he begins to feel less anxious and more ready to tackle challenging situations.

I find this special bond amazing because the love from another, human or animal, is the perfect antidote for stress. To know you are not alone when you feel defeated, and that there is a friend, a person or an animal, who recognises your vulnerability and offers you unconditional acceptance and understanding is so reassuring and uplifting. To me, Eran is a prime example of resilience. With the help of his family, his circle of supporters and Spot, he is learning to overcome his anxiety. By becoming more independent and going out into the community, doing the things he enjoys despite his challenges, Eran is refusing to accept a life circumscribed by his autistic differences. Bravo! Way to go, mate!

∽

April 2017

Tri came into my life as my support worker who almost didn't make it. Responding to an ad on the Melbourne University careers website to work with a young man with autism (me), Tri applied a little late, when Mum had already interviewed two other students. One of the applicants, Nisha, a science student going on to do a Masters in education, impressed us sufficiently to be immediately signed up. The other interviewee, a postgraduate engineering student, however, turned out to be a poor candidate. Mum became wary as she went through Tri's application. He was studying a Masters of business and finance, and she thought it safer to confine our search for students studying in the health sciences and humanities.

As it turned out, we were destined to meet. Not only was Tri most gracious in accepting a turn-down, but he wished us well and asked Mum to pass on his regards to me. Mum thought we needed to see him in person. Tri did not disappoint, in addition to his warmth and vitality, he was solicitous and completely respectful of my special needs. What cinched our decision was that Tri was prepared to have a go at facilitating me in communication and did a commendable job.

Tri put people at ease almost immediately. Because I do not speak, and because we were unable to communicate in the early days of our acquaintance, Tri took the initiative by regaling us with stories about himself and his family. We learned quite a bit about him in a short time. Tri comes from a solidly middle class background. He is the first born son in a family of two boys. His father is a successful businessman, director and major stockholder of a company in paper manufacturing in Ho Chi Minh City. The family had moved there from a small town after his little brother, some twelve years his junior, was born. Acceding to his father's wishes or more appropriately, dictates, Tri left home to do his first degree in Business at the University of Texas, Houston. To his surprise, Tri found that he liked what he did, and after he graduated, researched available postgraduate courses. He picked the University of Melbourne, I guess, because his girlfriend was studying in Melbourne. So he traveled again, this time half way round the world to Australia. It was like we were meant to meet.

Tri always came to our sessions armed with something to show me, like the video he made about his life in Houston, Texas, for his girlfriend (who was still in Vietnam at the time), or a game he enjoyed where the player gets to build amusement parks. I also began to catch the bug when Tri started playing the game with me. I am the addictive type, unfortunately or fortunately, because I am not independent with using computers, I hadn't been spending all my time at the console. Using available resources with some strategic planning, the player can build an amazing theme park with all the paraphernalia; sky wheels, roller coasters, zoos, water slides, aquarium, among other attractions. It's like Jurassic Park without the dinosaurs, and you can put in anything, including things you design and create limited only by your imagination. Tri played songs he loves, and helped me understand the games theory, the topic he was studying for his first exam just around the corner. We went out for walks and he looked out for me at every turn. I shared my writing in return, and when we started to type together, we would talk about books, movies and things we did. Tri made me smile whenever he told us about his adventures in the US as well as Australia, his sense of humour was infectious, prompting me to look at the lighter side of life.

In a way, Tri became my first real friend, someone close in age with similar interests, and more importantly, we liked each other although we're different. I guess he was drawn to me because I was an enigma. My autism is full on and on the surface, I couldn't look more disabled; no speech, hand flapping, toe walking, all grunts and squeals. Once I start to type, I begin to show another side of me. Tri told me I was "a regular dude", except when I started to blow my nose, another full on autistic feature. Tri came to support me at *Kevin Heinze Grow*, my transition program and people were impressed at the fine job he was doing. As Tri was becoming more interested in advocacy for people with disability, we asked him to attend the meetings at *Just Learning*, the advocacy organisation on student reengagement presided by my mentor and advocate, Emmy Elbaum. Tri was able to make a worthy contribution. An issue came up, on the vulnerability of people without speech in the care of support workers who might get impatient and short, Tri offered valuable suggestions including the 'mystery diner' or undercover customer/client, as well as making a video to highlight their/our plight.

Tri's energy and passion for what he does seems boundless. He often texted on the weekend to find out how we were going, and to tell us about his day, going to the market to get his favourite seafood which he offered to bring to the next session, driving for the day to visit Yarra Valley (an hour and a half away) then onto Geelong (taking another 3 hours one way), or trying out various activities. He had exacting standards, because one time he said he would like to be put back on his probationary pay level because he wasn't supporting my typing as well as he should. Mum refused to listen and continued to pay him at the increased level. One touching moment came when Tri confided in us an incident he was ashamed of. When he was a child, before moving from his home town to Ho Chi Minh City, there was a local man with intellectual disability who his friends picked on. He told us that after he got to know me, he was deeply ashamed that he took part in tormenting this man who, in hindsight, had done no wrong, but was just different and an easy target for the young bullies. I know it takes courage for anyone to admit to something they should not have done, and my respect and regard for Tri deepened. I also felt that putting his mind and heart into the care and support for me was like an atonement for the past.

Life is not meant to be easy, nor should we be complacent whenever things appear to be going our way. We were looking forward to the end of year, with plans for making the video over the holiday season. Mum was thinking of inviting Tri and his girlfriend to our Christmas celebration when calamity struck. Two weeks prior to the big day, Tri came for a session, very quiet, far from his usual upbeat self. After talking with him for a while, he confided to Mum that he had a call from his mother who informed him that his father was in hospital, diagnosed with advanced liver cancer, and he needed to come home. When Life throws us curved balls, we invariably feel helpless and lost, but the Chinese term for crisis is danger and opportunity. I guess it means that with every upheaval, there could be an upside. In summoning the necessary strength to deal with the problem, we may discover things that we haven't paid much attention to, and see other possibilities and Life with new eyes.

The following week was a whirlwind of activities. Mum took Tri and me to interview several people whom we thought should be featured on the video. Tri also had to settle things like contacting his course adviser, paying his bills and arranging for the return of the bond to his flat. There were quieter moments at home when we would talk and find comfort in sharing our uncertainty and fear. Mum and I could offer little besides our emotional support and some small gifts of money and books for his journey ahead. In return, Tri gave me his navy blue woolen coat, which fitted me surprisingly well.

Despite his own problems, Tri was worried that when he left, he would also leave a gap in the support and care of me. His concern for my welfare was touching, but the inevitable day arrived when we drove Tri to the airport. As I watched him disappear through the entrance, swallowed up by the crowd, I too was swallowed up by an emptiness inside. I felt sadness in the huge void in my life after his departure and in my concern for the heavy burdens Tri would be taking on, in the care of his ailing father, the financial and emotional support for his mother and little brother, and in joining in the running of his father's company. Tri had, without hesitation, accepted these responsibilities as the eldest son, and stoically put aside his dreams of completing his Master of Finance and working in Australia to build a better life for himself and his girlfriend. Before Tri left, he told us that he would find a way to come back because Melbourne was special to him, he had made friends and been met with kindness from many people. I would like to think, as atoms, once intertwined, become forever entangled even when they come apart, regardless of distance in space or time, that our friendship would bring us together again in future.

21

CHANGING LIVES

Amanda Marshall is the director at the *Kevin Heinze GROW* (acronym for Gardening for Recreation, Occupation and Wellbeing) centre, the transition program I started attending in 2014. She is the fulcrum through which the various groups, staff, trainees, students on placement, volunteers, community visitors and dignitaries, organisational and school projects, pivot around. With such a diversity of people, it must be a constant challenge to allocate time, resources and effort to meeting all their needs. Yet, we gravitate towards her because, apart from being the model of efficiency, Amanda remains a center of calm, able to keep an eye on or lend a hand to the activities that go on, as well as keep her head and focus at the same time.

Throughout my training at KHG, I have never seen Amanda fazed or frazzled, despite providing a service for a group of people with sometimes challenging behaviours. If she loses her cool, I have never seen it. After getting to know her better, I think the secret to her admirable cool-headedness and presence of mind come from the high value she places on each and every person who crosses her path, of never letting the label of a diagnosis obscure the individual's unique personality. Accordingly, she has a two-pronged strategy to tackle the challenge of how different people respond in different ways. Firstly, Amanda questions her cherished assumptions and beliefs, in her own words, come out of her 'assumption corner' to make room for understanding the motivation behind unacceptable behaviour. Secondly, she constantly reminds herself of the innate worth of all human beings. This mindset has become the cornerstone of her work and has been exemplified in people who have inspired her, such as, the principal of Croydon Village School where her daughter attended. This principal always managed to make allowance for students who lashed out or threw tantrums, by seeing the inherent value of all students. In helping these troubled youngsters to understand and manage their issues, they were able to change their negative behaviour to make positive contributions at school.

It must be hard to maintain congeniality and control as others around us are losing theirs. For instance, many of the trainees are on the autism spectrum, and have difficulty with changes, transitioning, and pressure to perform. One time, during morning tea, a trainee spilled a snack hot from the microwave onto the bench and floor. He froze, and you could tell he was overwhelmed, and distressed with the mess he had just created to the point of not knowing what to do. Sizing up the situation at a glance, Amanda said, "It's okay, no one died. Just get some paper towel and clean it up." With just a few words, she defused the crisis for the trainee, who was then able to clear up the aftermath and get on with his morning tea. Because the aim of the training program is transition to open employment, conscientiousness and punctuality are part of the values instilled. At morning tea, on the dot of 11.20am, the trainees are reminded to finish and get back to their jobs on the grounds. Because I communicate by typing, I am allowed some extra time to be able to talk to people. I guess some of the trainees make use of the opportunity to get some leeway by purposely coming to talk to me and then making the excuse that they will get back to work after our conversation. One time, Amanda had to tell a trainee firmly that he had to finish our talk, and go back outside. This young man objected and strenuously defended his right to keep going on his favourite topic because he was in the middle of his conversation with me. After exchanging some heated words, the trainee said everyone needed to be treated in the same way, and I should not have the privilege of more time to talk. Amanda deftly executed an about-turn by offering the trainee some homemade jam that Mum had brought in from the blackberries I picked on the weekend. This friendly gesture cut the argument short and the trainee, quite happily, began to thank her and me for the jar of jam.

While these incidents may not be earth shaking, they provide some indication of how Amanda works with people. At the critical moment, to model calmness and control, to give reassurance to those of us who are stuck in one mode of thinking, to help us shift from overload, panic or obsessive behaviour into positive response, and to fine-tune our awareness and learn the skills to deal with potential 'disasters', is something that calls for special qualities. How different this was from the lack of support I had received from many at high school. To me, she has certainly displayed unique perceptiveness of people with both a trust in herself and in the other person, however incomprehensible or difficult the behaviour may come across. Amanda said that whenever she is faced with some examples of challenging behaviour, she takes this as an opportunity to question her own assumptions.

From my own experience, questioning one's assumptions in the way Amanda has been doing is one of the hardest things in the world. I don't always have control over my body. When I have to do any of the kinds of things I need to deal with overload – flap my hands, hum, or sit on the ground – people inevitably look askance, some even give me the death stare. One time, I was riding on the train, one of my favourite pastimes, when a boy, aged in his early teens, continued to fix his gaze on me throughout our journey to Belgrave. It became nerve-wracking, because, try as I might, it was near impossible to restrain my hand-flapping or my involuntary grunts and grizzles as my uneasiness grew. As we got up to leave at Upper Ferntree Gully, to make our way to the National Park for a walk, this boy also rose from his seat and approached us. By that time, I was feeling extremely anxious. Much to our surprise, in a perfectly friendly way, the boy asked what I was doing. An explanation from Mum that I have autism and was trying to deal with sensory overload seemed to be satisfactory, as he wished me well. We made our exit, hugely relieved.

This incident jogged me into thinking how difficult it is to move out of my own assumption corner. Someone once said that there are two kinds of people in the world, (A) those who think there are two kinds and (B) those who think there is only one kind, all people are people. Group A distinguishes between the in-group and the out-group, or people less likely to be regarded as the friendlies, whereas Group B sees differences as just part of life and is comfortable with accepting everyone as a person. Because of my previous negative encounters with those who judged me, I was self-conscious about my differences and on the defensive. Hence, I came to the conclusion that the boy from the train was from Group A whereas he actually belonged to Group B, and was just trying to figure out my unusual behaviour. From questioning my assumptions about always being stigmatised for my differences, I also learnt that people may be curious about or afraid of me because they don't really know how to deal with my weirdness.

One of my own mentors, Dr. Michael Gordon, said that everyone we meet is, in some ways, our teacher, as they hold a mirror up to reflect back things in ourselves, the good and the beautiful as well as the bad and the ugly. I think this credo is

Amanda's personal philosophy as she said that she has been able to learn something from pretty much everyone she met. To her, everyone has some effect on how she sees the world, and helps her to foster the necessary courage and commitment to face what life throws up. Amanda considers herself fortunate to be constantly in the vicinity of people who have great faith in others, including her own teachers, breastfeeding counselors who mentored her, her daughter's principal at the Village School, people who cared for her brother, who was diagnosed with cancer and died two years later, the teaching colleagues she worked with at Emerald Secondary College, many of the adult students she taught, and of course, the people at *KHG*.

Amanda supported me in many ways to find my niche. I get the feeling that she knows quite a bit about all the trainees because she has a genuine interest in us. For instance, after a trip to Japan soon after I joined KHG, she told me about a trainee who did manga drawing and loved everything Japanese. I soon came to know this fellow trainee pretty well as we talked about our common interests in Japanese food and traditions and manga characters. By providing the opportunity for me to make good use of my skills, Amanda draws me out and gives me an arena for pursuing my passion. Because of constant overload, I am not so good at working as a team member at pruning, potting, preparing the soil, weeding and so on, so I was given a plot of my own in a quiet corner which I was able to look after and maintain. Amanda also saw that I love to talk on my voice output device. By setting an example herself, other staff, students and volunteers have also been coming specifically to chat with me during breaks. Amanda and I have also had many interesting discussions, I found out that we have some mutual interests in music, movies, books, alternative medicine (her sister is a naturopath), and in the countries we have visited and trips around Australia. In contrast, I am not so good at venturing out of my comfort zone, as Amanda dares to live her life fully, and continues to seek new experiences to stretch herself. She has already planned her next trip, to Scotland to visit her daughter, and will be spending several days alone at the Shetland Islands, a remote spot far from the madding crowd, to do some bird-watching, especially puffins.

When she learned about my love for writing, Amanda suggested that I could interview a volunteer at *KHG* and write this up for the newsletter. She paired me with Val, a wonderful lady who had worked at *KHG* for many years. Not only did I get to know this special person from an integral part of the *KHG* community, but my article was published in the *KHG* newsletter and read by all. As I was the only nonverbal trainee among my cohort, Amanda made a point of giving the other trainees the chance to watch my TEDTalk (December 2013). For months afterwards, people would come up and tell me how much they enjoyed watching the video. She kept up with my activities outside *KHG*, and from time to time, asked me to write about some special occurrences. For example, when I was called on by *Communication Rights Australia* (the advocacy organisation for those with little or no speech) to participate in the Review of the Program for Students with Disability in 2015 chaired by Dr. Graeme Innes (former Commissioner for Discrimination), Amanda requested that I write up this experience. All in all, Amanda seems to know just what to do to make me feel that, despite my difficulties with certain aspects of the program, I have also been making a positive contribution to *KHG*.

Amanda believes that she has always been attracted to the type of work that deals with differences. Despite the associated barriers and difficulties that continue to dog those of us with a difference, she loves to be part of the journey of people undergoing these challenging experiences, and to see the tiny glimpses of growth and development that come as a result. For myself, I know that my life has changed for the better with my experience at *KHG*. By giving me understanding and room to deal with my own issues, my self-confidence has grown. I am able to be more relaxed about my differences, to come out more readily from my assumption corner and be tolerant of the differences of others, and also to take pride in what I can do best. While I still have to live with my body, I am encouraged to think that autism is a two-edged sword. Because I am overwhelmingly sensitive to incoming data, the propensity for overloading can also give me additional information and help develop new insights to things and people. While I lack the ability to speak, my observational skills and capacity to perceive can be better honed. I am immensely grateful to Amanda as well as the *KHG* community for their passion in their work, taking pride and pleasure in being an integral part of a community that embraces differences and putting into action policy and practice that celebrate individual strengths.

22

INTO THE NIGHT

Do not go gentle into that good night. Rage, rage against the dying of the light.

Dylan Thomas

Sarah speaks

After easing into the program at *Kevin Heinze Grow* (*KHG*), Tim found some respite from the constant mental and emotional turmoil that had besieged him from his high school years. The setting, other trainees and staff, especially Amanda Marshall, the CEO, were very welcoming, and his differences were accepted, including the unconventional methods he used for managing his anxiety. Nevertheless, he found working in a group situation anxiety-provoking, with his hypersensitivities and overload causing huge problems. Hence, his times were spent mainly in solitary activities including watering, weeding and tending his own garden patch, with my support. Morning tea in the lunch room was fine, however, and Tim looked forward to the camaraderie, typing with my facilitation and talking to people, sharing the latest gossip, news and interests. He reveled in his new-found acceptance as well as status as 'resident writer'.

Towards the end of the first year of transition, on recommendation from a friend, the talented Michael Gilles Smith[1] met through Chris Varney, we both began treatment with Dr. Doris Were, kinesiologist, chiropractor and nutritionist. Doris also performed Network Spinal Analysis (NSA) where a series of light taps were made at precise points on the spine and back. According to Doris, these gentle touches cue the brain to develop strategies for healing. Healing waves that are created bring spontaneous release of spinal and body tension associated with mental and emotional stress accumulated in everyday life, and result in a reawakening of self-awareness and harmonious working between the body, mind and spirit.

After the first NSA session, I had felt the release of bodily tension with accompanying lightness of mind and spirit, and was gratified to hear from Tim that he had a similar experience. Doris also informed us that we had to keep up the treatment for the body to release built-up stress and for the continuation of mental and emotional healing. On the heel of the second and subsequent sessions, however, with the unleashing of physical tension, the lid that Tim had used to keep his emotions under control became unhatched, together with the release of an enormous reservoir of pent up negativity and associated issues. Once again, Tim's anxiety levels escalated and his depressive symptoms returned. His anger, apathy and agitation also threatened to get out of hand. It was difficult to get him to engage in any positive activities; as soon as we got out of the car at *KHG*, Tim would invariably make his way to the nearest garden bed, put soil on his head, then go straight to the nearest tap to spray himself with water. He even got into the pond once or twice. Although the staff continued to be most understanding and sympathetic, I decided to put a stop to Tim's attendance till he became better because he was unable to do very much besides 'stimming'. Instead, the work we had begun on Tim's issues now took place in earnest.

~

Tim speaks

Although I knew that I had stored an enormous amount of tension in myself, the NSA treatments I underwent seemed to dissolve whatever industrial-grade container I constructed for the purpose of putting a lid on my emotional baggage. With this dissolution, I found myself adrift in an angry sea of pent up feelings that surfaced with a vengeance. As the waves of uncontrollable emotions crashed on the rocks of my internal landscape with unbelievable force, my grip on myself also loosened and without any notice, I would be marooned in overwhelming anxiety, daunting fears and crippling self-hatred. Thankfully, help was at hand. It came in the form of those who never stop believing in me, and who are willing to walk beside me during my darkest hours.

I am, without question, indebted to Mum who helps me in every way on this voyage of self-discovery and reconciliation. Mum does everything. She is the chef, the washer-upper, the cleaning department, my personal wardrobe coordinator, as well as my social secretary and personal assistant. She is my teacher, my therapist and my advocate. She is the tinker, the tailor, the baker and the gluten-free bread maker. No one holds a candle to her tinkering and tailoring of the material and programs she devised for my learning and skills development, but, let's put it this way, there is room for improvement in the gluten-free goodies she bakes for my consumption! She is my chaperone and chauffeur. She also drives me up the wall with her insistence that I do things her way, some of the time. Her unconditional love for me knows no bounds.

My Dad also gives me his love which is as tall, strong and enduring as the mountains, and he takes on the task of teaching me the hands-on stuff, like chopping fire wood, building a fence, putting compost in the garden or washing and drying the dishes on the weekends. My parents' love for me, as well as the lifeline from Dr. Michael Gordon who stepped in with his professional skills and unconditional acceptance, saw me through this most difficult of times along my difficult journey of transformation and healing.

∼

Sarah speaks

In the days following consultation with Doris, it was as if a release valve had been blown wide open, and a tsunami of emotions flooded Tim, rendering him incapable of doing anything much except seek solace in obsessive rituals or hitting out in unprecedented ways. The soil and water stims occurred with alarming frequency, often up to five hour-long showers a day with wild splashing and squirting of water. After this time, the bathrooms would have to be completely overhauled as water that flooded the floor seeped beneath the tiles into the subfloor structures and caused large areas of damage to the ceiling plasters underneath.

I tried my best to put off the worry about the physical damage done and to refrain from stopping Tim, as any form of external interference or control, no matter how mild, would bring on a fresh attack of anxiety that led to more obsession and destructiveness. Instead, I made another decision to be led by Tim and to understand his behaviour from his viewpoint. We took long walks, several times a day, rain or shine, and came back refreshed and ready for more self-scrutiny and soul searching. We devoured books and movies, and it never ceased to amaze me how the right material would come, as if by miracle or synchronicity, that dovetailed precisely with what we were dealing with. We would analyse the emotional storms that Tim went through with regular and almost predictable sequences, using his behaviour and obsessions as signposts to guide us.

In October 2015, there was another major mishap. We were walking in the nearby parklands when, without warning, Tim collapsed and had his first epileptic seizure. He recovered well without noticeable adverse effects, and I put off seeking medical advice as we were due to depart for the family's trip to Korea in several days' time for Tim's brother's traditional wedding ceremony with his Korean fiancée. On our return, we informed Dr. Michael Gordon, who in turn contacted Professor Ingrid Scheffer. Since Ingrid only saw patients up to 18 years of age, she recommended a fellow neurologist, Dr. Saul Mullen. There were no abnormalities with the results of the electro encephalogram (EEG) Tim undertook, but Dr. Mullen advised anti-epileptic medication all the same. Tim was adamant, however, that he was not going to go down that path due to the side effects to his mental alertness and engagement with the world. Tim's decision was respected by Dr. Mullen and myself but caused consternation to the other members of the family, especially his elder sister who is medically trained. Again, in this case, I was acting on the principle that Tim would be the best judge as to how his body would respond. Dr. Mullen, to his credit, also thought that Tim was thoroughly capable of making decisions about his own life.

In a strange way, I could see a similarity between the electromagnetic storms that erupted through his brain with the emotional storms that swept through his mental landscape. Whenever Tim was laid low by seizures, which initially incapacitated and disoriented him for a couple of hours, on recovering, he would inevitably be assailed by strong emotions together with memories of specific traumas. It was as if the seizures were triggers that released these buried emotions and traumatic memories from which we were able to glean much information. The seizures would abate a couple of years down the track when many of these memories were unlocked and explored, with resolution found for their associated issues. Despite an occasion when Tim had to be revived and hospitalised when he had a seizure at the pool (on which more later), I was immensely grateful that there were no major medical problems otherwise. Through these hugely trying days that stretched into many months, I began to discern welcome changes, faintly at first, slight and insignificant on the surface, pointing to a slow but steady dismantling of a thick defensive wall, the accumulated debris of a lifetime of unresolved hurt and pain, tucked away in the knotted tension of the body and the deep recesses of the mind. These changes, I believe resulted from Tim's unrelenting work towards a better understanding of his issues, together with an accompanying shift in perception and awareness that brought about a healing process.

Tim speaks

With Mum's help, I began to examine my emotional juggernaut, constructed of unresolved anger, hurt and disillusionment, to delve deeper into the underlying difficulties. I was helped by Jung's[2] writing which my second sister's dinner time conversation had introduced me to: *symbols* as representations for things; *archetypes* as underlying universal patterns that give another level of meaning to what we do; the *shadow*, as the dark side or underbelly of our shortcomings and challenges, as well as the ideal self, the things we are reluctant or not ready to face. But love is what sustained me on the daunting quest to face the *shadow*, my dark side. In addition, without Mum's unfailing support and guidance,

I would never have ventured past the front door of the comfort and safety of my hobbit hole, to undertake the dark journey of self-discovery, confront terrifying enemies that took the form of overwhelming fears and suffocating self-rejection to face an unknown fate, as Frodo did in Lord of the Rings.

When looking at the debacle of my high school experiences *The Fool* is one of the archetypes I could see in myself. *The Fool* represents innocence and naivety as well as idealism, setting out on his journey of discovery, and is forever getting himself into strife.[3] When I first embarked on my quest for a mainstream high school education, I thought I would be able to carve a niche in an establishment that would provide me with the opportunities for learning, which would enable me to go on to tertiary studies. I came face to face with harsh reality in a very short time, but I don't think I ever lost that longing to be a student who not only achieves academic success but social acceptance as well, as I thought I would be able to follow in my siblings' footsteps.

The high school scenario provided me with ample fodder for seeing where I went wrong. I can see the archetype of *the Judge* in the Head of Integration, the 'Iceman', as well as in some of the staff who responded negatively towards me, when they rigidly applied school rules to my case, seeing only my autistic dysfunctions, and not as a real person with challenges. The Integration Head made lame excuses for depriving me of my right to communicate because he didn't think I fitted into the mold of the model student. By withdrawing the necessary props for me to type, I was unable to be seen and counted as a member of the student body. However, I could also see in myself, a reflection of their judgmental attitude, when I took on their assessment of me and felt I was a total failure in their criteria of a successful student. To make things even more complicated, the 'Iceman' had chosen to come across as caring and supportive in some ways, he enquired about my day whenever we chanced to meet, and framed and hung my artwork in his office. But then, he was paternalistic. Whenever I committed a transgression in his eyes, he enforced rules and delivered judgment and sentences in a final warning, last court of appeal manner, as *the Judge* would.

I also see myself as the *Cellophane Man*, the jilted husband in the musical *Chicago*,[4] whose wife cheats on him. This man not only forgives and supports his wife, he also begs her to come back although he knows she will cheat again. When the wife refuses, this character describes himself as a see-through person who everyone brushes-off and dismisses, the classic push-over. In my predicament at high school and other places where I was constantly ignored and denied a voice, I can certainly identify with this character's anguish and loneliness, but also respect the integrity and love he shows towards his wife, whose transgression he overlooks because he wants her by his side.

On the other hand, I can also see in myself, a resemblance to the *Standing Man*, an archetype of resilience, from *Bridge of Spies*.[5] This film is based on real life events in the exchange of prisoners in East Germany between the US and the USSR, just after the Berlin Wall was erected. In the film, the prisoner from the USSR, caught and accused of espionage in the US, said his defence lawyer reminded him of the *Standing Man*. This epithet was given to a nondescript friend of his father's, and who his father had asked him to pay attention to. One night, the secret police came and interrogated them. The 'Standing Man' kept getting knocked onto the ground, but he stood back up every time. In the end, they stopped the beating as they weren't able to get anything out of him. His indomitable spirit won the day. I guess my will to go on, in spite of all the beatings my spirit was subject to, gave me some degree of satisfaction that I went down with my head held high, but I came back up again to defeat my tormentors' objective to push me out.

In Year 5 at D Primary School, I often spent recess and lunchtime in the playground with other integration students, all supervised by a couple of support staff. There was a boy, Jason, in the year above, who was also nonverbal and on the spectrum. Jason appeared to be gentle and unassuming, harmless in every way, doing nothing more than walking around other kids on the play equipment, picking up the occasional stick to twirl in his hand or whip the grass. For some reason, his presence annoyed me, and I would spend my time making him feel thoroughly unwelcome. I would pick up handfuls of tanbark to throw at him, or stomp or crash on the ground close enough to startle him out of his peaceable meanderings. After reflecting on my high school years, I have learned to look back at these shameful acts, to understand more of my behaviour towards Jason.

The musical *Phantom of the Opera*[6] is a fascinating portrayal of the angst and anguish of the protagonist, nicknamed the Phantom because he wears a mask to hide his gross disfigurement, and makes his lurking presence felt in underhand ways. The Phantom resides in the labyrinthine lower levels of the Paris Opera House, and makes his living by writing letters to the management to demand payment by extortion and blackmail. On the other hand, he is a prodigy in music, engineering, and other areas. He also works as a composer, an inventor and a music teacher. The Phantom loves a young singer, whom he trains to become a diva, but although she values his singing lessons, she also fears him and is unable to return his love. The story of the Phantom resonates in many ways with me, and I can see several archetypes in his complex persona that I identify with, including the *Romantic*, the *Underground Man* (from *Notes from the Underground* by Dostoevsky[7]), the *Trickster* (Jung) as well as the *Killer*.

The *Romantic* yearns deeply to love and be loved, but in his insatiable desire for love, the *Romantic* will inevitably be faced with separation and rejection and the pain these conditions bring on their heels. I can see this *Romantic* in my own longing to be acknowledged, accepted and befriended, to carve a niche in the world of others who are 'normal', and to be considered, if not one of them, at least that I can hold my own. I can see that whenever I was rebuffed, even if by something as inconsequential as a person turning aside or an off-hand remark about my differences, I would suffer the agonies of rejection. The *Underground Man* is a pathetic figure, eaten up by resentment at the injustices he sees around him, especially those directed at him, and wallows in bitterness and despair. The *Underground Man's* largely ineffective way of dealing with his situation is to turn on the world in retribution for the slights and humiliation received, real or imagined. This is true in the Phantom, and also in myself trying to pay back the people who have judged me. However, in throwing tanbark, pencils and shoes and in running away from my Aide, I merely confirmed their thinking that I was beyond the pale. The *Trickster* is a paradox, a cunning and devious figure using underhand ways to achieve what he wants. However, as a clown or joker, the *Trickster's* powerful character draws us from our preoccupation with social convention and expectations, to look at life from a creative and fun-loving angle. Kikuchiyo, the seventh samurai in *Seven Samurai*, is the prime candidate for the *Trickster*. He was born a peasant but impersonates a samurai, joining the team in their mission to rid the village of marauding bandits. Kikuchiyo is a carouser and a drunk, winning smiles with his antics, but also winning respect and acceptance by his stalwart courage and fierce loyalty.

In my attempts to get suspended, and provide an escape from the intolerable school situation, I was a *Trickster* but I was still conflicted as I couldn't see the point of doing this indefinitely, and in the long run, I didn't really want to get kicked out. Michael Gordon is fond of a quotation, "Resentment is like taking poison, and then waiting for the other person to die." In reflecting on this saying, I began to realise that, ultimately, the person who suffers from negativity is none other than myself. I then started to catch myself in the throes of anger and resentment by seeing that I am also capable of hurting and showing disrespect for people. I was able to see that there is little difference between my throwing tanbark at Jason in Grade 5 with the people who judged and excluded me. This has helped me come to terms with the treatment I met with as well as the treatment I meted out.

Some of the destructive forces unleashed in the surge of rage and bitterness from being denied the recognition, power and love we feel we deserve can be seen as akin to those of the archetype of the *Killer*. In *Crime and Punishment*,[8] Dostoevsky's novel on the tortured mind of a murderer, the protagonist, Raskolnikov, an impoverished student, formulates and executes a plan to kill an unscrupulous pawnbroker for her money. In Raskolnikov is found the archetype of the *Killer*.

Energy found in the *Killer* archetype can similarly be seen in my destructive ways of dealing with gross disappointment at not being able to succeed academically and socially, and from my pain of being an *Outcast* at school. In Year 9, after I was able to type with support, I would give the Aide, Nicole, a relatively inexperienced but decent and caring young woman, a hard time by typing all sorts of insults directed at her and at other people at school. I also gave Mum a hard time at home when I lashed out at her, punched and broke windows, smashed walls and doors, and even ran away to make life difficult, but no one was more relieved than me, when I was found by the police hours later. It was my revenge against a cruel and uncaring world and at the time, I had felt perfectly justified in exacting retribution for my suffering. Energies of the *Killer* were also present when I threw tanbark at Jason in Year 5, and made his life miserable in the playground because I hated what he represented, another version of me, the 'me' that I came to loathe and despise, the 'me' that was judged and deemed a total write-off.

Like Raskolnikov, I know I am capable of hurting and humiliating others, but unlike Raskolnikov, I know I am incapable of killing. Raskolnikov justifies his actions by the argument that he can use the money to do good deeds to counteract the evil of the crime, while at the same time getting rid of a bad person. I too, have tried to rationalise my negative intents and behaviour by thinking that, after what I had been through, I was entitled to let those people who judged me know, I would not take their medicine lying down. I am also able to identify with Raskolnikov, who becomes riddled with self-pity, guilt and the fear of discovery, in my own sense of shame, self-hatred and despair at my urge to wreak destruction.

Like Raskolnikov who vacillates between confessing to the police and seeking a way out to avoid condemnation and punishment, I also struggle with the good and dark forces within myself. Raskolnikov is finally able to confess and takes his punishment of banishment to Siberia. Ultimately, his good side wins because he is deeply touched by a young woman, Sonia. Sonia, in the purity of her loving heart, is completely ready to forgive Raskolnikov, and in promising to accompany him to Siberia, Raskolnikov became reconciled to facing his unenviable fate. I too, find the love of my family and the support of my social network indispensable in my endeavours to do better. It has been the hardest thing for me, but in facing my *shadow*, I have come to understand myself better, and to know that I am also capable of doing good and making a contribution. After taking the leap into the *abyss*, I have come back with a renewed capacity to face my many challenges as well as the belief that I can work on becoming a better person.

Sarah speaks

When Tim decides on something, I know that he has made that choice after deliberation, and will always follow through. During a meeting (May, 2015) at *Just Learning Inc.*, the advocacy group working for student re-engagement, started up by our advocate, Emmy Elbaum, of which we are members, such an occasion came up. Tim said he would like to interview and write up stories about people who had stepped back from the brink after major challenges, to learn their secrets in dealing with life's curved balls. With the full support of Emmy and *Just Learning Inc.* Tim's project was given birth, and in the two years that followed, he completed the first draft of a manuscript of personal stories of people with the necessary resilience to bounce back after a crisis or life changing circumstances. It seems incredible that within this relatively short time, Tim had managed to achieve his dreams both in advocacy work as well as an aspiring author. Then again, I am all too familiar with Tim's stubbornness and tenacity, born out of the determination and readiness to tackle the obstacles that come his way. My hope is to continue in my role as his facilitator and support him in his many endeavours to prove to the world that autism need not be a stumbling block.

Tim speaks

Since I took up this writing project and got to know my interviewees, I have come to realise that these people who inspire me have come into my life for a purpose. In the mirror they have held up can be found the best ways to respond to adversity and to meet challenges, with fortitude and optimism, as well as with faith in the basic goodness of the world and an appreciation of the wonders of life. I also see in my interviewees the admirable qualities of Kambei, the noble leader in *Seven Samurai*, as a personification of the *Ideal Man*. Kambei's wisdom, high principles, compassion, concern for the welfare of his troupe as well as for the villagers who hired them, selfless devotion to duty, resolute stance in battle and resilience in setbacks, are qualities I also hope to emulate on my journey of self-exploration and transformation.

In writing up the stories of the inspiring people in my life, I have understood more of their admirable qualities. This group, including the ones I met more recently, embodies the *Warrior* archetype, and their resilience and courageous efforts for change dovetail with my own credo in the quest to achieve my goals. Julie Matheson is inspiring, in using her exceptional mind and heart to understand Laurence, her highly gifted son, and to explore different paths to provide every opportunity to foster his amazing talents, in the face of the obstacles erected by judgmental attitudes and envy towards both her son and herself. With Rosemary Crossley's heroic stance and unremitting efforts in her work to procure the right to communicate in people with complex communication needs, I have learned many things and tried my best to speak/type out and show people what we can be capable of when given the necessary support and the opportunity.

I have been inspired by Emmy Elbaum, my advocate, mentor and friend. Despite meeting the sorrowful fate that befell a child survivor of the Holocaust, Emmy passionately believes in the potential of each and every individual, irrespective of differences, to contribute to and live a full life. With this credo, Emmy has worked tirelessly to turn her anger at injustice and discrimination into positive action to help and advocate for vulnerable people. Eden Parris is my hero, in his superb efforts to negotiate for the necessary support for me at school, and in the judicious use of his passion as well as considerable advocacy skills to fight for the inclusion and fuller participation of people with little or no functional speech. Similarly, Chris Varney is my role model, for turning the challenges associated with autism into a focus on the strengths of people on the spectrum and to use this focus for a positive re-definition of autism. The students, instructors and volunteers of *Kevin Heinze Grow* have all taught me that life can be fulfilling and enjoyable, in the midst of the many challenges we all face. Amanda Marshall, who steered *Kevin Heinze Grow*, has brought me the gifts of confidence and self-belief with her continuing interest and support for me and my projects. In addition, she provides, by her own example, the philosophy of always questioning her assumptions to look for the reasons behind people's less than desirable behaviour, in order to become a better person and do a better job.

Michael Gordon, in my mind, is the archetypal *Sage* as well as *Wizard*, using his knowledge, skills and training in creating change and transforming lives. Michael's belief in the power of the human spirit can be seen from another memorable saying he gave me, from an admirable Tibetan monk who has this response to years of imprisonment in the hands of the Chinese, that what he found hardest was to feel compassion for his torturers. Michael's humanity and humility can also be seen in what he often said, that the most important things he has learned in his work came from his patients, including me. In his deep compassion for suffering, Michael has helped me in many ways to find and acknowledge the positive parts of myself that enabled me to keep going in the arduous process of examining and resolving my issues.

Most of all, I owe much to my family who have given me their loving care and help shape me into who and what I am. I know I share their acceptance of the differences and diversity in people, their compassion and a well-developed sense of social justice to do something to help, as well as their dictum that, a fine mind and a thirst for knowledge and as well as putting in the effort, can culminate in a rewarding life. Our family's drive for achieving our dreams has given me hope that, I too, will eventually be able to find my niche. As for Mum, my alter ego, wise

Counselor and trusted companion on my journey, it is her courage and perseverance that got me to where I am today. I see her putting off doing her own thing to devote her life to her children, especially to me. I see her cleaning up the mess, after my obsession with water and soil, for the umpteenth time, at all hours of the day and night, uncomplaining and unfazed. I see her love writ large, when after my meltdowns, she takes a deep breath and squares her shoulders, to ask, "So tell me what happened?" I know she will never stop the never-ending task of helping me, with whatever tools she can muster or devise, in the exploration of the dark corners of my mind, a process which helps me know myself. It is these times I think that Mum is the bravest person I know, Desmond Doss not withstanding.[9]

Sarah speaks

With the progress that Tim had made in understanding the meaning behind his suffering, I too am grateful for the many insights I have found from undertaking this healing journey together. Through our working partnership, Tim and I have come to believe that there is a similarity between trauma victims and the individuals affected by autism. There is a huge overlap between the symptoms of both groups brought about by the urgent need to dissociate from unbearable pain and unthinkable dangers, mental and physical, from the blows that life has dealt some of us. With this dissociation comes an enormous difficulty in accessing the essential functions that most of us take for granted, including speech, social engagement capacity and the ability to process incoming information and think rationally.[10] It is our hope that future research will be able to throw light on this intriguing association and lead to appropriate interventional strategies.

This model of autism has given Tim the means to take the edge off the negative definition and stereotype of autism. Rather than feeling himself to be an aberration based on the deficit model for which he felt nothing but pain and revulsion, autism, as explained by the Polyvagal theory (Porges, 2001),[11] comes about from our physiological adaptation to prolonged exposure to trauma and other extreme circumstances. There is nothing to feel shame or guilt about in the natural responses of our body to adversity, a biological response shaped by millions of years of evolution. With this redefinition, Tim has been able to see that the protective mechanism of dissociation, in response to imminent danger and trauma, has resulted in an inability to access the functions of speech, social engagement and information processing through language. But this dissociation has also brought to the forefront compensatory skills, including the fast track to seeing the world and how it works, with visual thinking, intuitive assessment of situations and phenomenal memory capacity.

∽

Tim speaks

I am awed to know that the people in my life exemplify, in one way or another, the archetypes of all the things I need to understand in myself. I also know that all the experiences I went through, good and bad, have molded me into who I am and will keep me moving forward to becoming the person I want to be.

In a way, my journey has come full circle. The inexplicable twist of fate that has afflicted me with severe autism has also brought about my confrontation with the pain of being an *Outcast* and the agony of self-rejection. However, with the therapeutic work that Mum and I undertook, as well as the professional help of Michael Gordon, I have been given the support to see things in a different light. In coming to terms with the discrimination as well as dismissal of me as a full human being from certain quarters, I know that I too, have been judgmental of myself and others like me. Time also heals, like the regeneration of the flora and fauna after a forest fire, out of the ashes, I too have been reborn. Out of the time spent in the dark night, I have emerged to become a better person, more able to follow the ideals I believe in, and more ready to put into action my dreams of working as an advocate for others in the same boat.

---

1. Michael Gilles Smith gave Tim some valuable tips on writing as well as an arrangement for an interview with an *Age* journalist for an article on the upcoming Autism Conference in Melbourne. Among his many achievements, Michael also served as speech writer to a former Prime Minister during his terms in office.
2. See Samuels A. (1986). *Jung and the Post-Jungians*. UK: Routledge.
3. The *Fool* is exemplified by the youngest samurai, Katsushiro, the novice, in Kurosawa's film, *Seven Samurai* (1954, Toho Production Company) in his hero worship of and devotion to the character of the *Ideal Man*, Kambei, the leader of the band of samurai hired by peasants to regain control of their village and their lives ruined by marauding bandits.
4. Marshall, R. (Director)(2002). *Chicago*. Producer Circle Co. Zadan/Meron Productions.
5. Spielberg, S. (Director) (2015) *Bridge of Spies*. DreamWorks Pictures.
6. Webber, A.L. (1986). *Phantom of the Opera* (Musical). West End, London.
7. Dostoevsky, F. (1864). *Notes from the underground*. UK: Vintage Books.
8. Dostoevsky, F. (1866,1956). *Crime and punishment*. UK: Random House.
9. For me, Desmond Doss epitomises supreme courage. His story is immortalised in the film *Hacksaw Ridge (*2016, Mel Gibson, director, Summit Entertainment*)*. Desmond Doss was a conscientious objector and worked as a combat medic in the US Army in World War II. He was treated with contempt, bullied and beaten by his fellow soldiers as well as court martialed by his superior officers for his refusal to carry a rifle or take part in arms training. In April, 1945, the bloodiest battle of the Pacific theatre took place in Okinawa on the Maeda Escarpment, or Hacksaw Ridge, so named because of its location on top of a sheer 400-foot cliff, fortified with deadly Japanese machine gun nests and booby traps. Although the mission was deemed to be suicidal, it was a deciding factor for Allied victory. When Doss's battalion was ordered to retreat, he refused to obey as he could not contemplate leaving his fallen comrades behind. Facing heavy machine gun and artillery fire and working completely on his own, Doss repeatedly ran alone into the kill zone to help the injured soldiers. Throughout the night, as

he lowered each rescued man down to safety, he prayed to God to "please help me get one more." He ended up with the rescue of approximately 75 men, including some wounded Japanese soldiers. Doss became the first conscientious objector to receive the Medal of Honor, the highest military award, for actions above and beyond the call of duty, as well as a swag of other medals.
10. The book by Holly Bridges (2016), *Reframe Your Thinking Around Autism: How the Polyvagal Theory and Brain Plasticity Help Us Make Sense of Autism*, UK: Jessica Kingsley Publisher, which we came across in 2016, is the only book to date that uses the Polyvagal model put forward by Stephen Porges (2001) in an interpretation of autistic symptoms. The Polyvagal Theory suggests autism is a learnt physiological response, hardwired by evolution, as a result of children being in a prolonged state of 'fight or flight' while their nervous system is still developing. This book explains the state of dissociation brought about by imminent danger/pain in terms of the breakdown of higher cortical functions, speech, social engagement and so on. The author incorporates recent neuroplasticity research to provide the tools to strengthen the child's brain-body connection and reverse the physical, social and emotional factors associated with autism.
11. Porges, S.W. (2001). The polyvagal theory: Phylogenetic substrates of a social nervous system. *International Journal of Psychophysiology, 42*, 123-146.

23
WORK IN PROGRESS

Tim speaks

I met Daniel Giles when I went to the first *I Can Camp* for young adults in 2014. Chris Varney, the Chief Enabling Officer of the *I Can Network*[1] and my mentor, had put me on as a speaker, and Daniel came up towards the end of the talk to introduce himself. Daniel also gave an *I Can* talk on his experiences as a child with autism with severe social and communication difficulties. He was given a gloomy prognosis by the professionals who did not think he would be able to live an independent life. However, through sheer perseverance and intensive effort, he has exceeded expectations, graduating from high school to undertake tertiary education, working as a graphic designer and living independently. Furthermore, Daniel has also gained a reputation as an advocate for autism and a motivational speaker; worthy achievements for someone who is just a few years older than I am.

Because there were so many people at this camp, nearly all unfamiliar, and because I was out of my depth with organised activities even at school, I was feeling totally overwhelmed. I remember going outside during a break to do my de-stressing ritual. I had a crazy urge to deal with my panic by digging my hands into the ground, then went to the nearest dorm and splashed water at the sink. Mum, as usual, helped to clean up the mess I made of myself and the room. After Daniel and I saw each other a few times through our involvement with different events, he told me that he had misunderstood my need to use the water and soil ritual for de-stressing and that it was a good learning experience for him. When my obsessions take hold, I usually don't think much about the consequences at the time, but afterwards, I always feel guilty when I realise that I have been a nuisance. I started to explain, however, I could see that Daniel was fine about the incident. From that act of honesty and generosity, I felt a desire to get to know him better. Daniel had also made overtures of friendship, making a point of talking to me in *I Can* events, sending me Christmas cards in his neat and painstaking writing, and sharing his specially ordered gluten free pizza with me during lunch meetings at *Youth Disability Advocacy Services* (*YDAS*) when he found out I also adhere to a gluten free diet.

Daniel and I were fellow committee members at the *YDAS*, an organisation that represents young people with disability and promotes their welfare. I went for an interview at the YDAS headquarters in response to an ad for membership on their steering committee, and Daniel was on the panel who interviewed me. Luckily they must have thought I would be able to make a contribution in advocacy work as my application was successful. However I didn't really get a chance to do much. I had always found it difficult to be at ease in a roomful of people I don't know well; a carryover from my difficult high school days. I was still suffering from the acute anxiety, a constant affliction which had intensified since high school. Since completing Year 12, I found myself paralysed with social phobia in unfamiliar situations, unable to take part in social activities or meet new people. My coping mechanism also became less effective as I invariably needed to deal with my fears even before I started. At *YDAS* meetings, with the inevitable overload, I was pacing around the room, resting my head on the table or lying on the floor. Sometimes, I also needed to go to the bathroom to splash water. In addition, social anxiety has drastically reduced my ability to type to communicate at events. I had joined *YDAS* in an effort to meet more people and contribute, however things got so dire that I resigned from my position on the *YDAS* steering committee and was forced to limit other social commitments. Instead, I made up by reading about disability advocacy as I still had an avid interest in what was going on in the field. Although my time at *YDAS* was brief, I learned much about advocacy. I also learned many things from being among a group of young people with various physical and other challenges.

I learned from Daniel's regular posts on Facebook that he was continuing his solid contribution to raise awareness for the autism community. Among his many projects, Daniel had organised some fundraising walks for autism, such as the 24-hour walk and the dawn to dusk walk in Bendigo, the country town where he lives. Daniel has well-developed interests in photography as well and took some beautifully evocative photos when he traveled that were posted online. A photo of a pair of shoes on a pier at the beach where he stayed, or the symmetry of electricity poles against the rolling landscape taken from the train window, are among my favourites. Daniel is a keen traveler as well. When I read that he had just made his first overseas trip to Bhutan via Singapore to attend an international autism conference as a speaker and representative from Australia,[2] I just had to talk to him again. I was rewarded with his prompt assent for a meeting.

In the environment of our home Daniel was very easy to engage, Mum and I spent time getting the low-down on his recent trip as well as other things. It comes as no surprise that Daniel is polite in the best sense of the word, that is, considerate of the needs of others. For instance, as I went in and out of the room constantly, he waited for me to return, and adjusted his seat when he talked so I could be included. He brought some gluten free brownies which he wanted to share for afternoon tea. During snacks, he asked if he could finish what he was eating first before answering our questions (we auties don't multitask easily.) I guess this politeness came from being entirely comfortable with who he is and he was not put off by my autistic traits or jumpiness, nor did he try to hide certain unconventionalities of his own.

What impressed me about Daniel is his willingness to meet challenges head on and, in the process, tackle his fears, hypersensitivities and other differences imposed by autism. For instance, one of the things Daniel did to raise funds for the *I Can April for Autism* campaign was to set himself the goal of spending more time with dogs. Like myself and others with autism, his hypersensitivity led to an aversion to dogs. He finds dogs' unpredictability in jumping up or barking difficult to manage. During this campaign, Daniel assiduously desensitised himself by seeking the company of his friends' dogs, and at the end of the month, posted a photo of himself walking a dog around the Lake in Bendigo. Another challenge Daniel took on with great determination saw him reaping unexpected rewards. He confessed that using public transport is a major difficulty due to the flow of people and noise invariably causing sensory overload. In addition to managing his sensory issues, he has to familiarise himself with the timetables and schedules, getting and validating his ticket, and putting all this information together so he can get on the right tram/bus/train. In Daniel's own words:

> "I was scared because it was busy and there seemed to be so much to do and so many things to think

about when catching public transport; such as having to not only buy, but also validate a ticket, and having to remember the best route to take. It was also difficult for me to try and work out all of the social etiquette to follow, and a lot of the time I couldn't get it right. When people told me to 'get a wriggle on' as I was trying to overcome these barriers, it made me feel like I was never going to be able to get around Melbourne independently.

I was able to overcome these challenges by just encountering people here and there who encouraged me and told me that I was doing a good job – people who would help me to break down big processes into little steps... Now I advise on disability access in Victorian public transport systems with the State Government to ensure they address not just the physical challenges experienced by people living with a disability while on public transport, but also ways to navigate changes and chaotic processes that might cause distress."[3]

Daniel did fantastically well, not just in working out how to use public transport, but also to turn this challenge into another of his strengths. In his advisory role to the transport department on more user-friendly services for people with special needs, Daniel is able to use his knowledge to help others in the same boat and to have a voice in making real changes in the area of public transport.

With his new-found strength, Daniel is justifiably proud that he was able to go on his first overseas trip to Bhutan recently. His stopover in Singapore actually afforded him the chance of taking in the sights by public transport on his own. He felt privileged that of all the international speakers, the Bhutan prime minister chose to come to his self-advocacy talk. In short, Daniel enjoyed the trip so much he has made plans for more international travelling in the immediate future.

Setbacks are commonplace for people like Daniel who refuse to stay in their comfort zone. How does Daniel navigate these pitfalls with his autism-associated challenges? For instance, when the Australians arrived in Bhutan, the bus that was going to take them from the airport to the capital city was supposed to take one hour. However, the Bhutan prime minister was also travelling, and the extra security meant that their bus trip ended up taking three hours. How did Daniel cope with unexpected changes in plan when it must already be difficult to manage an unfamiliar airport in a different country? In the past, Daniel has had misgivings with airport routines. The checks through security, immigration, and customs have been taxing especially after a long and tiring flight. On his first independent plane trip, his father and sister took him to the airport. Daniel recalls that he had panicked when the alarm went off for the security check. His sister wanted to help, but his father had insisted on letting Daniel handle this incident by himself, with complete faith in Daniel's ability to stay in control. Daniel said that because he had this opportunity to learn to navigate minor obstacles and setbacks, he became more able to face increasingly demanding situations later.

Daniel is grateful for the people who supported him by actually backing off to give him opportunities for independence. His father, of course, has played an important role on Daniel's journey for independence. Daniel started with Prep in a special school, and over a number of years, with dual enrolment or integration, gradually moved on to mainstream primary school full time. Daniel recounts that his Aide at the mainstream school was prepared to let Daniel have a go at doing things himself, standing back to support him only when there was a need. Daniel said that these opportunities helped build his confidence and self-reliance.

These days, Daniel has learned to be more philosophical when encountering obstacles. His strategy is to stay calm and remain optimistic about unforeseeable hindrances. After all, he said, "it's not the end of the world." Furthermore, in Daniel's opinion, the world will not always go the way you want, and acceptance of this fact enables him to go through life without accumulating too much unnecessary baggage. What about the people who don't really understand autism or our special physiology and are disrespectful or rude? I have experienced more than the usual share of negative reactions to my weirdness – from impatience to anger to shock. One time, Mum and I were watching a movie, and at the end, a lady sitting several rows in front came up and told us that she was appalled at my humming, and asked how it was possible to be enjoying the movie with such a racket. Mum explained that I have autism which worked as an apology of sorts. Irate strangers are not my cup of tea, but I have encountered worse situations when people who are supposed to be helping actually set out to work against our interests or set up roadblocks. For instance, I thought back to the times when I wanted to go to an event or join in an activity, and was told that there were prerequisites or guidelines which I don't qualify or it was impossible due to a lack of resources or the excuse that it would not be an ideal situation for me. I wanted to know what Daniel would do in such situations.

Daniel said that intolerance, derogatory remarks and active discrimination made him very sad. At the same time, he is adamant that he needs to forgive the very people who committed such acts. He quotes the saying that to live with hatred within you is to poison yourself and then wait for the other person to die. With this philosophy, Daniel has found that, the high way to deal with negative responses from other people, is to stay positive, and not to harbor bitterness or repay in kind. We should decry discrimination, but approach bigotry and bullying with compassion and understanding, to promote a peaceful resolution and reconciliation. Daniel adds that he still has a lot to learn, and forgiving those who hurt him is a work in progress, but he tries to live each day according to this precept.

I have immense respect for Daniel as a wise and wonderful friend. With Daniel's example, I now know that living according to our principles is the only way to achieve our dreams. When we follow our principles, we can live in harmony with our truths, and face the world by trusting ourselves. Although the world may not always go our way we can confront the obstacles in our paths with our inner resources and become better prepared for other challenges. The best thing Daniel has taught me is, by forgiving others when they hurt us, helps us to release our own pain and to live each day more fully. I can take heart by following Daniel in living a full life by leaning into the unknown, taking initiatives and facing risks rather than making excuses. To be comfortable with who we are is the only way we can get to where we want to go. Daniel's acceptance with the way things are, his perseverance in meeting his challenges to expand his horizons and to change the world for the better, his drive to follow his heart and his dreams, as well as his many achievements, are resounding testimony to this way of living.

---

1. *I Can Network, Humans on the Autism Spectrum,* (April, 2017). icannetwork.com.au/humans/
2. https://www.icannetwork.com.au/humans2017/daniel/
3. https://www.facebook.com/theicannetwork/photos/a.278436099008274.1073741828.215369978648220/675359799315900/?type=3&theater

24

HOPE SPRINGS ETERNAL

It was a bleak winter's day, overcast with rain-laden clouds, and the cold wove a way through my woolen jumper and overcoat. A flame stood at the entrance of our destination, resembling the larger eternal flame at the Shrine of Remembrance. Mum and I were approaching the Jewish Holocaust Centre; part memorial, part museum. We entered and were given a kind welcome by Dr. Michael Cohen, the director of community relations, who had arranged a meeting for us with Maria Lewitt, a Holocaust survivor. I could find no better example of resilience than those who had gone through the Holocaust, who had lost family and loved ones, who had witnessed and been subjected to extreme discrimination, deprivation, and the constant threat of violence, deportation and death. I wished to learn their secret, how were they able to go through the horror and extreme dehumanization of their treatment, what gave them the courage to live on, what kind of perspective of the world and of people would emerge after such unspeakably traumatic experiences? From a different angle, how would we fare under similar circumstances and how would we measure ourselves against such extraordinary courage and heroism with our more mundane challenges? Moreover, with my writing aspirations, to be meeting Maria, a literary giant with a reputation as an acclaimed author and poet, was nerve wracking to say the least. That I was jittery would be an understatement.

I need not have worried. With the help of a cane, Maria walked in with firm steps. She was slightly built, but radiating a kindness and warmth that made her appear larger than her diminutive frame. She put us at ease from the beginning and made us feel thoroughly welcome. When she was informed by Michael that we would like to meet and talk with her, she said she turned 91 a few days ago and added that our meeting was her birthday present. Throughout this meeting, whenever I became overloaded, needing to rest my head on the table, or to lie down on the floor, she enveloped me with concern, understanding and respect.

Maria had taken pains to bring memorabilia of the past, including photos of herself as a toddler, and as a child with her older sister, another one of her mother, and of the park in Lodz, Poland, where she was born, as well as a drawing, sketched by her architect son, of the house where she was in hiding during the war years. There were stairs leading to the cellar where they hid, and in the front were rabbit hutches. The Nazis used dogs to sniff out Jews and other people in hiding, and the rabbits served as legitimate excuses for the barking of the dogs; stark reminders of the dangers of discovery.

She also brought a book she had written, *Just Call Me Bob*, written for young people with reading difficulties, and gifted this to us because it was out of print. In this book she slipped her poem, *Smugglers*, written about the process of disembarking and going through immigration and customs when first migrating to Australia. I had read this poem before we met, and the furtive and almost illicit feel in the piece had resonated with my own feelings of being a fringe dweller in a society consisting in the majority of able-minded and able-bodied people. Meeting Maria, I was struck by the contrast between her outward appearance of respectability, conventionality and serenity, with her insights and depth which hinted at a familiarity with more weighty issues; the darker side of life that would 'leave a trail of unsuspected contraband' of 'the heavy cargo of our past'.[1]

Maria's protected and privileged childhood years ended in 1939 when she turned 15, with the invasion of Poland by the Nazis. Almost overnight, the situation became extremely dangerous for Jews. Anti-Semitism was rampant, and Jews were not allowed to be on the main streets, to go to the theatre, library, or to participate in recreational or social activities. Maria said that schools were forbidden to Jewish children, and teachers who taught Jewish students faced the death penalty if found out. Even doing routine things, such as crossing the road, could get you shot.

My own experiences with discrimination, with at least a veneer of benevolence, were mild in comparison. "As Tim is not able to do the 20km compulsory bike ride, sorry but we think he is not ready for school camp." Or "We have no resources at the school for training staff to facilitate his typing, perhaps another school or dual enrolment at the special school would better meet his needs." However, for the ill-fated Jews of Nazi-occupied Europe, the bitter pill of discrimination was not even sugar coated, they had to swallow daily doses of continual mocking, baiting, humiliation, as well as every conceivable danger to life and limb. Maria's father, who always had time to read through her school work, and have talks with her, was brutally kicked to death by a Nazi early in the war, and those in his funeral procession were pelted with rocks and jeers of "Down with Jews. One less, good riddance."[2]

I wonder how any person could take the extreme dehumanisation meted out to the Jewish people under Nazi Germany, and stay sane. In my experience, constant belittlement and lack of acknowledgement reduced me to a state of fear and anguish. I was always on the defensive, angry with those who looked askance at me, yet angrier at myself for being an 'apology of a human being'. Watching Maria's equanimity in recounting the terrible wrongs done to her and her family, I felt tears sting my eyes as her compassion and humanity washed over me with every word. What moved me deeply were her refusal to become bitter and her steadfast faith in the inherent goodness of the human race. Is this the secret to happiness then, a stubborn belief that things will work out and tomorrow brings a new day and a new beginning?

What enabled Maria to live through this terrible time? She emphatically stated that because there was no other choice, she had to find ways to lighten her burden with any means available. Unlike those less fortunate, her mother, sister, and other members of the extended family were with her. Through the daily terror of family and friends disappearing, harassment, beating and persecution of Jews everywhere, she willed herself to find reminders of hope; a beautiful vista of the sky, the patterns of nature, and other things most of us take for granted, like a bunch of lilies or a table cloth from the family home, the semblance of normality. If only I had had half as much courage! Then perhaps I could have withstood the onslaught of attacks against my differences. Mostly they came from ignorant people too busy with their own agenda of upholding the reputation and standards of a school famed for academic performance. They feared, I guess, that I would sully the school's reputation with my autism, lack of speech, hand flapping and other telltale signs of an overloaded nervous system. In hindsight, I should take note of what one of my mentors, Dr. Michael Gordon, said, so that my alienation and pain can be put to some use. Michael said that how we are treated by others can be reflected on to give us the impetus to act in the way we would like to be treated. That is, when we encounter prejudice, it should just be another reminder to learn to be more tolerant of others' differences.

∼

I think that from Maria's traumatic war experiences were born the relentless drive to find hope in every situation, her courage and instinct to keep going. These fortified her resolve to migrate and rebuild a second life in Australia after the war. With her strength, intelligence and the link provided by her husband's second cousin, she forged a new life. It must not have been easy: uprooted and without a working knowledge of English, although she speaks French and Russian in addition to her native Polish. Later Maria took classes at the Council of Adult Education. This intense desire to learn had its roots in what her father once said. He told her that the Nazis could take many things from them, including the beautiful artwork on their walls, but one thing they could not take was "what we had learned".

Her writing indicates not only a proficient command of English, but also an outstanding and eloquent ability to use language to portray the complex political, social and emotional landscapes of what she had gone through. Maria has worked as a volunteer in the Centre in the past 26 years, and she gave us a short, guided tour which focused on the displays of the photos of her family and friends. Her new life must have been remarkable because, as she told us in her modest way, she was awarded a Medal of the Order of Australia (OAM) some time ago for her services.

∼

We felt very lucky to meet a truly inspiring person in Maria and departed with many gifts from this memorable meeting: her amazing story, the inspiring poem and book, as well as her autobiographical novel of the war years, *Come Spring*, which she bought from the Centre bookshop especially for us, inscribed, "To Tim, with Best Wishes, Maria". Most of all, her indomitable spirit of resilience and hope was emblazoned in my mind. I felt I could hold up my head now, embraced as a fellow human being by Maria's unconditional understanding and love. Although the mid-winter weather was in full force as she insisted on walking out to wave us goodbye, spring, the season of renewal and hope, had arrived for me.

---

1. Lewitt, M. *Smugglers*. Unpublished poem. https://www.enotes.com/homework-help/maria-lewitt-poem-smugglers-438949
2. Lewitt M (2002) *Come Spring*, Melbourne: Scribe Publisher, p.10

25

KOREA: RESILIENCE IN ACTION

South Korea is a land of contrast, as I discovered when my family and I travelled there in 2015. My first impression, when we land at Incheon International Airport, tired and disoriented from our 18 hour trip, was a highly developed technological society, fast-paced and digitally advanced. At the same time, there remained a charming interior imbued with traditional values as evidenced by much bowing and *kamsa hamida* (thank you) from shopkeepers, restaurateurs, and even bus drivers. Throughout our eight-day visit to attend my brother and his Korean fiancée, Minhee's, traditional Korean wedding, this impression was reinforced time and again.

Asan, Minhee's home town is about a two and a half hour bus ride from Incheon. The hotel we checked into, the Onyang Hot Spring Hotel, has every modern amenity, including Wi-Fi, yet is a remodeled palace, built in the Joseon Dynasty, 16th century, where the royal family would come to make full use of the mineral hot springs that bubble up from deep underground. We passed through the grand arched entry complete with inscribed plaque and columns and a sweeping tiled roof that inclines upwards at the edges. A small ornamental garden greeted us, with a fishpond and beautifully pruned trees and shrubs that set an elegant contrast amidst the bustling city traffic just outside the gate.

Mr. Li, Minhee's father, took us to visit the traditional Oeam Folk Village, an important cultural heritage attraction, first established in the 16th century. The village of thatched roof houses, persimmon trees, well swept laneways and open grounds with traditional threshing and grinding mills, weaving looms and other folk objects, contained several distinguishing features. We saw extensive rice fields with waving stalks heavy with ripening pods, the pond with an original timber wheel turning with water from the Seolhwasan Mountain in the backdrop, and 600 meters of preserved original stone walls. In the display area where some of the original buildings still stand, we were shown large earthenware jars (for *kimchi*, the traditional spicy pickles) next to some thatched tent-shaped constructions for their storage. Further along, we visited a thatched-roof house where *kimchi* was being made using modern equipment, and stored in large freezers. If not for the stainless steel vats and freezers, partially hidden from view, we would have thought we had stepped back centuries in time. Minhee handed us cups filled from bottled drinks she bought, which I thought was lemonade. It was not Sprite but a delicious cool sweet concoction made from rice found liberally at the bottom of the cup.

Besides the mineral hot springs, Asan is famous for being the birthplace of Admiral Yi Sun-Sin, the legendary national hero who I grew to admire the more I learnt about him. Admiral Yi was extraordinary by any standard. Without any previous naval battle experience, Yi had 23 successful naval encounters; never losing a single battle at sea. Through the use of brilliant strategies, he successfully repelled the Japanese invasion in the late 16th

century with only meager resources and a vastly outnumbered naval force. What is even more remarkable is that Admiral Yi was suffering from poor health, the result of being the victim of a plot by jealous rivals at court who convinced the King to arrest Yi, strip him of his titles and subject him to torture and imprisonment. Yi was undeterred by his cruel and humiliating treatment and once again, on his release, offered his loyal services to the state as a low-ranked infantry soldier. Yi was reinstated to the commanding post after a disastrous sea battle, where his successor General Won Gyun lost all but 13 of the 150 warships (saved by another commander Bae Seol who fled the battle.) The most watched Korean film, *The Admiral: Roaring Currents*,[1] tells the story of the famous battle of Myeongnyang where the 330 invading Japanese ships, including 133 battle ships, were stymied by only 13 Korean warships with the help of a flotilla of small fishing vessels. Yi, by the use of outstanding military tactics, taking advantage of the familiar coastline and natural forces of wind and current as well as the courage and patriotism of his people, drew the Japanese attackers into the treacherous waters. Breaking their vanguard by destroying 31 of the Japanese warships without losing any Korean ship, the Japanese were finally forced to retreat.

A charismatic leader and man of exemplary character, Admiral Yi won the love and loyalty of his people by, amongst other things, personally fulfilling the dying wishes of those under his command, fighting amongst them when exposed to great danger and showing sympathies for the hardships suffered by the peasants. The spirit of the Admiral, resilience after personal humiliation and difficulties, courage in the face of huge obstacles, selfless devotion to his country and its people, and diligence to duty, lives on in many ways.

One shining example is the patriotism of the Koreans. Our first expedition was organised by Mr. Li to the Independence Hall of Korea in Cheonan, a memorial and museum that documents the (one-time only) colonisation of Korea by Japan in the years from 1910 to 1945. In seven exhibition halls with numerous artifacts, monuments, panoramas, videos and visual displays, the brutality of the oppressors together with the patriotic resistance of the Korean people were showcased. Exhibition Hall six features a life-sized display of the March 1st Movement, an uprising in 1919 from people of all walks of Korean society. We saw many nationalistic Korean visitors joining in waving the Korean flag and chanting the pro-Korean independence cries with the models at this exhibit.

In Seoul, Minhee took us to the War Memorial which devoted a large section to the Korean War of 1950-1953. The exhibits, displays and videos as well as our English-speaking guide led us into the experience of what it felt like to hold cherished ideals and fight for one's country, amidst the most difficult terrain, inclement weather and hostile conditions imaginable. In the Hall of Visual Experience, we sat in the freezing cold in front of the replica of a frozen landscape with snowflakes drifting down. In the eerie darkness, the walls reverberated with ear-splitting bombs accompanied by the sharp cackle of gunfire. On the screen, a documentary showed the Heungnam evacuation with soldiers and exhausted refugees moving along in the bitter cold. The devastation of the war, evident in the carpet bombing by the North Korean and Chinese Communist forces aided by the Soviet Union, prompted US General Douglas McArthur to say that, in his opinion, it would take a hundred years to rebuild the country. Yet, in 2012, South Korea, with a population of 50 million and half the size of the state of Victoria, was ranked 13th in the world economy. As another guide proudly told an American touring party, Seoul, with its technological, scientific, industrial and cultural development, would not be found wanting in comparison to other major world cities including New York or London.

We also saw another Korea. At Sudeoksa Seon Monastery, famed for its renowned Buddhist scholars and texts, the ancestral tablets of Minhee's family are kept. Passing through each arched gateway on the ascending path, there was an increasing sense of peace as we entered a world dedicated to spiritual practice. Cradled against the mountain, the serene splendor of the temple buildings stood out against the majestic backdrop of pine trees. On entering, we were introduced to the Buddhist worldview as represented by the relics, statues and scrolls of poems and texts on exhibition. In a street market nearby, Minhee offered us a local delicacy, silkworm chrysalis, braised in soy sauce which she ate with relish. They were soft with a texture hard to pinpoint – I wouldn't say this was going to be my all-time favourite. Apparently after the Korean War, food was so scarce that people resorted to eating the silkworm chrysalis. Another tradition, odd to our ways of thinking, is to bring gifts of toilet paper and bleach to house-warming parties. Because of the hard times after the war, toilet rolls and bleach were luxury items by Korean standards, and these gifts have persisted to the present day. From these stories, we can sense the depth of privations suffered by the Korean people after the harsh years of the Japanese occupation and, on its heels, a civil war which tore across the country.

How did the reconstruction and economic rebirth miracle occur? Always keen to learn from others' experience of resilience, I felt that it came largely from the indomitable spirit of the people. This was exemplified by their high level for endurance of hardship, exceptional work ethics and national pride, in addition to the foreign aid that came from the US as well as other countries. We were astounded and shocked when Minhee first told us, some time ago, about the typical day of Korean students, consisting of formal school from 7.30am to 3pm, followed by private tutorials till 10pm after which they would spend several hours doing their homework, going to bed around 2 am to wake up again at 6.30 am for the following day's classes. Minhee who worked for the Korean Trade Association (equivalent to Austrade) in Melbourne, was responsible for organising their job fairs. In the months leading up to a job fair, she would work every day till around 8pm, and late as it was, sometimes bring home letters and pamphlets to work on, as well as distribute brochures on some Saturdays and Sundays. In the week before the job fair, her work hours could extend to 11pm or even 12am, and she would invariably work all night on the day before the fair, and in addition to the full day of the fair, amounting to a 36-hour non-stop work day.

Confirmation of the Korean work ethic came unexpectedly in Seoul. At the downtown hotel where we stayed, we could hear repair work going on across the road throughout the night, and in the morning, with a group still hard at work, a large section of the pavement had been transformed from broken rubble the day before with newly laid pavers. I think that if it is in the best interest, Koreans will see that the job gets done to a high standard no matter how difficult or how labourious. So it is not surprising that a revitalised, highly efficient and robust South Korea has been rebuilt in half the time predicted by General McArthur.

My impressions of South Korea are memorable and vivid: the solemn and timeless ritual of the traditional wedding with the bride and groom resplendent in the Korean *Hanbok*, bowing and offering each other tea; the futuristic Design and Technology Centre shaped like a flying saucer while, across the road, street vendors sold *hotteok*, the traditional pancake with sweet filling fried to an enticing golden brown; steaming bowls of hot noodles accompanied by several varieties of *kimchi*; pavilions and reflexology walks with different textured pebbles dotting the foliage in city parks. More importantly, we were moved by the generosity of Korean hospitality; Mrs. Li, who took time off from her 60-hour work week, to welcome us into her apartment and ply us with fruit and rice cakes she still finds time to make herself, her final hugs and gifts to us at the Asan bus stop where she saw us on our way, and Mr. Li, who took several days off work, hiring a minibus to take us to historically and culturally significant heritage sites, was always the first to pay for lunches or fares and the last to take any rest or refreshment.

South Korea also reminds me of Byeong, a worker from the local council, who looks after me every week. Byeong is Korean, an experienced marine engineer who migrated to Australia with his family. Byeong's father, a conscript at 19 in the South Korean army, was wounded and spent 3 years as a Prisoner of War in North Korea, and had instilled many values that have helped his son adjust to his adopted country. Unable to find work as an engineer, Byeong works in respite care, conscientious and uncomplaining. In his new line of work, he finds satisfaction in caring for others and in understanding the needs of those who require assistance. I am also beginning to see this indomitable spirit as exemplified by the South Korean soldiers who crawled along the heavily bombarded frozen wasteland into enemy lines, without a thought to their personal safety but ready to sacrifice their lives for freedom. Likewise, the sailors under Admiral Yi, giving up all thoughts of returning home to loved ones, determinedly fought for their king and country, guided by the Admiral's words; *Those who fight to save their own lives will die, and those who fight to save others will live.*

Yes, the Korean national spirit lives on because its people take pains, through memorials, traditions as well as personal stories, to keep alive their history of the huge personal costs and self-sacrifices of previous generations who fought to achieve a better world for those who follow. I came away from my visit, inspired anew in my quest for the ways and means to overcome obstacles and find inner strength to keep going on my own journey in the face of many challenges. If ever an entire country can be mobilised to show resilience and the determination to work towards the realisation of common goals, Korea would fit the bill. It gives me hope that as a community, we can strive towards the achievement of an equitable and just society, with the well-being of all people, no matter how different, as the ideal to work towards.

---

1. Kim, H-m. (2014). *The Admiral: Roaring Currents*. Seoul: Big Stone Pictures.

26

FINDING OUR VOICE

> *I had found what I was looking for – a [person] like myself but one who in [their] search for meaning had discovered a worthwhile object for [their] life; who had paid every price and not counted it as a sacrifice; who cared nothing for compromise, nothing for [their] pride, nothing for ourselves or the opinion of others; who had reduced [their] life to one thing that mattered to [them], and was free.*
>
> John Le Carre, *The Secret Pilgrim*

Tim speaks

I met Anne Carson in the most fortuitous way, at a dinner to celebrate the completion and publication of a book put out by one of her creative writing groups in 2013. Mum was involved in this project in which Anne was the creative writing therapist and editor. The project consisted of gathering a collection of stories of ordinary people caught up in extraordinary circumstances, specifically, the experiences of families living with autism. There were about eight mothers and two disability workers/teachers in the group, and each contributed one or several pieces to this powerful anthology. As a budding writer, at Year 12, I was nervous to meet so many published authors for the first time, but the evening was pleasant enough. I found Anne very approachable and welcoming. We met in person again, in October, 2016, when a continuation of the project was underway, sponsored by Ondru, an organisation dedicated to raising awareness and creating social change through art. Anne, as a director of Ondru (meaning 'one' in Tamil), was aiming to compile a vocal rendition of the anthology for the purpose of turning these into an artistic representation through music and dance.

With the opportunity to talk in more depth, I sensed a presence about Anne, an impression of coming from some refined plane where poets and artists reside. However, her genuine warmth and thoughtfulness put me at ease. I felt that she would always find time to listen to people, irrespective of their differences. Anne displayed no signs of discomfort as I squealed and hummed, lay on the floor, left the room abruptly for extended periods, or exhibited any amount of autistic mannerisms. In addition to accepting me the way I am, she was most astute in observing that I appear to be extremely sensitive to light and sound. I had the impression Anne was curious, in an empathic way, about my autistic behaviour and rituals and how I navigate the world.

I find it most unnerving when I need to face the outside world, a world that appears almost alien, particularly when I am thrown into the arena with unfamiliar people. With Anne, who had taken pains to get to know me, I felt surprisingly comfortable at close quarters. She knelt beside me as I lay on the carpet, to get a better sense of my humming. She felt that my vocalisation was a vital part of my communication and of who I was, and was keen to get a recording of it. After a lifetime of stares, turning askance, or even outright hostility from the general public to my vocal output, hand flapping, and other mannerisms, I have always felt very defensive about my differences. To meet someone who not only accepted my odd demeanor, but expressed a genuine interest in me on a personal level was very reassuring. After exchanging a greeting with her and some small talk via my typing, I was ready to bare my soul. Anne's assured sense of who she is and her place in the world, as well as her passion and skills for linguistic and artistic expression must have come from meeting life with uncommon courage. I sensed her story would be one outside the box. I felt a kinship with Anne, especially in the journey she embarked upon to self-discovery.

To chart Anne's many achievements, which include being an award winning poet, writer, artist, teacher and therapist, is to trace a unique trajectory. Anne recalled she had a privileged and relatively sheltered upbringing, completed her education in private schools and majored in Sociology at University. From early life, she had been affected by sensory hypersensitivities, which could cause obvious discomfort, but also led to a heightened ability to see things other people might miss. I believe this sensitivity was put to good use in the development of a keen mind with unusual awareness and perceptiveness. The early experience of being different from others also led to Anne's interest in people who are atypical including those on the autism spectrum as well as other marginalised groups, and this curiosity has since led her to explore the lives of these people more fully. As she had done well in University, the steps towards a career in the academia appeared paved, with a bright future on the horizon.

On graduating, however, Anne made an uncharacteristic decision. Forsaking the life of comfort and security, she forged her own path in a new direction by leaving university and working for some years as a Youth Worker. After training as a Social Worker she worked for 10 years in the area of Domestic Violence. Facing burnout she decided she needed to recreate herself and left the city behind. In a mud brick house in an isolated rural location with no electricity and no running water, Anne embarked on a back to the basics lifestyle. She accepted the challenges to meet her basic needs, including chopping wood for cooking and heating, and using candles for lighting in the evenings. Surrounded by the bush and her solitude, she found the necessary space and time to develop her creativity and poured her soul into writing poetry, painting, and other artistic pursuits.

In a mud brick cabin amidst the bush, in a landscape sculpted by wind, sun and rain, you would be surrounded by nature at its starkest and its best. While the setting may be idyllic, there is nothing romantic about the ongoing chores, chopping wood, fetching water, or repairing any damage, that go into meeting your basic needs. Still, I imagine she took satisfaction from seeing and enjoying the fruit of her labour and the simple pleasures of watching a sunset or a flock of birds darting across the sky. After living for seven years under the primitive conditions which she came to relish, Anne emerged as a person who had 'found her voice.' Through the act of giving up her old life, in the profound stillness of the bush, Anne was able to discover that essential part of her selfhood. During and after this hermetic phase of her life, Anne continued to explore herself in poetry, writing and works of art. After this period, she returned to the city, eager to pursue her calling as a writer and poet full time.

The search for personhood can be a daunting process. I see a similarity in a bush walk I undertook with Mum in Gippsland. Hiking through an old growth forest, brushing past the sweeping fronds of tree ferns, I breathed in the clean sharp air, redolent with the scent of eucalypt. The silence was broken only by the rustling of trees, the hum of insects and the occasional call of birds. There, we could hear it, the distinctive song of the lyrebird, off in the undergrowth nearby, but when we walked in the direction of the song, it stopped, re-emerging a little further off. This hide and seek game continued for some time until it dawned on us that this would be the closest we could get. I often feel that an essential part of us is like the lyrebird, beautiful, mysterious and elusive. What makes someone with undeniable talents, an assured social niche, not to mention a promising career, do the hard yard, to court challenges which are self-imposed? How did Anne deal with the reactions, concern and consternation of her family and friends by this inexplicable move? Where did she summon the courage to defy expectations to follow the road less traveled? Did the motivation come from a persistent inner calling that cannot be ignored?

As mentioned in previous chapters, my own search had begun some time ago. I was catapulted into it in my school years where I often felt like I was trapped in a gigantic theme park ride in a malfunctioning buggy, with very little control over its speed or direction and precariously close to losing my grip. The movement, noises and voices of students in the corridor, or outside shooting basketball, playing dodge ball, or just laughing or chatting with their friends inevitably brought an overwhelming sense of anxiety and sensory overload in me. Whenever someone noticed me, I felt like the Hunchback of Notre Dame amongst graceful athletes. One of the girls in my Year 8 class used to say hi and smile at me. One time, when she walked past without acknowledging me, I felt wracked with pain as if I had been physically punched. Social isolation and the nagging feeling of being in the wrong place became inescapable facts of my high school life.

However, in dealing with being different, I had begun my own journey of self-discovery. After the initial settling in, since I was very much on my own, I cultivated a habit of tuning into my own internal landscape, examining how my mind and recalcitrant body work, making sense of raw sensations, emotions, thoughts, and detecting the occasional rumbling of some subterranean forces from deep within myself. With time, I was aware that a part of me was observing everything with a kind of detached interest and without judgment. In the observer mode, I was able to bypass the urge to belittle myself or decry other people's lack of attention. In addition, although the observer was aware of social standards and others' expectations, he was not too concerned about people's acceptance or rejection, but just rode things out. Over time, I learned to see past the me on the outside, autistic trimmings and all, to get better acquainted with the essential person that makes up who I am. I also became more ready to question the conventional expectations about what it takes to be socially acceptable and to know we have the power to adopt or discard these standards. Letting go, getting up and picking up the pieces to put myself together again, I realised I have stretched and grown just a little more. In fact, shaking up the old me, painful though it is, led to a reshaping and reinvention of the person I want to be.

I am also reminded of a recurring dream of a lone eagle soaring high in the sky. Gliding like the eagle for a timeless moment, I would wake up feeling refreshed and liberated. This dream came after a primary school excursion to the Healesville Sanctuary, a wildlife nature park. There was a show put on by a wedge-tail eagle and her trainer. The trainer was in the center of this open air arena, while this dark brown fierce-looking eagle was perched on a tree branch at the side. At a signal, she flew and retrieved an object on the other side of the arena, and then went straight to the trainer to get a morsel of food from his hand as a reward. I can still recall the air current created by the flap of her powerful wings as she flew just above our heads. Now, years later, I can see that I had identified with the eagle which had come to represent an aspect of myself, unfettered, free, in her element with the earth and sky. I sense that my essential nature is capable of soaring like an eagle. However, the rounds of daily living in a body which does not respond well to instruction or intention, the obligation to fit in with people's expectations, not to mention other responsibility and commitments have obscured the meaning of who I really am, similar to the tamed eagle which had been brought up to respond to the trainer's commands. In performing for food with the training instilled and the habituation to a captive life, the eagle has forgotten her true nature, just as we have when tethered to our upbringing and enculturation.

Tuning into our body and soul's internal rhythms is never easy amidst the myriad tasks of acquiring and maintaining an enviable lifestyle in our competitive consumer society. That's why it has to take Anne tremendous courage and tenacity to embark on her sojourn. To strip back the various layers of ourselves, and to know that the external paraphernalia and possessions that we have become identified with can be re-assessed and even jettisoned requires concerted effort. To discover what makes life worth living and to pursue our aspiration call for strength of heart and will-power. In the rediscovery of who we truly are and want to become, we can stay tuned to the rhyme and reason of our being to follow our dreams. In the process, Anne found her voice, and life would never be the same again.

27

HOPE REVISITED

Never shall I forget the small faces of the children whose bodies I saw transformed into smoke under a silent sky.

Elie Wiesel, *Night*

Tim speaks

I pushed the door leading into the Jewish Holocaust Centre and took in all the points of interest, those I had remembered on my first visit approximately nineteen months ago, and others I have just noticed on this revisit. From the flame and exquisite sculpture at the entrance, to the galleries with their displays of photos, records, screens replaying videos of the experiences of Holocaust survivors, a panoramic model of a recreation of the death camps, all available space was used to preserve the experiences of the Jewish people who had gone through the tumultuous upheaval of World War II and the horrors of the Holocaust. I felt I had stepped into a time capsule.

On a wall near the entrance foyer, the photos of the children who had lost their lives looked faded, yet, here and there, some bright eyes and expressive faces evoked their owners' presence, and captured for posterity their innocence and unique individuality. Photographic reminders made the loss of these young lives all the more poignant. I felt my senses reeling, assaulted by a barrage of emotions. Chief among them was anguish for the cruel twist of fate that brought about their deaths, and outrage at the grievous injustice. I was completely overwhelmed by the enormity of the suffering depicted – here were people disowned, dispossessed and disintegrated, their loved ones and families torn asunder and murdered. I had to lie down before sensory overload overtook me.

I was spinning in the whirlpool of incessant raucous signals; the brightness of the spot lights, shuffling and footsteps, background voices, noise of the traffic outside and the imprint of the carpet on my torso and limbs where they touched the floor, a jumble of sensory data my overtaxed mental apparatus was doing its best to process. I could only wait for a clearing of the brain fog. Gradually, the sensory onslaught gave way to dawning comprehension of the talk presented to a school group in an alcove nearby. "Any questions?" asked the speaker. The uncomfortable silence that followed seemed interminable before a boy raised a question about the dietary practices of the Jewish people. I wondered if this group of young students was just as overwhelmed as I was by seeing the human faces of those destroyed by the insane machinery of Hitler's Final Solution. Would questions bring understanding of the systematic and devilishly efficient attempt to obliterate six million people, more than a quarter of the entire population of Australia?

About a year and a half ago, on my first visit to the Centre, when

I met and interviewed Maria Lewitt – child Holocaust survivor, author, poet, volunteer Centre guide, Member of the Order of Australia, among her many achievements – I had several pressing questions. For me, it boiled down to two crucial issues; firstly, how did Holocaust survivors come to terms with the horrors and extreme dehumanisation of what they went through, where did the courage to keep going come from and what worldview or mindset would develop from such traumatic experiences? Secondly, how would an ordinary person like me measure up under similar circumstances? However, when Maria started to recount her wartime experiences, in the context of what happened to the Jewish people after the Nazis overran Lodz, her hometown in Poland, I could not think of any questions appropriate for the occasion. Although I made feeble attempts to grasp the significance of Maria's account of her life during this time, nothing prepared me for the sheer scale of the tragedy that befell her, her family and her people. In the months that followed, grappling with my unasked questions, I ploughed through any material I could find on the Holocaust as well as other extreme experiences, and reread Viktor Frankl[1] in one man's search for meaning, my own.

Terror comes in many guises. When I was eight years old, I had felt terror. When I was in Year 2 in Special School, I had a holy terror of a classmate who screamed, scratched, kicked and bit almost continually. She never seemed to mind the teacher or the teacher's aide, and often had to be dragged into the classroom by two adults prying her hands off things she clung on to. To make her sit still in a designated spot, some adult had to constantly sit nearby to stop her jumping off the floor or chair and taking off. No one could handle her, not even the principal. What's more, she was unpredictable. I never felt safe in that class and dreaded the hours at school before Mum came to collect me at the end of the day. When a commotion occurred, it was like being hit by a tornado; I would lie on the floor with hands covering my ears. With eyes closed, I would mentally will myself a thousand miles away. It was worse in the playground where there were fewer adults to supervise the kids. The cacophony of noise and movements was nerve racking, and there were simply no places to hide.

One day, I managed to avoid another kid just spinning around, but found myself next to this girl. I don't know if I did anything to upset her, but she was quicker than me, turned around and bit me on the shoulder. For someone who is as sensitive to touch as I am, where even a pat on the back feels like being belted, the pain was excruciating. When her teeth tore into my flesh they also seared into my brain; I started to feel numb and was weak for days afterwards. Years later, I read that when we are facing danger or are traumatised, our instinctual self-preservation kicks in, but if we can't do fight or flight, the only remaining option is to deaden our feelings to lessen the inevitable pain. This incident spurred Mum to redouble her efforts to find a mainstream school which would take me as a full time student. The following term found me at a small country school about a hundred kilometers from Melbourne. Because I had escaped the daily bedlam and torment, I sometimes felt guilty about those left behind, especially a couple of quieter boys in the class whom I liked. But at least I felt vastly relieved from the ordeal of having to face the constant terror caused by my classmate in special school.

Looking at the faces of the murdered children at the JHC, I had a glimmer of comprehension of what it would be like to be deprived of all the things that sustain us and make life worth living; our home, our circle of family, friends and loved ones, adequate food, clean water, cherished possessions. When these essentials are taken, what remains of life? Moreover, when individuals are deprived of freedom, denied every basic human right, subject to forced marches, enduring long hours of hard labor on a meager diet that barely keeps body and soul together, exposed to the elements in threadbare clothing and in footwear that wear feet away, minded by cruel and capricious guards, under the constant threat of severe punishment or death, what coping strategies can possibly be adequate? Maria had encapsulated this by saying that if all other ways are unavailable or unthinkable, the only way is to ***keep going***.

What makes people keep on going in extreme situations? In all of us is a strong will to live, but why do some of us give up, and for those who refuse to knuckle under, what gives them the incentive to persevere in the face of the insurmountable difficulty rather than opt for an easier way out? Aron Ralston, a seasoned, solo mountaineer, climbing in one of the most remote mountains in Utah, accidentally got his arm crushed by a dislodged boulder entrapping him in a canyon. As he recounted in his autobiography, *Between a Rock and a Hard Place*,[2] Ralston did everything he could to conserve his energy and to wait for help, but after five days and nights when his strength waned, he started to stare death in the eye. When life and death hung in delicate balance, what enabled Ralston – and other brave souls – to pull back from the brink and keep going to find a way back to life?

Viktor Frankl, who survived Auschwitz, believed that the identification of the underlying purpose of our lives, and an active faith in the positive outcomes of that purpose combine to produce the necessary strength to keep going under extreme conditions. Finding the meaning to our suffering, therefore, helps us to face the direst plight with courage if not equanimity.

When Ralston was contemplating how to meet death, he reported seeing an image of a child whom he knew was going to be his son. From this precognitive vision, with the reassurance of a future where he would be a father, he was able to think of unprecedented ways to keep going. Steeling himself against the pain, Ralston unflinchingly forced the bone in his entrapped arm to break and using a utility knife blunted by repeated chipping of the rock that trapped him, succeeded in cutting off the remaining arm tissue to finally free himself. With uncanny presence of mind, he applied rudimentary first aid to the wound and, although weak from his 127-hour ordeal and loss of blood, rappelled down and then walked to get to rescue. With the momentous thought of being able to father his future child, Ralston found the meaning to achieve the near impossible.

I was roused from my reverie by Mum who said Maria had arrived, and there she was, as I remembered her. Time seemed to have stood still. I sat up, tried to compose myself, to type, to say how happy I was to find her unchanged and well. Although her voice appeared softer, Maria radiated the same unconditional acceptance and warmth. Her mind sharp as ever, she talked to us as old friends, and even alluded to some of the things I had written about from our previous interview. With Maria within sight and hearing, everything fell into place for me. Looking at her, feeling her presence, knowing that despite the hardship she had endured during the war years, Maria has unfailingly reached out and touched people with her kindness, inspired others with her resilience, and used her gifts of writing to convey her hope in finding a better future. At that moment, I knew that whether you live to nine or ninety, what really counts is what you do with the hand of cards that life dealt you, no matter how appalling. If you are able to make just one iota of difference to other people for the better, your life has meaning and it is a life worth living.

---

1. Frankl, V. (1946). *Man's Search for Meaning: An Introduction to Logotherapy*, Boston, MA: Beacon Press.
2. Ralston, A. (2004). *Between a rock and a hard place*. US: Atria Books.

28

CHAMPION FOR COMMUNICATION

 *Communication falls into the same category as food, drink and shelter - it is essential for life, and without it life becomes worthless.*

Anne McDonald, *The Right to Communicate* 1992

Tim speaks

It was a rare privilege to be meeting Doug Biklen, whose life work to promote communication and equal opportunity for those with little or no functional speech has been nothing less than inspiring. Doug has also been at the forefront for the right to an inclusive education for young people with disability since the early 1970s. Early in his career, the fact that autistic students lacking in communication skills were at a distinct disadvantage in mainstream educational settings became very plain to him. It was after reading the book *Annie's Coming Out* by Anne McDonald and Rosemary Crossley that he began to explore facilitated communication (FC) or typing with support as a method of communication. Since then, Doug has done groundbreaking work in the practice and research in assisted typing as a viable means to communicate for those with little or no functional speech.

Believe me, life can be a monumental struggle when you can't speak, not even to make a simple request for your most basic needs. Severe autism has rendered me, among other challenges, without a voice. With an intensive learning program starting at 2 years of age, I have made certain progress. However, even after years of discrete trial learning, speech therapy, occupational therapy, as well as other methods in the armamentarium of autism treatment and education, I have not been able to communicate using my own voice or other independent means (I also have dyspraxia, severely curtailing speech and writing ability). Hence I will never forget the first time I was taught to type at the age of nine on our first visit to the DEAL Communication Center. This was the first time I was able to use my own words. That simple communicative act, a thing most people take for granted, was, for me, momentous and life changing.

Doug exuded kindness with an abundance of erudition and wisdom gained from years of working in the field of disability and academic environments. I wanted to know more about his proposition that intellectual disability (ID) is a metaphor. I had done some homework and taken mental notes of an entry in the *Harvard Educational Review Blog* by Doug, Chris Kliewer and Amy Petersen (25 March, 2015)[1] entitled 'At the End of Intellectual Disability', an eloquent and powerful presentation of the guiding principles underpinning his work which was cogently summed up by Doug in person. Doug's explanation, a radical viewpoint that the term ID is a value judgment imposed on people who then become disadvantaged and marginalised, was focused, sound, and convincing and, furthermore, was said with a reasonableness backed by scientific training, an argument hard to refute even by hardened critics.

> "Intellectual disability (the current nomenclature replacing *retardation*) is someone's claim made about the *other*; it is both a hypothesis and a judgment of innate deficiency assigned from a position of cultural power, privilege, and authority. Intellectual disability is a metaphor: It is *as if* this person with limited spoken language has no concepts about which to express. It is *as if* her mind is slowed, impaired, or deficient.
>
> Yet, at some point in history, the metaphoric nature, the *as if* of assigning intellectual disability, was obscured within the argot of professions scrambling to construct a science of human deficiency. Intellectual disability is not science. It is a culturally agreed upon lens that insidiously Photoshops select scenes of an individual's life, the dataset so to speak, into a particular frame."

What I admire about Doug is his humanity and his principles, reflected in his respect for those he works with, in the attitude of taking the person into consideration first and foremost, even if some of us may not be doing things in expected ways or according to the dictates of social convention. In the absence of a valid means to accurately know someone's intellectual capacity, Doug thinks we need to presume that people are functioning at the level of intelligence that enables them to understand things appropriately, regardless of their responding in ways that may be different because of their disability. Furthermore, Doug is adamant that a different perspective, in presuming competence, would bring forth from us, the students, things that cannot be achieved under the gauntlet of low expectations and stigmatisation.

> "Our consideration of the end of intellectual

disability began years ago and has continued in excellent classrooms around the world, in the living rooms of family homes, and in other locations where the delimiting contours of intrinsic deficiency have been set aside. We are participants among communities whose most vulnerable members are interpreted as rightful, valued, and thoughtful citizens. Supports are provided in order to foster opportunity and connectedness. When success occurs, those supports are enhanced; they are not removed for purposes of assessment. Expectations do not exist in traditional graded fashion, whether low or high, but rather in an open format with possibility as the primary guide."

If ID is a metaphor, I typed, what about autism? Doug went on to say that autism is a different concept, a list of characteristics or ways of being. If you have enough of the items on the list, then you may be labeled autistic. Autism has been described as a spectrum with a great deal of variation between individuals along it. But of course there are many disagreements about the term autism, with some so-called experts assuming that a person who is on the spectrum and doesn't have useable speech must be intellectually impaired or unable to appreciate that other people have different perspectives than them; this latter phenomenon has been referred to as lacking a 'theory of mind.' Doug rejects these pessimistic notions as brutally damaging.

Without warning, I was assailed by strong emotions. I had to lie down, had to wait for my mind to come up with a definition for this sudden intense onslaught. Like an MC opening an envelope to announce the results, a mental picture emerged of a time when I was nine years old, in the school psychologist's office. It was this psychologist who, with the results from one assessment, probably a morning of her time, pronounced me severely autistic and intellectually disabled to the world. For me, on the other hand, it was akin to a life sentence, without hope of appeal or reprieve, relegated to the limbo of no-man's land, a place where some deviant members of the human species, those without voice, are forever condemned.

I guess this memory came in strong contrast to how Doug would work with people like me. There is a huge gulf between some professionals whose only concern is to categorise and label. The psychologist had totally disregarded me, making her pronouncement in front of me, *as if* I was not there, *as if* I did not have any ability to understand things, *as if* I was inanimate, without thoughts or feelings. In the labels she applied and in her peremptory dismissal of me, I was once again reminded that even with all the hard work that I had put into getting a head start with learning, I was an abysmal failure. However, given a method of communication at that momentous visit to DEAL Communication Centre days afterwards, I was one step closer to achieving my dreams. With Rosemary's instructions, whilst it was still an uphill effort, I was able to prove to the world that I am intelligent and capable of learning, and I seized this opportunity as a drowning man thrown a lifeline.

I had grasped the means to communicate as the key for unlocking the door to the external world, but it was hard going. Held in the stranglehold of an errant body that just refused to obey my mental instructions, I could only think of the vivid image of a diving suit from *The Diving Bell and the Butterfly*. Over the years, I have tried in different ways to make my body more amenable, and can certainly attest to the strength of mind and will that goes into learning to drive your body in a direction that it never registers. Mum and I read books on the Lock-in Syndrome, spinal and other debilitating injuries, and ultra-marathon training and we'd practice. We did qigong and body awareness and we'd practice. Mum gave me back, shoulder and arm massages and we'd keep practicing. With practice, I certainly got better at typing, but sometimes I get discouraged as no matter how hard I try, especially in self-correcting, my finger seems to have a mind of its own, and persists in hitting an adjacent key time and time again.

All the hard work we put into acquiring a means to communicate makes no difference when some people refuse to see us as having the capability to communicate. I get totally incensed when people make disparaging remarks about us *as if* speech is the sole standard for intelligence. According to these critics, facilitated communication consists of nothing more than we the users being manipulated to type what the facilitators want us to type. To back up their denigration of FCT (Facilitated Communication Training) as a reliable means for communication, the opponents have relied on outdated research to support their position on the lack of validity and veracity of this method. However, I took comfort in hearing Doug explain that the kind of research used, message passing and so on, had flaws and were designed in ways that disadvantaged the participants. For those of us who have worked hard to adopt this method as our means for communicating, the issue of validity is only of theoretical interest. What is of utmost importance is not to be denied the opportunity to communicate. Speaking from first-hand experience, what drives my deep desire to communicate is the pressing need to tell others what I have to say. Furthermore, I have definitely not been trained to use this method for the purpose of taking dictation from the facilitator.

In addition, to counteract the negative viewpoints, Doug and his colleagues have been busy with first-rate research into validating assisted typing, primarily on the issue of authorship. Doug mentioned statistical analyses of texts for similarity of styles across different facilitators. Current advances in technology including eye scanning and brain imaging may also potentially be useful. Moreover, Doug has worked with people who have actually become independent typists or have acquired the ability to speak before and during typing which all goes to providing ammunition for the use of assisted typing as a springboard for self-expression. Until better communication methods are found for those with little or no functional speech, Doug believes that it is imperative to provide some means to communicate and to continue with research to refine current and explore other reliable methods.

We, already struggling with the difficulties imposed by lack of speech, are also deterred by obstacles put up by others who refuse to see us as full human beings with similar needs and the capacity for communication. I asked Doug how he dealt with setbacks and criticisms. He made two points. What keeps him going is firstly that the work to provide a reliable means to communicate is vital to those without independent speech or writing, and secondly, that when you have allies, it makes a big difference to how you can overcome disparagement and mental fatigue. At no point could I detect any signs of denouncement, exasperation or outright condemnation that I often felt in the attacks from the opposing camps. Needless to say, in meeting Doug personally, I have derived inspiration from a great educator with the humanitarian interests of people like me in mind, and reassurance that he will continue the good fight to champion our rights to communicate.

My journey towards communication has been long and arduous, but I am one of the lucky ones. With assiduous practice, I am now approaching independence, able to type with just a light touch on my shoulder or back, which goes far in establishing that what I type comes from me, and not my facilitators. With communication, a whole new world is opening for me. With continued improvement in assisted typing, I have been able to attend and complete mainstream high school, make friends, join advocacy groups, present at forums, give a TEDTalk, and even to go to University. With the work of Doug and others like him, being provided with a means to communicate, and with the belief in our communicative competence, we can be optimistic towards achieving a meaningful life and a worthwhile future.

---

1. hepg.org/her-home/issues/harvard-educational-review-volume-85-number-1/herarticle/at-the-end-of-intellectual-disability

29

AN UNEXPECTED ENCOUNTER

 The most beautiful thing we can experience is the mysterious.

Einstein

Tim speaks

Einstein once said, there are two ways to live, one is to live as if nothing in life is a miracle, the other is as if everything in life is a miracle. I had an appointment with death one Sunday in May, 2016, and I think that my perspective of life has changed, edging closer to seeing the miraculous in everything. What I am about to disclose is not your typical Near Death Experience, there was no tunnel, no warm welcome by deceased family or friends, and no ferry ride across the River Styx either. Nonetheless, it was an intensely personal and immensely moving encounter with the Unknown, which was also the reason why I had not been able to find the wherewithal to write about this experience until much later.

Growing up with severe autism means that my point of view will always be different from most other people around me. Whilst they see the world through their prescribed definitions and lenses, I am inclined to see patterns and movement, timbre and tone, all calibrated to blend together into a grand panorama. Whilst they talk as if what they are saying is reality, I don't feel that the cacophony of sounds in their speech can ever accurately describe the actual experience of things.

The day started like most days, I had a shower around 6am, or I should say, I went through my rituals with water which concluded about an hour later. Then we walked the dogs for another hour. A simple breakfast and, at 9am, my second sister came to take me to the pool, as I love water. The local pool was a familiar place and it was already pretty crowded with kids taking lessons, families enjoying a leisurely Sunday swim and dedicated athletes churning up and down the lanes. I got to my spot at the smaller pool with the water slide and settled into my usual routine, splashing water on my head, occasionally diving to submerge myself, reveling in the sensation of being suspended in the water. Of course, I also immerse myself into the patterns of light on and beneath the surface of the water that never fail to give me shivers of delight.

Suddenly, without warning, I found my control slipping and my consciousness shifting. I saw my body from above, convulsing, twitching, and drowning fast. Seeing my body thrashing in the throes of a mental electrical storm, I realised that I was having a seizure. I felt it was beyond my capacity to help myself when the thought dawned that the pool was not a good place for epileptic fits. My awareness of the world around me then started to fade, and I found myself wrapped in a dense grey fog. A little light was uniformly dispersed through the grey goo, but not much was visible as the fog shrouded everything. I could have been suspended in this grey and lifeless world for an eternity when my attention shifted to a shaft of light penetrating the thick grey mist and growing ever brighter. Drawn to the light, I was suddenly enveloped by a warm and loving Presence. With a rush of reciprocating emotions, I recognised this radiant Spirit as my Guide whom I have known for a long time. Words are inadequate to portray the peace, well-being and joy of this reunion – I felt that I had come home in His loving embrace

I remember the scenarios of my inter-dimensional trip as clearly as if it were a day-old event, despite the passage of many intervening months. On the other hand, this ineffable experience can only be recaptured through a memory, and through a condensation of the actual event via the use of language, much like water droplets on a window pane, or dew on a leaf that come from the transformation of invisible moisture in the air to visible liquid form. However, the purpose of this visit with the Unknown, and some of the accompanying emotions will remain with me as a vivid reminder of my glimpse into some vistas of this miraculous universe.

The best way to describe the next stage of my journey is a "beam me up Scottie" mode of transportation as, enveloped in the matrix of my Guide's energy field, I was able to float along, passing through a world of remarkable wonders. The whole landscape felt alive, and appeared to be made out of energy. As we made our way through the initial denser layers to more refined levels, I noticed the subtle changes in the gossamer-like patterns of energy to ever more brilliance and vividness in colour. I've never felt more alive, but what I saw has much in common with virtual reality. What came to mind are some three-dimensional representations of the cerebral landscape in films, with neurons represented by sparks of light, and their firing in electrical impulses travelling along dendritic networks as beams of multi-coloured light. The reality which I found myself, and was part of, was very similar, with millions of incandescent points of light like miniature supernovas emitting a dazzling array of energy beams in brilliant hues from the entire chromatic spectrum. The iridescent world around me appeared infinite, with networks of energy criss-crossing in marvelously complex and extraordinarily beautiful patterns.

I was very conscious of my Guide's presence, and His thoughts were transmitted in a form of mental energy that was received instantaneously by me without any need for speech. My thoughts were also picked up by my Guide as soon as I formulated them. Incredible as it seemed, I found myself quite at home using thought transference to communicate. I certainly didn't miss my usual mode of communication by typing with support. With adequate time to adjust to the new surroundings, I found that the body I was occupying was like a more complete version of myself. This body was made of lighter and finer substance, infinitely more comfortable and much more to my liking, not dissimilar to a top range Armani suit in comparison to second-hand ill-fitting gear picked up from the local op shop which my earth body was beginning to resemble. For instance, at no time did I suffer from the hypersensory challenges of stimuli being too bright, too loud, too harsh or too intense as I do in my earth body. What's more, the bonus of being completely able to control this fantastic upgrade of a body was sheer delight. Whatever and whenever my intentions were directed, the desired effects were instantly produced and perceived. In addition, I found that my mind was working as it never had before, what to me were mental gymnastics in the past was now effortless.

My awareness had also changed, as I was able to see certain events as well as the same event from different points in time simultaneously. Furthermore, I was not only able to look at the different parts that make up an event, but also, the total picture of interconnection with other events in its entirety were all uploaded onto my mental screen at the same time. It is as if when riding a bike, I would be able to see the spokes of the wheels turning, feel the wind on my face, sense my body doing its act, respiratory apparatus breathing, heart beating, muscles pumping as I pedal and balance the bike to move on the road, in addition to every detail of the passing scenery synchronously. It was an amazing feeling because, being autistic, I am extremely challenged when it comes to multi-tasking. Let me explain further. There is a book about two dimensional beings, known as *flat-landers*, who are unable to understand what the third dimension looks like from their world.[1] For instance, a house to us is made of rooms with walls, floor, roof, windows, doors and so on. To two dimensional beings, the same house will be flat, like a drawing on paper, with walls, floor and roof appearing as lines, with windows and doors as rectangles or squares. What I was able to get from this Guided tour was like, I was suddenly able to see things from some other dimensions with a very different and added perspective to the one I am used to as an inhabitant from the three-dimensional plane, much like *flat-landers* moving up to a three dimensional world. With these new-found skills, I was subsequently able to both observe and participate in the main feature of this visit.

As we rode on energy beams passing through the millions upon millions of incandescent points of light, I saw, on closer look, that the points of light were actually people, or beings. Whenever I brushed past their energy fields as we went along, I could sense their thoughts and feelings giving me some idea of what kind of people they were. Some of them I was unable to assign a known source, as the mental and emotional contents of their field appeared unfamiliar, almost alien. There was no time for pursuing these lines of thinking, however, as my Guide directed my attention to what appeared to be a building. On entering, we found ourselves in a vast hall, but without any kind of structural boundaries, as it seemed to stretch on forever, in every direction. I was guided to an enclosure that resembled a small theatre, and I remember thinking, with the preview I had up to that stage, this show had got to be good.

If what had happened up to that moment was mind-boggling, the next scenario was light-years beyond my usual frame of reference. There is a Chinese term, 'float-sink' which actually means to be suspended or immersed, that captures the gist of this core experience in some ways. The theatre was a three dimensional screen/stage, and the screen/stage began to come alive with images, scenes, complete with actors, action and accompanying sound tracks. When I had time to adjust to the surroundings, I realised, with a shock, that the unfolding 3-D movie around me was actually a story of my own life, but with a difference. There appeared to be multiple tracks of the story, but I was able to take in all the different renditions simultaneously. On the one hand, I could see the actual events unfolding, but it was more than being the protagonist as well as a member of the audience, I was also able to become part of all the other actors in my life story and to access the thoughts and feelings of each. In addition, the context and background information to what we were thinking and feeling were available whenever I paid closer attention. On the other hand, I also felt that I was standing above it all, and could see the big picture as the story emerged and the main themes, in terms of the purpose of my life, came across. On this level, I was like, producer, screen writer, director, actor, audience, film critic, light and sound engineer as well as whole other roles all rolled into one in my life story. It was as if I was playing an advanced interactive computer game with more sci-fi like technology than even the most cutting edge version could provide. As the events in my life played out, wherever I directed my attention and **intention**, the story was, more or less, subject to my control, as on this advanced level, I was able to edit, insert and rewrite things whenever I wanted, simply by using my thoughts alone.

An Unexpected Encounter | 261

∽

Although I was able to see many different aspects of my life, I will focus on just one example. From my upper primary years onward, there has been quite a bit of tension between my second sister and me. She has always been a good sister, trying her best to take care of me and do things with me. Because she was closest in age to me, just four years older, Mum would take us out together to do fun things when we were young, like roller blading, rowing, or picnicking in the park. We share some traits. With some sensitivity issues, though not as severely as mine, she would block out her surroundings by loud music whenever she did desk work, like I do with my humming, and she didn't like to try unfamiliar food, or was famous for mashing up food so the consistency and texture made it more palatable. It was also difficult for her to adjust to changes in routine, and overloading in her case meant she didn't want to go on holidays, or eat in a restaurant, and she would prefer to bury her nose in a book. We have common interests in books and computer games which she kindly let me play with her. From a young age, she was my role model as well as companion.

However, all this changed when I reached Grade 5, as she would head off with her friends to do their thing. Even when she was at home, she would be studying in her own room. I didn't like this one bit, as I missed her companionship. It's hard for me to have friends my age because I don't talk and it's not easy to type with just anyone, as I needed the support from familiar communication partners. Besides, as I am not independent, who wants your Mum with you when you're hanging out with friends? Things got even worse, because in early high school, I felt like an outcast. When my second sister was busy with her own life, I felt that she was deliberately ignoring me, and why should I have to deal with this at home when I got truckloads of it at school already! I am ashamed to owe it, but I got to a point where I didn't want to take it anymore, and was going to pay her back. I waited till she was at Uni, then I ripped and shredded pages out of a textbook she just bought. What made my revenge even more inexcusable was she bought the book (over $100) from her own funds because she felt that Mum and Dad had already footed the bill for all her other resources. Of course, she was furious with me, and our relationship, already strained, deteriorated even further.

When the story of my life was played out, with the compassionate support from my Guide, I summoned the courage to look into the relationship between my second sister and me, and was even more ashamed. My second sister was the baby of the family before I came along, and everyone adored her, but when I came on the scene, the limelight fell from her onto me. Because she was only four years old, growing up with me along-side, she missed Mum's attention which shifted primarily onto me. As Mum's concerns with my struggles to master milestones and deal with other challenges became more and more time consuming, my second sister got jealous. Nevertheless, she tried to include me in her life by playing with me, and was protective of me whenever I couldn't do things other kids my age did. When adolescence hit, she was understandably more involved with her friends, and it was difficult to juggle school, friendship and other interests with her role as my big sister.

From my expanded perspective, I could clearly see that my second sister had her own struggles, and, although her challenges were different from mine, life was not a bed of roses for her either. I could also see her love for me despite our differences as well as the murky emotions underlying our sibling rivalry. However, instead of getting stuck in a quagmire of my disappointing behaviour, guilt and recrimination, an amazing thing happened. With my Guide's compassionate assistance, I could see that I was in a position to do something about this situation. At this advanced level, aided by a higher perspective, I was able to play the game of life differently as I sat at the control. Although I wasn't able to erase what had already happened, with my new found understanding, I could change some of the parameters of the situation by forgiving myself and her, and in forgoing my own preoccupation, give my second sister back the love and concern for her welfare that I have always known, but was unable to feel because I got too caught up with my own issues. With this intention, I could take myself to a future where my second sister and I were able to be friends once more, and what laid between us in the past, instead of bogging us down, would increase our understanding of and love for each other as well as for ourselves.

My second sister once said that if she had a child with severe autism, she would kill it. I felt hurt and resentful about this remark. However, from the higher perspective, I could see that not everyone was prepared to go through the grueling and onerous task involved in bringing up a child with severe autism, especially when someone like my second sister, who already had to forgo a substantial amount of the attention and nurturing any child has a right to expect, missing out because of a sibling with disability. I could also see that I am extremely lucky to receive the unconditional love and care of Mum, who tries her best to give me a life worth living, despite the obvious challenges. I could see the enormous difference Mum has made, not only to my life, but to many others as well, because we are all connected in a gigantic human network, that reminds me of the diversity and density of neuronal connections in the brain. I came to realise the meaning of the saying that a butterfly fluttering its wings can cause a tornado on the other side of the world. Mum's love for me and the family spread along this human connectivity web to create ripple effects that can be felt by many many other people we are linked to. I could see that the decisions we make have similar ripple effects that ultimately come back to us, and that the results of our choices have huge impact on our lives. I was also able to accept, under Guidance, that our suffering is a wake-up call to examine our lives in order to develop the skills and know-how to get to a higher level so we don't make the same mistakes again. I was completely overwhelmed and deeply moved by everything, but the most important thing to emerge was I needed to take the lessons I've learned back to live my life in better ways. With these thoughts still reverberating, my Guide indicated that my visit was coming to an end. I was, once again, rejuvenated and renewed in the warm and loving enfoldment of His energy field as we parted ways.

Suddenly, I found myself looking at the ceiling of the swimming pool as my consciousness returned to the body I had left behind. Mum's face came into focus, and my second sister was crying beside her, as the paramedics put me on the stretcher. I was taken by ambulance to the nearest hospital, accompanied by Mum, but either because I was very tired or still floating on cloud nine, I felt completely at peace, and was able to sleep through it all. Apparently, I was not under water for long, as I was pulled out of the water by a savvy swimmer. Luck, providence or synchronicity was at work because there was a pediatric surgeon at the pool with his young family who came to offer his help. In addition, the lifeguard on duty had just done a refresher course on first aid. Both of them administered CPR while someone rang the ambulance which came within the record time of a quarter of an hour. When I arrived at the hospital emergency department, I checked out fine in every way. I typed that I want to go home, but the doctor said I needed to stay for observation because water in my lungs could cause an infection. I was discharged after 24 hours as I passed all the check-points again, as I knew I would.

My brush with death was the most profound and impactful experience of my life. I have changed for the better, and hopefully will continue to do better in applying the lessons I learned from my visit to the Beyond. As someone once said, a story is never finished, it simply stops in interesting places. I feel that I can close a chapter in my book of life and, with everything I've learned, proceed with my newly acquired understanding onto the next level of the game.

---

1. Abbott, E. (1884). *Flatland*. UK: Seeley and Co.

EPILOGUE

Tim speaks

I have been told that writing is like giving birth, that going through labour creates something that is part of me, and yet will lead an independent existence when I share this with others. I think I am ready to let go, and let others make their own way through the story I've given birth to. Writing up my experiences was first suggested by my mentor, psychiatrist Michael Gordon, who said I would be able to provide a unique view on autism. This process has given me the opportunity to stand back and reflect on those experiences, not unlike sentry outposts that provide rest breaks as well as strategic positions for taking stock after the hard grind of our journey. If we stay at a position that lets us take in the view, we may reach a different level of understanding or develop a new outlook on who we are and where we are heading. On the other hand, if we tarry too long at one spot, we may stagnate or even go backward, so the journey continues.

Sarah speaks

Intimate involvement with autism is an experience that I was not prepared for, but since Tim was born, as his mother and primary carer, I have been able to learn many things as well as to unlearn some of my firmly held notions and cherished beliefs. In the years following Tim's diagnosis, with the necessity and impetus to understand his challenges and help him achieve a satisfying life, the enormity of the task has often been overwhelming, but I also feel that I am privileged in getting a unique and personal perspective on the enigmatic condition of autism. Together, Tim and I have charted our course through numerous treatment and intervention regimes, but found that the most effective starting point is to listen and learn from ourselves. Looking back, this arduous journey has brought many gifts, and not least among these, a readiness to tackle our problems. Furthermore, this process has enabled me to see how our challenges provide opportunities to question our entrenched notions, to embrace different ways of seeing the world as well as to appreciate the personal transformation that accompanies perspective shifts. So in hindsight, no matter how helpless or lost I have felt, I would not trade places with parents who have not had close encounters with autism. I would not be the person I am today if it had not been for Tim coming into our family. I know now that this is a blessing in many ways.

Ever eager to rise to his challenges, 2018 is another milestone as Tim makes tentative steps towards a Bachelor of Arts degree. With an inclusive milieu that gives him support and acceptance of his differences from the academic as well as 'student success' staff, even with the inevitable sensory overload and anxiety, Tim revels in the time spent at Uni as well as on the required reading and assessment tasks done at home. Looking back to when we first became aware of Tim's differences, I feel we have cause to celebrate his successes (as well as less notable non-successes) over the years.

On the one hand, the fight for inclusion and recognition of people who function differently in mind and body will be ongoing. On the other hand, it is comforting to know that progress has been made. Within the framework of inclusion for all students, the Department of Education has instigated one relevant advance in eligibility for programs for students with disability (PSD) with the re-direction from cognitive assessment to functional needs as a revised model for funding.[1] A pilot study has been conducted using this model with future implementation in all schools across the state. These gains, great and small, are enabling all of us to take, in Tim's words, "a few steps forward in a thousand mile journey."

---

1. The Department of Education has been implementing recommendations from the Review into the Program for Students with Disability (PSD Review, 2016) chaired by Dr, Graeme Innes, former Disability Discrimination Commissioner, to which Tim has made submissions under the auspices of *Communication Rights Australia*.

    From the PSD Review - Recommendation 23: "Develop and implement a strengths-based, functional needs approach to assessing student need, to support the achievement and participation of students with disabilities."

    https://www.education.vic.gov.au/about/programs/Pages/Inclusive-education-for-students-with-disabilities.aspx

ACKNOWLEDGMENTS

We wish to thank our editor, Anne Carson, for her insightful efforts and superb skills for helping us to achieve our vision to share our story. We have been greatly helped also by Anne's expertise at every stage in preparing for publication.

We are grateful to Emmy Elbaum, our mentor, advocate and friend, and *Just Learning Inc.* in providing dedicated commitment, encouragement and support for this writing project in so many ways. Emmy has never spared herself, further cajoling her friends in reading and reviewing the manuscript. Special thanks to Belinda Frisch and Dr. Mike Steer for their eloquent and perceptive reviews.

We are also indebted to Dr. Wenn Lawson for his generous efforts in reading and editing chapters of the manuscript. Appreciation goes to Ruben Ayers for his constructive feedback and assistance in many aspects of preparing the manuscript for a wider audience.

Julie Matheson, kindred spirit and fellow traveler, has done wonders with creating and putting the finishing touches to photos as well as offering an empathetic ear.

Many thanks to the inspirational people whom we have had the great good fortune to meet and talk to, whose examples we have learned much from.

Finally, this project has been underscored by the love and support from our family. Special thanks to Erica for her sage guidance and generous assistance especially in presentation, formatting and printing.

ADDITIONAL RESOURCES

Anne McDonald Communication Centre: Teaches Augmentative and Alternative Communication to individuals with little or no speech

http://www.annemcdonaldcentre.org.au

Communication Rights Australia: Human rights advocates for those with communication support needs

www.communicationrights.org.au

Disability Discrimination Legal Services: Community legal centre specialising in disability discrimination legal matters

http://www.ddls.org.au

AMAZE: Formerly Autism Victoria, AMAZE is the Victorian peak body for those on the autism spectrum

http://www.amaze.org.au

ASPECT Autism Spectrum Australia: Australia's largest non-profit autism-specific service provider

www.autismspectrum.org.au

Children and Young Adults with Disability Australia: Australia's peak body for children / young adults with disability

www.cyda.org.au

I Can Network: Empowering people on the autism spectrum

www.icannetwork.com

MORE ABOUT TIM

Tim's Website
https://www.timhchan.com

Tim's TedTalk
www.youtube.com/watch?v=Woy-XzC-UVs

www.ingramcontent.com/pod-product-compliance
Lightning Source LLC
Chambersburg PA
CBHW051937290426
44110CB00015B/2015